THESE STONES WILL SHOUT

A new voice for the Old Testament

by Mark Link, S.J.

Argus Communications A Division of **DLM,** Inc.
Allen, Texas 75002 U.S.A.

ACKNOWLEDGMENTS

Scripture quotations in this publication, unless otherwise indicated, are from the *Good News Bible*—Old Testament: Copyright © American Bible Society 1976; New Testament: Copyright © American Bible Society 1966, 1971, 1976. Used by permission.

Excerpt from "The Trial That Rocked the Nation" by John T. Scopes, *Reader's Digest*, March 1961. Reprinted by permission.

Excerpt from "The Lutheran Pope," *Newsweek*, July 23, 1973. Copyright 1973 by Newsweek, Inc. All rights reserved. Reprinted by permission.

Excerpt from "Protestant Misuse of the Bible" by Charles Clayton Morrison. Copyright 1946 Christian Century Foundation. Reprinted by permission from the June 5, 1946, issue of *The Christian Century*.

Excerpts from "Dinosaurs Before Adam?" by Robert E. Gentet, *Tract #670*. Copyright 1963. Reprinted by permission of Ambassador College, Pasadena, California.

Excerpts from *Is the Bible Really the Word of God?* by the Watch Tower Bible and Tract Society of Pennsylvania. Copyright 1969. Reprinted by permission of the Watch Tower Bible and Tract Society of Pennsylvania.

Excerpt from "In Darwin's Century" by Loren Eiseley from *Adventures of the Mind*, reprinted from *The Saturday Evening Post*. © 1958 The Curtis Publishing Company. Reprinted by permission.

Excerpts from "Deadend for Expanding Universe?" by Ronald Kotulak, *Chicago Tribune*, 1973. Reprinted, courtesy of the *Chicago Tribune*.

Excerpts from "Creation" and "Noah Built the Ark" from *God's Trombones* by James Weldon Johnson. Copyright 1927 by The Viking Press, Inc., © renewed 1955 by Grace Nail Johnson. Reprinted by permission of Viking Penguin Inc.

Excerpts from *The Last Temptation of Christ* by Nikos Kazantzakis, trans. by P. A. Bien. Copyright © 1960 by Simon & Schuster, Inc. Reprinted by permission of Simon & Schuster, a Division of Gulf & Western Corporation, and Mrs. Helen Kazantzakis.

Excerpt from "Carbon Copy Man" by Bill Barry, *Chicago Sun-Times Midwest Magazine*, March 11, 1973. Reprinted by permission of Bill Barry.

Excerpt from ". . . Half Plant, Half Animal" by Ronald Kotulak, *Chicago Tribune*, March 21, 1976. Reprinted, courtesy of the *Chicago Tribune*.

Excerpt from *Strength to Love* by Martin Luther King, Jr. Copyright © 1963 by Martin Luther King, Jr. Reprinted by permission of Joan Daves.

Excerpt from "Man's a Born Killer . . ." by Arthur J. Snider, *Chicago Daily News*, September 1–2, 1973. Reprinted with permission from Field Enterprises, Inc.

Excerpt from *The Seven Storey Mountain* by Thomas Merton. Copyright © 1948 by Harcourt Brace & Company, Inc. Copyright renewed © 1976 by Trustees of the Merton Legacy Trust. Reprinted by permission of Harcourt Brace Jovanovich, Inc., and Curtis Brown, Ltd.

Excerpt from *Studs Lonigan* by James T. Farrell. Copyright © 1932, 1933, 1934 by Vanguard Press, Inc. Copyright renewed 1960, 1962, 1963 by James T. Farrell. Epilogue and author's introduction to epilogue copyright © 1978 by James T. Farrell. Reprinted by permission of Vanguard Press, Inc.

Excerpts from *The Bible as History: A Confirmation of the Book of Books* by Werner Keller, trans. by William Neil. Copyright © 1956 by Werner Keller. Reprinted by permission of William Morrow & Co., Inc.

Continued on page 236.

PHOTO CREDITS

Gene Ahrens/Freelance Photographers Guild, Inc.   132

J. Baker/Shostal Associates, Inc.   226

The Bettmann Archive, Inc.   121

Biblical Archaeology Review   98, 109, 114

Courtesy of the Trustees of the British Museum   17, 40, 48L, 102, 146–47, 154, 155, 156, 164, 173, 175T, 193, 217

Brown Brothers   8, 9

Chicago Tribune   41

Robert deGast/Photo Researchers, Inc.   25

Diane Dybsky   141

Stephen L. Feldman/Photo Researchers, Inc.   204

Georg Gerster   120

Weems Hutto   180

Courtesy of the Israel Department of Antiquities and Museums   97T, 175B

Israel Government Tourist Office   51, 52, 84, 87, 89, 95B, 105, 117, 118, 119, 128, 129, 138, 152, 166, 197, 198, 200, 220

Israel Museum   95T, 96, 169, 178

Leo M. Johnson/Corn's Photo Service   23

Algimantas Kezys   37, 56

Ken Lambert/Freelance Photographers Guild, Inc.   136

H. Lanks/Freelance Photographers Guild, Inc.   125

Jean-Claude Lejeune   59, 81, 139

Archie Lieberman   11, 82, 163

Mark Link   26, 65, 88, 122

Llewellyn/Freelance Photographers Guild, Inc.   143

Alexander Lowry/Photo Researchers, Inc.   134

Margot Lubinski/Freelance Photographers Guild, Inc.   171

Tom McHugh/Photo Researchers, Inc.   28–29

David Muench/Freelance Photographers Guild, Inc.   210

Courtesy of the Oriental Institute, University of Chicago   34, 44–45, 48R, 49, 67, 97B, 158, 176, 184–85, 189, 190, 191, 194T, 195R, 196, 202

Photoworld, Inc.   29, 113

Curt Salonick   20

Raymond Schoder   6–7, 16, 18 (Courtesy of the Oriental Institute, University of Chicago, Statuette Orinst. A 7119), 19, 72R, 73TR, 73B, 77, 100–101, 104, 127, 130, 142, 165, 194–95, 203, 206, 209, 215, 222, 223

E. Streichan/Shostal Associates, Inc.   cover

Arthur Tress/Photo Researchers, Inc.   159

James Vorwaldt   115, 212–13, 225

Wolfe Worldwide Films   47, 66, 68, 72L, 73TL

The Archives of the YIVO Institute for Jewish Research   43

CONTENTS

A New Voice for the Old Testament

John Henry Newman once said:
"I read the Bible to know what people ought to do,
and my newspaper to know what they are doing."
Paul Tillich made a similar observation.

We might add a further observation
made by Maurice Zundel: "You can understand
the Bible only on your knees."

These Stones Will Shout
tries to present the Jewish Scriptures
in a way that not only remains faithful to them,
but in a way, also, that relates them
to what people today are doing and thinking.

More importantly, *These Stones Will Shout*
tries to present the Jewish Scriptures
in a way that leads to a prayerful reflection
of them.

When *These Stones Will Shout* appeared in 1975,
the author said that his method and approach
grew out of a classroom teaching situation.
The same is true of this revised edition:
it represents nine years of classroom experience.

For those interested in teaching this book,
the following aids are available:
a highly detailed *Teacher Manual,*
a *Blackline Master Kit,* and a *Poster Activity Kit.*

The author concludes his observations
as he did his original edition.
He tried to follow the scholars at a distance.
With each page he wrote,
he saw the desirability to qualify something.

Yet, he knew that if he did
he would end up with just another scholarly effort—
a poor one at that.
And so he decided to risk all
for the pearl of great price.

If he has failed the scholars,
he begs their understanding.
If he has failed his readers,
he hopes another will succeed where he has not.
If he has failed the Bible,
he trusts in the forgiveness
of what he understands to be a forgiving God.

Easter, 1980   Mark Link, S.J.

5

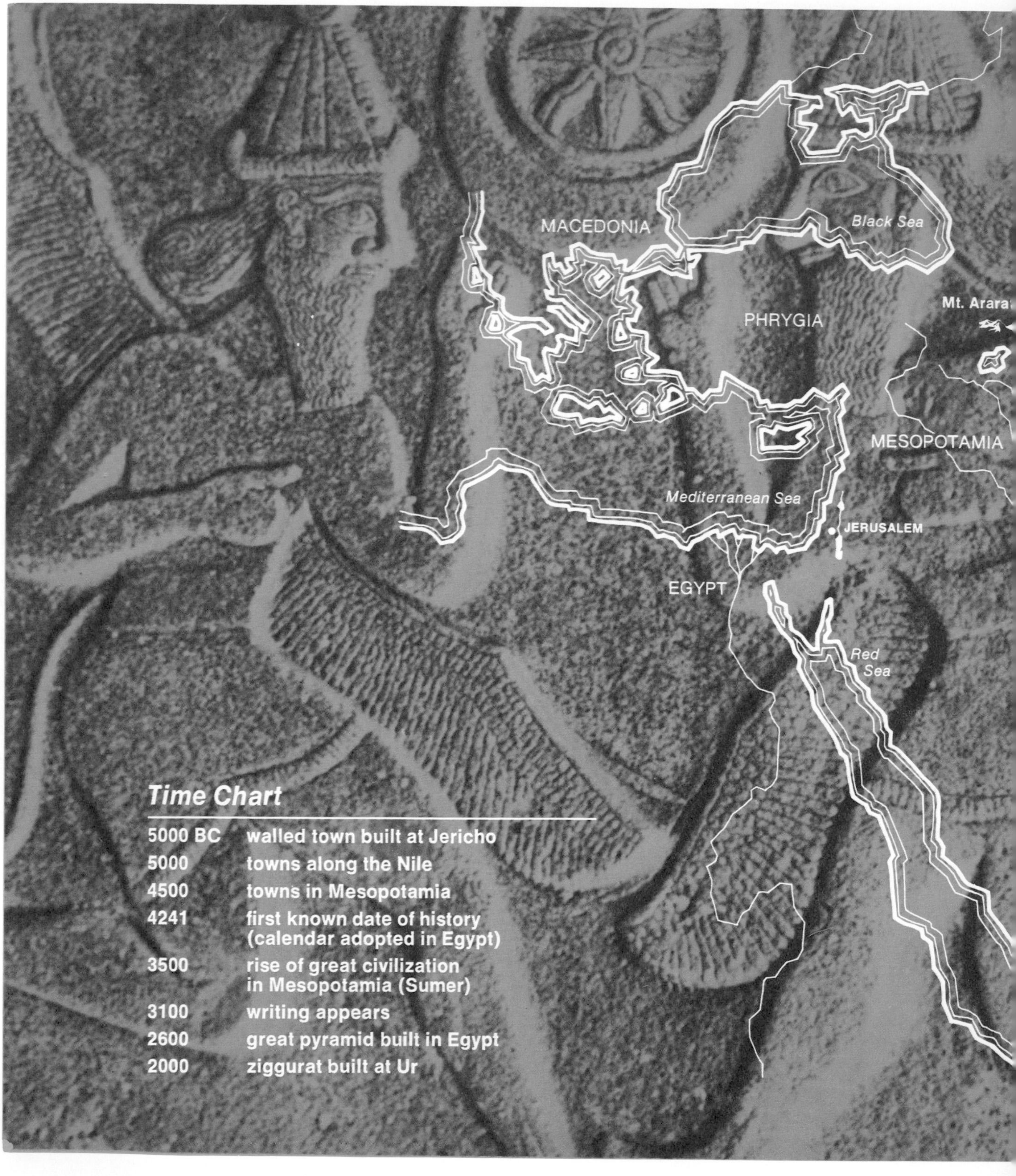

MACEDONIA

Black Sea

PHRYGIA

Mt. Ararat

MESOPOTAMIA

Mediterranean Sea

● JERUSALEM

EGYPT

Red Sea

Time Chart

5000 BC	walled town built at Jericho
5000	towns along the Nile
4500	towns in Mesopotamia
4241	first known date of history (calendar adopted in Egypt)
3500	rise of great civilization in Mesopotamia (Sumer)
3100	writing appears
2600	great pyramid built in Egypt
2000	ziggurat built at Ur

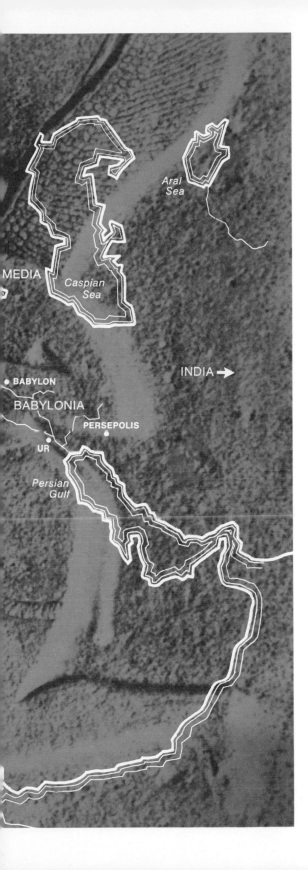

BIBLICAL PREHISTORY

Books

Genesis 1-11

1

The Confrontation

It all started rather harmlessly.
On March 21, 1925,
the Tennessee legislature passed this law:

It shall be unlawful for any teacher
in any of the Universities, Normals,
and all other public schools of the state,
which are supported in whole or in part
by the public school funds of the State,
to teach any theory that denies the story of the
Divine Creation of man as taught in the Bible,
and to teach that man has descended
from a lower order of animals.

No one expected much would come of this law.
It was merely in the books
to pacify those who interpreted the Bible literally.
Within days, however,
the American Civil Liberties Union
voted to test the constitutionality of the law.

John Scopes, a biology teacher
who taught evolution to his classes,
agreed to submit to arrest.
Clarence Darrow, the famous criminal lawyer,
agreed to defend Scopes without a fee.

On the other side of the fence,
the World's Fundamentalist Association
hired the renowned William Jennings Bryan
to assist the prosecution.

Darrow (left) and Bryan (right) pose at the Dayton trial.
Because of huge crowds and the July heat,
the judge moved several sessions out-of-doors.
Scopes was found guilty and fined $100.
Bryan collapsed and died in Dayton
a few days after the trial.

A fundamentalist and three-time nominee for
President on the Democratic ticket,
he would counter the prestige of Darrow.

THE TRIAL

On July 10, 1925, the trial began in Dayton.
To everyone's surprise, one of Darrow's first moves
was to call Bryan as a witness.
Here is a report of what happened.

The Trial That Rocked the Nation
JOHN T. SCOPES

Darrow read from Genesis:
"And the morning and the evening
were the first day."
Then he asked Bryan if he believed
that the sun was created on the fourth day.
Bryan said he did.

*"How could there have been morning
and evening without any sun?" Darrow inquired.
Bryan mopped his bald dome in silence.
There were snickers from the crowd,
even among the faithful. . . .
"And you believe that God punished the serpent
by condemning snakes forever after
to crawl on their bellies?"*

"I believe that!"

*"Well, have you any idea
how the snake went before that?"*

*The crowd laughed, and Bryan turned livid.
His voice rose
and the fan in his hand shook in anger.*

*"Your honor," he said, "I will answer
all Mr. Darrow's questions at once.
I want the world to know that this man who does
not believe in God is using a Tennessee court
to cast slurs on Him. . . ."*

*"I object to that statement," Darrow shouted.
"I am examining you on your fool ideas
that no intelligent Christian on earth believes."*

STILL A PROBLEM

The dispute over the Bible is far from over.
It leaped back into the news in the mid-1970s
when Missouri Synod Lutherans
voted to adopt a stricter interpretation of the Bible.
The vote received a great deal of coverage
in the popular news media.

*It is now absolute dogma within the sect
that a man named Jonah
was swallowed by a whale and lived to tell the tale.
In addition, all the miracles in the Bible
occurred precisely as reported.
And Adam and Eve were real people created by God,
which means
that the theory of evolution is fantasy. . . .*

*For the moment, the future is uncertain
for at least one million Missouri Synod Lutherans
whose ideas of Christian orthodoxy
do not include Biblical literalism. . . .
As soon as the convention declared . . .
fundamentalism to be the standard for the church,
more than 400 delegates marched on the podium
to deposit their names in dissent.*

Scenes like this gave the trial a carnival atmosphere.
Preachers held forth on street corners,
and peddlers hawked their wares among the crowds.
A local drugstore renamed itself
"Monkeyville Soda Fountain."

Who Decides?

The problem of biblical interpretation
is as old as the Bible itself.
Peter wrote concerning Paul's letters:

There are some difficult things in his letters
which ignorant and unstable people
explain falsely,
as they do with other passages of the Scriptures.
So they bring on their own destruction.

2 PETER 3:16

Early Christians resolved major biblical disputes
by deferring to church leadership,
which they believed to be divinely guided.
This way of resolving disputes
ended for many Christians, however,
with the advent of the Protestant Reformation
in the 16th century.
The effects were far-reaching,
as this Protestant report explains.

Protestant Misuse of the Bible
CHARLES CLAYTON MORRISON

The conference of Luther and Zwingli . . .
to unify the German and Swiss Reformation,
broke down . . .
over the failure of the two leaders
to agree on the interpretation
of a single Biblical text: "This is my Body."

From that day on the misuse of the Bible
has vitiated the spirit of Protestantism . . .
and divided it into sects.

2
Literal
Interpreter

Modern Bible readers split into two main groups.
For the sake of clarity,
we may refer to them as literal interpreters
and contextual interpreters.

Literal interpreters
focus primarily on the *text* of the Bible.

Contextual interpreters focus equally on the *text*
and *context* (historical, cultural, and literary)
in which the Bible developed.
Within each group there is some flexibility.

An example of flexibility among *literal* interpreters
is shown by the positions taken by
Jehovah's Witnesses and the Church of God
concerning the word *day* in the creation story.
Jehovah's Witnesses hold
you may interpret the word *day* to mean "era."
Church of God members hold
you must interpret it to mean 24 hours.

Thus, Church of God members,
following a strict biblical timetable,
hold that creation took place in the year 4004 B.C.
Moreover, they believe it took place
in the course of six 24-hour days.

People ask: "How can you hold
that creation took place about 6,000 years ago,
when science proves the earth is millions of years old?"
The literal interpreters answer, "Read your Bible!"

10

The earth became chaotic and void.

In the beginning,
when God created the universe,
the earth was formless and desolate.
The raging ocean that covered everything
was engulfed in total darkness,
and the power of God was moving over the water.
Then God commanded, "Let there be light."

GENESIS 1:1–3

Literal readers say the word *then* holds the key.
It shows that
"the heavens and the earth" already existed
before God began his six days of work.
The six days, therefore,
refer only to *preparing* earth for human habitation.

PREHUMAN ERA

But this still leaves a problem.
How do we explain the existence of fossils, ferns,
and dinosaurs that are millions of years old?
Shouldn't they also be 6,000 years old,
if God created them?

Again, the literalists feel they have an answer.
They believe the earth had a prehuman habitation—
an angelic civilization.

Dinosaurs Before Adam?
ROBERT E. GENTET

Ezekiel 28 and Isaiah 14 tell of the time
when the great archangel called Lucifer—
who ruled the earth before Adam's creation—
rebelled against his Creator and fought God's
loyal angels for control of the universe.
In his rebellion, he led away
one third of the angelic world (Revelation 12:4). . . .

It was at this time
the archangel Lucifer became Satan!

This great battle for control of the universe
caused great destruction upon the earth.

Animal and plant life of the types that then lived
were destroyed, rapidly buried, and fossilized.
The earth became chaotic and void. . . .
The first six days recorded in Genesis I
describe the surface of the earth
being reformed out of a chaotic condition!

To support his theory,
Gentet cites Carl Dunbar's *Historical Geology,*
which notes that dinosaurs vanished suddenly,
not gradually, as the theory of evolution requires.

It was as if the curtain
were rung down suddenly on a stage . . .
and rose immediately
to reveal the same setting but an entirely new cast,
a cast in which dinosaurs do not appear . . .
and the leading parts are all played by mammals.

Gentet feels that his explanation fits the facts.
The *great battle* ended up in a global wipe-out:
total and sudden destruction of all forms of life
on the planet earth.

11

Indeed, this was the "curtain"
that came down suddenly on the stage.
It rose just as suddenly
when God decided to create a human civilization.

The literal interpreters also feel
they can answer Darrow's first question to Bryan:
"How could there have been morning and evening
without any sun?"

Here's how Jehovah's Witnesses respond.

Is the Bible Really the Word of God?
WATCH TOWER BIBLE AND TRACT SOCIETY

Genesis 1:1 shows that the "heavens,"
which include the sun, moon and stars . . .
were already created
before the "first day" ever began.
Yet, prior to the "first day"
the earth itself was in darkness.

The Bible does not state
what prevented the sun's rays
from reaching the planet at that point. . . .

The Book of Job, in describing the earth's formation,
at one point speaks of it as having
"the cloud as its garment and thick gloom
as its swaddling band." (Job 38:4-9)

To illustrate:
One planet in our solar system, Venus,
is completely blanketed
by an unbroken layer of clouds.
Even with their powerful telescopes,
astronomers have never seen its surface.
Though Earth's "swaddling band"
may have been of different composition,
the present state of Venus at least illustrates
what may have been the condition of its neighbor
planet Earth up until the "fourth day."

One thing is certain: A notable change
took place in that fourth period. . . .
God evidently caused the "swaddling band"
high above the earth to become translucent,
thus dispelling the darkness beneath.
So, by God's creative force the sun, moon and stars
were now "made" to be visible
from within the earth's atmosphere.

CREATIONIST

Because they believe the creation story
took place as the Bible describes it,
the literal interpreters reject the theory of evolution.

They take a creationist view of life,
namely, that the various "kinds" of life on earth
came directly from the creative hand of God.
They do stress, however,
the importance of the word *kinds.*
The creationist does not rule out variations
within a specific kind.
Here is one statement of this position.

Why the New Creation-Evolution Controversy?
WILLIAM F. DANKENBRING

At a recent convention
of the National Association of Biology Teachers
in California, it was evident that evolutionists
assumed that the Genesis "kinds"
referred to every last species and variety
as being individually created. . . .

Simply because each "kind"
reproduces after its own kind
does not mean that there can be no variation
within an original Genesis kind.

There are many varieties of dogs, horses and cats.
Yet, each of these varieties
is still a member of the same original kind. . . .
These variations . . . are merely new varieties
arising within the original Genesis kind.

EVOLUTIONIST

Readers who interpret Scripture less rigidly
are open to the possibility of evolution.
Thus, they can read with serious reflection
this imaginative description of human origin.

In Darwin's Century
LOREN EISELEY

*In all that prehuman world there had been
no animal capable of looking back or forward.
No living creature had wept over another's grave.
There had been nothing to comprehend the whole.*

*For three billion years that rule remained unbroken.
At the end of that period
there occurred a small soundless concussion. . . .
The event itself took place in silence,
the silence of cells multiplying at an enormous pace
under a small bone roof,
the silence of some great fungus
coming up at night in a forest glade. . . .*

*For three billion years,
until some ageless watcher
might have turned away in weariness,
nothing moved but the slime and its creations.
Toward the end of that time,
a small unprepossessing animal sat on his haunches
by a rock pile on a waste of open ground.
He clutched a stick
and chewed the end of it meditatively.
He was the first of the great explosion.
In his head was the first twinkle
of that tenuous rainbow bridge that stretches
between the earth and the city of the Gods.*

Evolutionists suggest
that man is part of an evolutionary process
that has been going on for billions of years—
and still goes on.
Among evolutionists
there are both theists and nontheists.

Nontheistic evolutionists do not, necessarily,
see a God involved in this process in any way.
Some speak of a "life force" at work,
but it is in no way a *personal* God.

Theistic evolutionists, on the other hand,
see the process intimately linked to a personal God.
Strangely enough, Saint Augustine (fifth century)
seems to have had a sense of the process of evolution.
He suggested that God could have created
a primeval form or seed
from which our universe and life slowly emerged.

Though Augustine's theory was rejected in his time,
some modern scientists think along similar lines.

Deadend for Expanding Universe?
RONALD KOTULAK

*Most astronomers believe in the "big bang" theory
of the creation of the universe.
According to this concept,
all of the matter in the universe was condensed
into a primeval fireball about 10 billion years ago.*

*The ball exploded [bang], and all the matter
has been expanding outward ever since,
forming the stars, planets,
and galaxies in the process. . . .*

*What has perplexed scientists, however,
is whether the universe
would continue to expand indefinitely
or if it would stop expanding at some point
and begin to come together again.*

*The only way it could contract would be
if there was sufficient matter in the universe
so that the collective gravity of this mass
would be strong enough to brake the expansion.
Like a ball
at the end of an outstretched rubber string,
all of the matter would then snap back
into another fireball. . . .*

Scientists are divided
on the answer to this question.
Some think
there is enough matter in the universe
to reverse the expansion process.
Others think the discovery of "fossil" elements,
like deuterium (residue from the "big bang"),
suggests that the amount of matter
may not be sufficient.
If this is true,
the universe will continue to expand,
while slowing down gradually,
as great galaxies burn themselves out
to become giant graveyards of cooling cinders.

A second question perplexes scientists.
Ronald Kotulak puts it this way:

*Astronomers are still stumped
by the imponderable question
of where the original fireball came from. . . .*

*For all their studies, scientists have not been able
to come up with a better answer than
that posed by many of the world's major religions:
At one point matter was created.*

STILL OPEN-ENDED

Teilhard de Chardin, a priest-scientist,
accepts the possibility
that God could have created in the way described.

A paleontologist and theologian, he blends
both science and theology, discerning God
to be the author and destiny of the process.

In the final analysis, however,
we are dealing in theory.
When it comes to "earth's infancy,"
says J. H. Umgrove in *The Earth's Shifting Crust,*
we are still in the dark.
"Probably not a single step can be placed
on solid ground."

Creation "Fossils"?

All that the two scientists wanted to do
was to get rid of the "faint static"
from Bell Lab's big radio telescope in New Jersey.
They even got down on their hands and knees
and scrubbed pigeon dung from the big horn,
thinking the slight radiation it gave off
might be the culprit.

Then, a chance phone call to a Princeton professor
ignited a chain of events
that left the scientific community stunned.

End Only 100 Billion Years Away
RONALD KOTULAK

*That nuisance static turned out to be a whisper
from space and ancient history.
It was a message*

*left over from the creation of the universe
about 18 billion years ago
and it confirmed the "big bang" theory
of how the universe was created.*

The next step was to try to identify
the elements in space producing the static
and believed to be "fossils" from the "big bang."

The discovery of deuterium among the fossils
suggests insufficient matter in the universe
to brake its present outward motion
and cause the galaxies to rush together again
in what is known as the "big crunch."

Eventually, the universe will grind to a halt.
In the words of poet T. S. Eliot, "The world ends
not with a bang but a whimper."

14

3
Contextual Interpreter

Contextual interpreters view the Bible
differently than do their literal colleagues.
They believe that the key to understanding it
lies not in adherence to the *text* alone.
Equally important is an understanding
of the historical and cultural *context*
in which the Bible developed and was written.

This is especially true of early accounts
that deal with *prehistory*,
that foggy period of time
between the appearance of humans on earth
and their first attempt to tell their story.

For example, when the Bible says
that Adam lived 930 years,
did the biblical writer intend this literally?
Or when the Bible says the snake talked to Eve,
did the biblical writer intend to teach us something
about the previous condition of snakes?

Or when the first chapter of the Book of Genesis
says that man was created last,
and the next chapter says that he was created first,
wasn't the biblical writer aware
that this report is contradictory, if taken literally?

The contextualists firmly believe
that the Bible is the word of God
but is expressed in the words of humans.
They believe that God inspired the biblical writers.
God, however, did not dictate what to say.

The biblical writer
was a person uniquely open to God's revelation
and uniquely inspired by God to express it
in the language and idiom of his time.

GO BACK IN SPIRIT

Contextual interpreters believe
that they must read the Bible within the context
of its historical times and cultural background.
This gives a better understanding
not only of the words, but also of the special meaning
certain words and symbols held in ancient times.
Pope Pious XII told Catholic biblical scholars:

*You must go back, as it were,
in spirit to those remote centuries of the East.
With the aid of history, archaeology, ethnology,
and the other sciences,
you must determine accurately what modes
of writing the ancient writers would likely use,
and in fact did use.*

In other words, scholars must approach the Bible
from the viewpoint of ancient times,
and not impose their own 20th-century viewpoint.
This is simple in theory but difficult in practice.

MODERN SCHOLARSHIP

In recent years, however, remarkable advances
have been made in biblical interpretation.
New sciences, like biblical archaeology,
have cast new light on passages and stories.
Never, since the biblical time itself,
has so much new information been available.

As a result,
a whole new understanding of the Bible is emerging.
The biblical scholar is like a person
who has been walking in the fog.
Now the fog is lifting,
and the scholar sees, in beautiful detail,
things once seen only in vague outline.
To illustrate, consider the Book of Genesis.

Biblical Archaeology

The science of biblical archaeology
selects from the remains of the past
any evidence that sheds light on the Bible.

Illustrations from Biblical Archaeology
D. J. WISEMAN

On the basis of this evidence,
it is now possible
to paint a picture of Old Testament times
on a canvas
which a hundred years ago was almost blank.

Archaeologists dig, sift, study, and catalog
every people-produced object they come across.
It is a tedious, painstaking task.

CREATION STORY

In the beginning,
when God created the universe,
the earth was formless and desolate.
The raging ocean that covered everything
was engulfed in total darkness,
and the power of God
was moving over the water.

Then God commanded,
"Let there be light"—
and light appeared. . . .
Then he separated the light from
the darkness, and he named the light "Day"
and the darkness "Night."
Evening passed and morning came—
that was the first day.

Then God commanded,
"Let there be a dome to divide the water
and to keep it in two separate places"—
and it was done.
So God made a dome,
and it separated the water under it
from the water above it.
He named the dome "Sky."
Evening passed and morning came—
that was the second day.

Then God commanded,
"Let the water below the sky come together
in one place,
so that the land will appear"—
and it was done.
He named the land "Earth,"
and the water . . . "Sea."
And God was pleased with what he saw.
Then he commanded,
"Let the earth produce all kinds
of plants . . ."—and it was done. . . .
God was pleased with what he saw.
Evening passed and morning came—
that was the third day.

Then God commanded,
"Let lights appear in the sky
to separate day from night . . . ;
they will shine in the sky
to give light to the earth"—
and it was done.
So God made the two larger lights,
the sun to rule over the day
and the moon to rule over the night;
he also made the stars. . . .
And God was pleased with what he saw.
Evening passed and morning came—
that was the fourth day.

Then God commanded,
"Let the water be filled
with many kinds of living beings,
and let the air be filled with birds." . . .
And God was pleased with what he saw.
He blessed them all. . . .
Evening passed and morning came—
that was the fifth day

Then God commanded,
"Let the earth produce all kinds of animal life:
domestic and wild, large and small"—
and it was done.
So God made them all,
and he was pleased with what he saw.
Then God said,
"And now we will make human beings;
they will be like us and resemble us.
They will have power over the fish,
the birds, and all animals. . . ."
So God created human beings . . .
blessed them, and said,
"Have many children, so that your descendants
will live all over the earth
and bring it under their control. . . ."
God looked at everything he had made,
and he was very pleased.
Evening passed and morning came—
that was the sixth day.

These clay tablet fragments found at Nineveh
are part of a series
that contain a Babylonian account of creation.
Although the Nineveh tablets
date from about the 7th century B.C.,
their story goes back to the 20th century B.C.
Scholars believe that the Babylonians
borrowed it from an earlier Sumerian story.

And so the whole universe was completed.
By the seventh day
God finished what he had been doing
and stopped working.
He blessed the seventh day
and set it apart as a special day.

GENESIS 1:1–31; 2:1–3

17

This remarkable four-faced deity was just one of many Babylonian gods. Archaeologists retrieved it from the sandy grave where it lay buried for nearly 4,000 years.

LITERARY PATTERNS

A careful analysis of the Genesis story turns up something that many Bible readers miss. Each day is described in almost identically the same pattern:

an introduction,
a command,
the accomplishment of the command,
an affirmation of goodness,
an identification of the day.

Going further, we discover that the overall week also follows a fixed pattern:

FIRST DAY   God created light, and separated it from darkness.

SECOND DAY   God separated the waters above the dome from the waters below it. (Hebrews viewed the sky as a thin dome, holding back the waters "above" [rain] from the waters "below" [sea].)

THIRD DAY   God separated the waters below from the dry land and clothed the land with vegetation.

FOURTH DAY   God populated the sky with sun, moon, and stars.

FIFTH DAY   God populated the air and sea with birds and fish.

SIXTH DAY   God populated the land with people and animals.

SEVENTH DAY God celebrated. He blessed the seventh day and made it holy, because on it he rested.

This overall pattern emerges:

FIRST STAGE   Three days of separation
SECOND STAGE   Three days of population
THIRD STAGE   One day of celebration

LITERARY FORM

These fixed patterns warn us that we are dealing with a special kind of writing, not scientific description or an eyewitness report. Rather, we are dealing with a poemlike story, designed to aid memory and to teach. (Ancients learned almost everything by word of mouth.)

What truths did the biblical writer intend to teach? The truths emerge only if we "go back in spirit" to the historical times in which the writer lived.

18

MANY GODS

When the biblical writer lived,
the worship of many gods was as widespread
as is the worship of one God today.

Almost every object in nature
was worshiped by some group or nation.
The biblical writer testified to this fact
when he warned:

Make certain
that you do not sin
by making for yourselves an idol
in any form at all—
whether man or woman,
animal or bird,
reptile or fish.
Do not be tempted to worship
and serve what you see in the sky—
the sun, the moon, the stars.

DEUTERONOMY 4:15-19

The biblical writer's point is this:
There is only one God!
He makes his point by having the "one" God create
the false gods that ancient peoples worshiped.

In the process of teaching this key truth,
the biblical writer touches upon another error
widespread among ancients.

Archaeology shows that Babylonian astrologers
believed the heavenly bodies controlled people.
The Genesis writer reversed this view.
He taught that God intended the heavenly bodies
to serve people,
to "mark" their seasons and to "light" their earth.

HAPHAZARD EVENT

Also widespread in biblical times
was the belief that the world came into being
through a haphazard act of feuding gods.
For example, a Babylonian creation story,
called *Enuma Elish,* expresses this belief.

Stone tablets of the Babylonian story
were found at Nineveh by archaeologists.
Some interpreters think the biblical writer
consciously set out to refute the Babylonian story.

The biblical writer
follows the Babylonian sequence of creation.
But he departs radically
when it comes to the creator.
He portrays God creating the world by design
and with loving care.

The Babylonian account describes the world
coming about after a bloody battle
between two rival gods: Marduk and Tiamat.
From the lacerated and slain body of Tiamat,
Marduk fashions the world.

The biblical writer's point is this:
God created the world not by whim or chance
but by loving design.

These Assyrian/Hittite gods,
in an apparent feuding posture,
turn back the clock of history
nearly 3,000 years.

19

EVIL MATTER

Next, many people in biblical times
believed that parts of creation were evil
because they were created by evil gods.
As late as the 12th century A.D.
this idea was still widely circulated.

Those who taught it maintained that people
were composed of two contradictory elements:
matter (from Satan) and spirit (from God).

Against these theories,
the Bible teaches that God created everything:
and everything God created is good!
The biblical writer makes this point
by having God affirm the goodness
of all that he creates, especially people.

GRAND FINALE

The key point about creation is left to last.
The biblical writer describes God
as blessing the last day and resting on it.
Why this conclusion?

First, he wants to teach that the Sabbath
should be observed in a special way.

Second, and more important, he wants to teach
that God, who created us in his image,
intends that we should enjoy creation with him
in a kind of eternal enjoyment, forever.
The reason God created us
is not that we should be his pawns
and the created world his personal chessboard,
but that we should be his children
and the created world our home—forever.

Biblical Singer

God's interest in people
excited the heart of the Hebrew psalmist.
Strolling out into the star-filled night,
he would climb a hill, face the sky, and sing:

O LORD, our Lord,
your greatness is seen in all the world! . . .

When I look at the sky,
which you have made,
at the moon and the stars,
which you set in their places—
what is man, that you think of him;
mere man, that you care for him?

Yet you made him inferior only to yourself;
you crowned him with glory and honor.
You appointed him
ruler over everything you made;
you placed him over all creation:
sheep and cattle, and the wild animals too;
the birds and the fish
and the creatures in the seas.

O LORD, our Lord,
your greatness is seen in all the world!

PSALM 8

4

The Bible God

Some people are surprised that chapter 1
of Genesis ends with the sixth day of creation.
Chapter 2 opens with the seventh day.

Chapter 2

1 *So the whole universe was completed.*
2 *By the seventh day*
   God finished what he had been doing
   and stopped working.
3 *He blessed the seventh day*
   and set it apart as a special day. . . .
4 *And that is how the universe was created.*

   When the LORD God made the universe,
5 *there were no plants on the earth*
   and no seeds had sprouted,
   because he had not sent any rain,
   and there was no one to cultivate the land;
6 *but water would come up from beneath*
   the surface and water the ground.

7 *Then the LORD God*
   took some soil from the ground
   and formed a man out of it;
   he breathed life-giving breath
   into his nostrils
   and the man began to live.

8 *Then the LORD God*
   planted a garden in Eden, in the East,
   and there he put the man he had formed.
9 *He made all kinds of beautiful trees*
   grow there and produce good fruit.

HOW IT HAPPENED

Two questions arise.
Why put the chapter division after the sixth day?
Why a "second" creation story?

The biblical writers did not divide their works
into chapters and verses.
Later scholars did this to facilitate Bible study.

Some modern scholars feel
that some of the divisions were unfortunate.
For example,
they feel that the first chapter of Genesis
would better be called a "Preface to the Torah,"
not a chapter of Genesis.
They note that the early books of the Bible,
especially the first five books, called the Torah,
were passed on orally for centuries.
Only later were these oral traditions collected,
recorded, and edited in the form they now have.

Most scholars agree that the Torah
went through four major editing stages.
They identify them by the following names.

Yahwist (J)	around 900 B.C
Elohist (E)	around 700 B.C.
Deuteronomist (D)	around 600 B.C.
Priestly (P)	around 500-400 B.C.

Scholarship shows that the "first" creation story
was written during the Priestly stage
as a kind of liturgical "Preface to the Torah."

It prepares us for all that follows.
It explains how God—

   made all things,
   planned them,
   made them good,
   intended us to enjoy them forever.

Thus, the main body of the Torah
actually begins with the "second" creation story,
which dates from the Yahwist stage.

Brother Star, Sister Earth

Occasionally, we are struck
with a special awareness of our unique kinship
with the rest of creation.
Here's one young person's experience.

The Brothers Karamazov
FEODOR DOSTOEVSKI

The vault of heaven, full of soft, shining stars,
stretched vast and fathomless. . . .
The mystery of earth was one
with the mystery of the stars. . . .

Alyosha stood, gazed,
and suddenly threw himself down on the earth.
He did not know why he embraced it. . . .
But he kissed it weeping,
sobbing and watering it with his tears. . . .
What was he weeping over?

Oh! in his rapture
he was weeping even over those stars,
which were shining to him from the abyss of space,
and "he was not ashamed of that ecstasy.". . .

He longed to forgive everyone and for everything,
and to beg forgiveness.
Oh, not for himself, but for all men,
for all and for everything. . . .
Something firm and unshakable
as that vault of heaven had entered into his soul.
It was as though some idea
had seized the sovereignty of his mind—
and it was for all his life and for ever and ever.

He had fallen on the earth a weak boy,
but he rose up a resolute champion,
and he knew and felt it suddenly
at the very moment of his ecstasy.
And never, never, all his life long,
could Alyosha forget that minute.

YAHWIST STORY

The Yahwist creation story
differs greatly in style from the Priestly "preface."
It is less formal and more earthy.
It portrays God as a potter,
molding man's body out of clay.

Underlying the story is an important teaching:
the intimacy that exists between God and people.

To begin with, man is described
as being created before all other creatures.
Second, he is described as being composed
of two elements: *clay* and the *breath* of God.

In the context of the story, *clay* points to
our kinship with the rest of God's creation.
The *breath* of God, on the other hand,
points to our kinship with God himself.
God and people are related as intimately
as a person is to his own breath.

REVOLUTIONARY TEACHING

The second creation story highlights a teaching
that makes the religion of the Bible
totally different from all other world religions.
Other religions may stress God's knowledge,
his infinity, or his power.
But the Bible stresses God's intimacy with people.

GOD'S OWN IMAGE

The God of the Bible is a "God of Intimacy."
He created people in his own "image" (first story)
and breathed into them
his own "breath" of life (second story).
God and people are related with an intimacy
that can be best explained
by comparing it to the intimacy
that exists between a parent and a child.

"LORD, I put my hope in you;
I have trusted you since I was young."
Psalm 71:5

Relating to God

The Book of Psalms
is the prayerbook of the Old Testament.
More than any other book,
it lets us penetrate
the mind and the heart of the ancient Hebrew.

A recurring theme in the Book of Psalms
is the intimate relationship between God and people.
Sometimes the psalmist finds it a source of joy,
sometimes an occasion for concern,
but always a mystery.
Here are some of his reflections.

LORD, you have examined me
and you know me.
You know everything I do;
from far away you understand all my thoughts.
You see me, whether I am working or resting;
you know all my actions.
Even before I speak,
you already know what I will say. . . .
Your knowledge of me is too deep;
it is beyond my understanding.

PSALM 139:1–6

In times of trouble I pray to the Lord . . .
but I cannot find comfort.
When I think of God, I sigh;
when I meditate, I feel discouraged. . . .
I think of days gone by . . .
and this is what I ask myself:
"Will the Lord always reject us?
Will he never again be pleased with us?"

PSALM 77:2–7

Sovereign LORD, I put my hope in you;
I have trusted in you since I was young.
I have relied on you all my life;
you have protected me since the day I was born.
I will always praise you. . . .
You have sent troubles and suffering on me,
but you will restore my strength. . . .
You will make me greater than ever;
you will comfort me again.

PSALM 71:5–6, 20–21

The LORD is my shepherd;
I have everything I need.
He lets me rest in fields of green grass
and leads me to quiet pools of fresh water.
He gives me new strength.
He guides me in the right paths, as he has promised.
Even if I go through the deepest darkness,
I will not be afraid, LORD,
for you are with me. . . .
I know that your goodness and love
will be with me all my life;
and your house will be my home as long as I live.

PSALM 23:1–6

23

5
Who Told Them?

BIBLICAL INSPIRATION

How did God inspire the biblical writers?
Were these writers inspired the way a poet is?
Or did God inspire them in a more direct way?

Consider this imaginative scene
from a modern novel about biblical times.

Inspired by the Yahwist creation story,
poet James Weldon Johnson wrote "Creation."
A portion of it reads:

Then God walked around,
And God looked around
On all that he had made. . . .
He looked on his world
With all its living things,
And God said: I'm lonely still.

Then God sat down—
On the side of a hill where he could think;
By a deep, wide river he sat down;
With his head in his hands,
God thought and thought,
Till he thought: I'll make me a man!

Up from the bed of the river
God scooped the clay;
And by the bank of the river
He kneeled him down;
And there the great God Almighty
Who lit the sun and fixed it in the sky,
Who flung the stars to the most far corner
of the night,
Who rounded the earth in the middle of his hand;
This Great God,
Like a mammy bending over her baby,
Kneeled down in the dust
Toiling over a lump of clay
Till he shaped it in his own image;

Then into it he blew the breath of life,
And man became a living soul.

The Last Temptation of Christ
NIKOS KAZANTZAKIS

Jesus took a long stride and entered the house.
He saw Matthew next to the lamp,
still holding the open notebook on his knees.
He stopped. Matthew's eyes were closed:
he was still submerged in all that he had read.

"Matthew," said Jesus,
"bring your notebook here.
What do you write?"

Matthew got up and handed Jesus his writings.
He was very happy.

"Rabbi," he said,
"here I recount your life and works,
for men of the future."

Jesus knelt under the lamp
and began to read.
At the very first words, he gave a start.

Kazantzakis then has Jesus confront Matthew,
asking him where he got all the information
he had put down in writing.

"The angel revealed it to me,"
Matthew answered, trembling.

"The angel? What angel?"

"The one who comes each night I take up my pen.
He leans over my ear and dictates what I write."

*but men were under the control
of the Holy Spirit as they spoke the message
that came from God.* (2 Peter 1:21)

Jesus taught:

*"The Holy Spirit inspired David to say:
'The Lord said to my Lord:
Sit here at my right hand.'"* (Mark 12:36)

ILLUMINATION

Basically, inspiration means
that the primary author of the Bible is God;
the human author is God's instrument.
From early times,
this was a firm and constant belief among Jews.
New Testament writers shared the belief,
and used the word *inspiration* to describe it,
but did not explain its meaning.

In the course of history,
there have been two extreme positions proposed
as to how God inspired the biblical writers.
The first is that God dictated to them,
much as a businessman dictates to his secretary.
The second is
that they were inspired in a "religious" way,
much as a songwriter is inspired in a musical way.

Modern scholars reject both extremes.
Generally, they hold that the biblical writers
were given some special illumination by God,
which enabled them to communicate faithfully
what God wanted them to convey.

The main concern of early Jews and Christians
was not *how* the biblical writers were inspired,
but *that* they were inspired.

The poet Samuel Taylor Coleridge
speaks for all believers when he says:

*I know the Bible is inspired
because it finds me at greater depths of my being
than any other book.*

LED BY THE SPIRIT

There are many theories about how God
communicated *instruction* to priests,
counsel to the wise, and *messages* to the prophets
(Jeremiah 18:18).

Although the Old Testament gives no explanation,
we do find New Testament writers referring to it
in several places. Paul writes:

All Scripture is inspired by God. (2 Timothy 3:16)

Peter says:

*No prophetic message
ever came just from the will of man,*

6

Bone of My Bone

Oriental women go about their daily chores today much as they did in ancient times.

GOD
It is not good
for the man to live alone.
I will make a suitable companion
to help him.

NARRATOR
...Then the LORD God
made the man fall into a deep sleep,
and while he was sleeping,
he took out one of the man's ribs
and closed up the flesh.
He formed a woman out of the rib
and brought her to him.

MAN
... Here is one of my own kind—
Bone taken from my bone,
and flesh from my flesh.
"Woman" is her name
because she was taken out of man.

NARRATOR
That is why
a man leaves his father and mother
and is united with his wife,
and they become one.

The man and the woman were both
naked, but they were not embarrassed.

GENESIS 2:18-25

This colorful story of woman's origin
brings to a close the second creation story.
Inspired by its imagery,
Gordon Higham penned these words:

Woman was not taken
from man's head to be ruled by him,

nor from his feet to be trampled upon,
but from his side to walk beside him,
from under his arm to be protected by him,
and from near his heart to be loved by him.

CONTEXTUALIST VIEW

Hebrew society, like most ancient societies,
was dominated by men.
Women belonged to a depressed minority.
They existed primarily to bear children—
male children at that.

Contextualists interpret the story of woman's origin
as a rejection of this social situation.
By portraying woman
as coming from the same substance as man,
the biblical writer sought to teach
that man and woman are equal in dignity.

This idea was so revolutionary
that even later biblical writers struggled
to assimilate it into their human thought patterns.
The feminist movement of recent years
testifies that even modern man
has not fully understood this biblical teaching.

LITERALIST VIEW

Literalists hold that woman was created exactly
as the biblical writer depicts the event.

Is the Bible Really the Word of God?
WATCH TOWER BIBLE AND TRACT SOCIETY

*The creation of the first woman as recorded
in Genesis has been scoffed at by some. . . .
Yet they will read
with great interest and seriousness
an article such as appeared in* Life *magazine
of September 10, 1965. It dealt
with experiments on plant cells by biologists
and contained the following statement:*

*"It is not absurd
to imagine the day when a single tiny cell
taken from the skin of the world's greatest genius
might be grown into a second individual
who is in every respect identical."*

Jehovah's Witnesses
refer to reports such as the following.
Though experimentation is still in early stages,
a few experts predict
that it may someday be realized at a human level.

Carbon Copy Man
BILL BARRY

*A Clone is a human child
created from a single asexual body cell;
the child is the exact duplicate
of the person from whom the body cell was taken.
The simple, painless scraping of a human arm
produces enough healthy body cells
to make a thousand clones—
all perfect carbon copies of the man or woman
from whom they were created. . . .*

*If Cloning had been achieved twenty years ago:
John F. Kennedy, shot to death in Dallas
on November 22, 1963, could still be alive today,*

*in the person of his Clone—
not a son, but an exact copy of himself. . . .*

*In 1961, across the Atlantic at Oxford University,
zoologist J. B. Gurdon undertook
certain experiments with the African clawed frog.
From one frog, he extracted an unfertilized egg cell,
destroyed the nucleus with ultraviolet radiation,
and preserved the womb-like cytoplasm.
From a second frog's intestine,
he extracted the nucleus of a body cell,
and planted it in the preserved cytoplasm.*

*Soon after, a tadpole was born,
identical in every respect to the second frog,
from which the body cell had been taken.
Virgin birth had occurred in the animal kingdom. . . .*

*Nobel geneticist Joshua Lederberg . . .
suggests that Clones bred from one person
would be so similar neurologically,
they would communicate almost with the ease
of reading each other's minds.*

The Mind
TIME

*Another prospect is to alter genes
so that babies will be born with rote knowledge—
language skills, multiplication tables—
just as birds apparently emerge from the egg
with programs that enable them to navigate.*

The Second Genesis
ALBERT ROSENFELD

*When this kind of biochemical sophistication
has been attained . . .
man's powers will become truly godlike.
Just as man has been able, through chemistry,
to create a variety of synthetic materials
that never existed in nature,
so may he, through "genetic surgery,"
bring into being new . . . species of creatures
never before seen or imagined in the universe.*

27

The development of creatures
"never before seen or imagined in the universe"
is no longer a biochemical dream.

... Half Plant, Half Animal
RONALD KOTULAK

An organism
that nature hasn't dared create—
half plant and half animal—
has been produced
by a team of English scientists. . . .

The work of the British scientists
closely follows another genetic breakthrough
pioneered by California scientists.

Using newly discovered enzymes,
the California researchers
have been able to break the species barrier.
They can extract the genetic material
from one species and splice it into
the genetic code of another species.

And consider another recent report.

Fierce DNA Debate
WILLIAM HINES

It is possible to "train" bacteria to make insulin,
an essential drug for many diabetics.
General Electric is working on a bacteria strain
that could "eat up" oil spills and die out
when there is no more oil to scavenge.
These are great promises.

But each could conceivably backfire. . . .
What if the insulin-producing bacteria
got loose and invaded human bodies,
throwing normal persons into insulin shock?
What if oil-eating bugs
got into natural crude deposits?

These scientific advances raise a question:
Is this the kind of *dominion*
God intended us to exercise over creation?

28

Uncreation

An anonymous poet
ponders the kind of dominion over creation
we have exercised so far.

In the beginning was the earth.
And it was beautiful.
And man lived upon the earth. And man said:
"Let us build skyscrapers and expressways."
And man covered the earth with steel and concrete.
And man said: "It is good."

On the second day,
man looked upon the clear blue waters of the earth.
And man said: "Let us dump our sewage
and wastes into the waters." And man did.
The waters became dark and murky.
And man said: "It is good."

On the third day,
man gazed at the forests on the earth.
They were tall and green. And man said:
"Let us cut the trees and build things for ourselves."
And man did. And the forests grew thin.
And man said: "It is good."

"Let us cover the earth . . ."

On the fourth day,
man saw the animals leaping in the fields
and playing in the sun. And man said: "Let us trap
the animals for money and shoot them for sport."
And man did. And the animals became scarce.
And man said: "It is good."

On the fifth day,
man felt the cool breeze in his nostrils.
And man said: "Let us burn our refuse
and let the wind blow away the smoke and debris."
And man did.
And the air became dense with smoke and carbon.
And man said: "It is good."

On the sixth day,
man saw the many kinds of people on the earth—
different in race, color, and creed.
And man feared and said: "Let us make bombs
and missiles in case misunderstandings arise."
And man did. And missile sites and bomb dumps
checkered the landscape.
And man said: "It is good."

On the seventh day, man rested.
And the earth was quiet and deathly still.
For man was no more.
And it was good!

"And man was no more . . ."

Something to Ponder

Dr. Martin Luther King wrote in *Strength to Love:*

*Our scientific power
has outrun our spiritual power.
We have guided missiles and misguided men. . . .*

*Science gives man knowledge which is power;
religion gives man wisdom which is control.*

29

7

Blaming the Snake

Man's a Born Killer . . .
ARTHUR J. SNIDER

*"Man has been violent since his remote ape-like ancestors descended from trees
and there is little prospect that his innate desire to kill for dominance ever will change."*

*This gloomy assessment
was laid before anthropologists
gathered here from around the world. . . .*

*"We have to face the truth and accept one basic, unpleasant fact,"
warned Dr. Norman MacDonald. . . .
"Man being what he is, violence is forever."*

"The only hope for humans to live in peace is to first be honest with ourselves and accept the fact that biologically man is a killer, the greatest predator the world has ever known," he said.

*"We deceive ourselves if we call murder inhuman,"
said Dr. MacDonald. "It is characteristic of man."*

"It may be inhumane, but it is not inhuman."

*"From the time he fashioned a club
as his first weapon, man has insisted on developing more powerful weapons
so that now, instead of killing individuals or groups, he can annihilate a planet."*

WHAT HAPPENED?

If the Bible is correct,
and God did make people "very good,"
what caused them to change so radically?
And if God and people are so intimately linked—
almost as a parent to children—
what happened to destroy that intimacy?

These questions cried for an answer in early times.
They still cry out for an answer today.
The biblical writer faced the question immediately
after he described the creation of woman.

NARRATOR *The snake was the most cunning animal that the LORD God had made. The snake asked the woman,*

SNAKE *Did God really tell you not to eat fruit from any tree in the garden?*

WOMAN *We may eat the fruit of any tree . . . except the tree in the middle. . . . God told us not to eat the fruit of that tree or even touch it; if we do, we will die.*

SNAKE *That's not true; you will not die. God said that because he knows that when you eat it, you will be like God and know what is good and what is bad. . . .*

NARRATOR *So she took some of the fruit. . . . Then she gave some to her husband. . . . As soon as they had eaten it, they were given understanding and realized that they were naked.*

GENESIS 3:1–7

SYMBOL STORY

Contextualists interpret this as a symbol story.
Its purpose is to answer the question:
If God made people good,
how did evil enter their hearts?

The key symbol in the story is the snake.
Even in modern times,
the snake suggests an evil image for most people.
The snake was even more repulsive to Hebrews.

Archaeology reveals that snakes played a bizarre
role in the worship ceremony of the Canaanites,
Israel's ancient enemy. Thus the snake made an
ideal evil symbol for the biblical writer.

Another key symbol is the act of *eating*.
Recall that the snake promised:
If you eat from the tree,
you will be like gods, who *know* good and evil.

Eating is equated with *knowing*.
To know, for ancient peoples, was to discover
by experience, not to learn from books.
To eat is a symbolic way of saying Adam and Eve
learned evil by the experience of becoming evil.
They both shared in some derelict act.

What was this evil act?
Some literal readers think it was disobedience
to God's command "not to eat from the tree."
Others say it was pride: wanting to be like gods.
A few think it involved sex.

Contextual readers say the question lies outside
the biblical writer's intention.
The main point he wishes to communicate is this:
People broke faith with God in some way.
What they did is really irrelevant.

A second question is often asked:
Did the biblical writer intend the snake
to represent a real tempter apart from people,
or merely a temptation within people?
Again, Bible readers disagree.
Regardless of how you answer the question,
the writer's primary point remains unchanged:
People, freely, chose to break faith with God.
Thus, they are directly responsible
for the entry of evil into their lives.

SELF-ALIENATION

After Adam and Eve sinned, the Bible says
they "realized that they were naked" (Genesis 3:7).
Why this strange statement?

Archaeology shows
that nakedness was a sign of disgrace and defeat.
Excavations have uncovered stone slabs
showing enemy soldiers, defeated in battle,
marching naked before their conquerors.
The Genesis writer apparently took this idea
and gave it a deeper meaning.

An awareness of nakedness after sin
(not there before it) seems to imply
that a change took place in the consciousness
of the first couple as a result of sin.
Somehow, they are uneasy with themselves.
They are alienated from themselves,
no longer at peace with what they have become.

In modern times, a similar observation
has been made about contemporary man.

A Visit with India's High-Powered New Prophet
PAUL HORN

The main feeling you get today—
you can even see it in people's faces—
is that nearly everyone is uptight.
Tense vibrations are everywhere. . . .

Actually, they just reflect the sum
of conflicts and hostilities and tensions
on the individual level. . . .
Maharishi Mahesh Yogi of India . . .
believes such a tense atmosphere
and the wars that result from it
could never happen
in a world peopled by individuals
at peace with themselves.

He says, "For the forest to be green,
the trees must be green."

The Night I Prayed

Young Tom Merton
had just graduated from high school
and was traveling alone in Europe.
His father had died the year before,
and Tom was leading a wayward life.
One night, in the silence of his room,
he underwent a soul-stirring experience.
He describes it in his autobiography.

The Seven Storey Mountain
THOMAS MERTON

I was overwhelmed
with a sudden and profound insight
into the misery and corruption of my own soul . . .
I was filled with horror at what I saw,
and my whole being rose up in revolt
against what was within me,
and my soul desired
escape and liberation and freedom from all this
with an intensity and an urgency
unlike anything I had ever known before.

And now I think for the first time in my whole life
I really began to pray—
praying not with my lips and with my intellect
and my imagination,
but praying out of the very roots of my life
and of my being,
and praying to the God I had never known,
to reach down towards me out of His darkness
and to help me to get free
of the thousand terrible things
that held my will in their slavery.

GOD ALIENATION

The sin story continues:

NARRATOR *That evening*
they heard the LORD God
walking in the garden,
and they hid from him
among the trees.

GOD *Where are you?*

MAN *I heard you in the garden;*
I was afraid and hid from you,
because I was naked.

GOD *Who told you that you were naked?*
Did you eat the fruit
that I told you not to eat?

MAN *The woman you put here with me*
gave me the fruit,
and I ate it.

GOD *[to woman]*
Why did you do this?

WOMAN *The snake tricked me*
into eating it.

GENESIS 3:8–13

Two points stand out in the sin dialogue.
First, Adam and Eve show an estrangement to God.
They conceal themselves, because they are naked.
Thus, another result of sin is implied:
alienation from God.

Second, when God questions Adam,
Adam immediately points his finger at Eve.
Eve, in turn, blames the snake.
Each attempts to shift the blame to the other.

The conclusion of the first sin story is this:
Evil did not enter the world through some force
over which people had no control.
People, themselves, are to blame for it.

8

Thorns and Thistles

God, why do you permit men to starve,
hunger, die from syphilis, cancer, consumption?
God, why do you not raise one little finger
to save man from all the . . .
suffering on this planet?

Ancient peoples, also, cried out in anguish
about suffering and death in the world.
They asked their holy people:
If sin (moral evil) is the fault of the people,
who caused suffering and death (physical evil)?

NATURE ALIENATION

After the sin dialogue,
the biblical writer has God confront each involved.

TO SNAKE   *From now on*
you will crawl on your belly. . . .

I will make you and the woman
hate each other; her offspring
and yours will always be enemies.
Her offspring will crush your head,
and you will bite their heel.

TO WOMAN   *I will increase*
your trouble in pregnancy
and your pain in giving birth. . . .

TO MAN   *The ground*
will be under a curse. . . .
It will produce weeds and thorns,
and you will have to eat wild plants.
You will have to work hard
and sweat
to make the soil produce anything,
until you go back to the soil
from which you were formed.
You were made from soil,
and you will become soil again.

GENESIS 3:14–19

This conversation
between the Creator and his creatures
dramatizes a further alienation caused by sin.

Sin alienates one not only from God
and from oneself, but also from nature.
The earth
now resists human dominion over it.

One even loses dominion over one's own body.
It falls under the dominion of suffering and death.
Thus, the biblical writer answers the question:
How did suffering and death (physical evil)
enter the world?
They entered not through some defect in creation,
but through a sinful misuse of it.

Does the writer imply suffering and death
are punishment for sin?

Or are they the result of sin,
just as hunger is the result of not eating?
The writer seems to leave this question open.

Later books of the Bible, especially the Book of Job,
will probe more deeply the mystery of suffering.
For the present,
the biblical writer merely says this:
Suffering and death entered the world
not through a defect in creation,
but through a sinful misuse of creation.

SIGN OF HOPE

New Testament writers showed special interest
in God's remarks to the serpent.
They interpreted them as the first indication
of a savior for the human race.

Referring to the story, Jesus says:

*"From the very beginning he [the Devil]
was a murderer. . . . He is a liar
and the father of all lies."* (John 8:44)

John says of Jesus:

*The Son of God appeared
for this very reason, to destroy
what the Devil had done.* (1 John 3:8)

In other words, enmity between people and evil
has existed from the beginning.
But people (in the offspring of Jesus)
will eventually crush evil.

END OF A DRAMA

The biblical writer brings down the curtain
on the first sin story this way:

*So the LORD God
sent him out of the Garden of Eden
and made him cultivate the soil
from which he had been formed. . . .
He put living creatures and a flaming sword
which turned in all directions . . .
to keep anyone from coming near
the tree that gives life.*

GENESIS 3:23–24

Archaeologists have cleared up the confusion
that once surrounded these strange creatures.
Cherubim are legendary winged animals
with a human head.
Found at entrances to ancient buildings and cities,
cherubim were supposed to ward off evil intruders.

Paul-Emile Botta, a French archaeologist,
first unearthed them in the 1840s
while excavating the palace of Sargon II, an ancient
Assyrian king. Flanking the palace doorway,
they were carved in gigantic stone slabs.
Their discovery attracted worldwide attention.
The 16-foot slabs now reside
in the famous Louvre museum in Paris.

Similarly, archaeologists point out
that the tree of life is also an ancient symbol.
It refers to a legendary plant,
thought to confer immortality (freedom from death)
on those who had access to it.
It might be compared to the fountain of youth,
which legend says
Spanish explorers hoped to find in Florida.

When we connect these two symbols,
we understand the biblical writer's point.
Cherubim keep people away from the tree
in the garden
because people are no longer worthy to eat from it.
They are now subject to death.

LEVELS OF MEANING

Perhaps what is most striking in these stories
is the depth of meaning they contain.
Just as Jesus gave deeper meaning to his parables,
so Old Testament writers
gave deeper meaning to some of their narratives.

Obviously, there is the *literal* meaning—
the actual meaning of the words themselves.
For example, the story of the creation of woman
merely describes her as coming from man's side.

But beyond this literal meaning
is a deeper, *intended* meaning.
By describing woman
as coming from the same substance as man,
the biblical writer *intends* to teach
that man and woman are equal in dignity.

Legendary Watchdog

Standing an impressive 16 feet tall,
this colossal winged animal with human head
stood guard at the outer gate
of the 8th-century B.C. palace of Sargon II.

The Assyrian king's 209-room residence
was unearthed in the early 19th century
by French archaeologist Paul-Emile Botta.

The animal's fifth leg
was added by the ancient artist
for visual purposes.
When viewed from the front,
the creature appeared in perfect symmetry.
When viewed from the side,
it gave the impression of balance and motion.

9
And God Grieved

CAIN   *Let's go out in the fields.*

NARRATOR   *When they were out in the fields,
Cain turned on his brother
and killed him.*

LORD   *Where is your brother Abel?*

CAIN   *I don't know. Am I supposed
to take care of my brother?*

LORD   *. . . Your brother's blood
is crying out to me from the ground. . . .*

NARRATOR   *Cain went away from the LORD's
presence and lived in a land . . .
east of Eden.*

GENESIS 4:8–10, 16

FURTHER ALIENATION

The main purpose of the Cain story
is to teach that when one breaks faith with God,
he soon breaks faith with others as well.

Thus, the story extends the biblical writer's theme
that sin alienates. Sin alienates not only

person from self	(Adam's nakedness),
person from God	(Adam's hiding),
person from nature	(curse), but also
person from person	(Cain's violence).

Cain's act of violence begins a tidal wave of sin
that now floods the world.

DISINTEGRATION

The biblical writer teaches this in a poetic way:
he lists two genealogies (family trees).

The first begins with Adam and ends with Noah.
Fantastic ages are assigned to the men named.

Adam lived 930 years.
Seth lived 912 years.
Lamech lived 777 years. (Genesis 5:1-32)

The second family tree starts with Shem,
Noah's son,
and ends with Terah, Abraham's father.

Shem lived 600 years.
Eber lived 464 years.
Terah lived 205 years. (Genesis 11:10-32)

The purpose of the family trees is twofold.

First, they build a literary bridge
between Adam, the father of all people,
and Abraham, the father of the Hebrew people.

Second, they advance the "sin" motif
in the Book of Genesis.
They do this by showing the steady decline
in human life spans
from the start of each family tree to its end.
Although the "pattern of decline" is not perfect,
the "decline" is definite and dramatic.

In brief,
the biblical writer uses the two family trees
as a literary device.

First, they establish the continuity of life
from Adam to Abraham.
Second, they show the disintegration of life
as it travels from Adam to Abraham.
Declining age spans are signs
not only of the spread of sin to all life,
but also of the disintegration of all life by sin.

CORRUPTION

A baffling report of marriages between
"human women" and "supernatural beings"
appears in Genesis 6:1-4.
This episode is still the subject of much debate.

A few recent fundamentalist popularizers
have suggested that
the story is documentation
that ancient astronauts once visited Earth
and intermarried with its dwellers.

Some contextualists
interpret the narrative as another sin story.
Good people ("supernatural beings")
and bad people ("human women") intermarry.
Good and evil intermingle
and become hopelessly entangled.
The disintegrating effect of sin spreads to everyone,
even the good.

Following this report, the biblical writer
portrays God looking down on the world
with a heavy heart.

When the LORD saw
how wicked everyone on earth was
and how evil their thoughts were . . .
he was sorry
that he had ever made them
and put them on the earth.

GENESIS 6:5-6

Perhaps William Shakespeare
had this paragraph in mind when he wrote:

Man, proud man!
drest in a little brief authority . . .
Plays such fantastic tricks
before high heaven
As make the angels weep.

MEASURE FOR MEASURE

10
The Flood

"The floodgates of the sky were opened."
Genesis 7:11

Noah Built the Ark
JAMES WELDON JOHNSON

And a little black spot begun to spread,
Like a bottle of ink spilling over the sky,
And the thunder rolled like a rumbling drum;
And the lightning jumped from pole to pole;
And it rained down rain, rain, rain,
Great God, but didn't it rain!
For forty days and forty nights
Waters poured down and waters gushed up;
And the dry land turned to sea.
And the old ark-a she begun to ride;
The old ark-a she begun to rock;
Sinners came a-running down to the ark;
Sinners came a-swimming all round the ark;
Sinners pleaded and sinners prayed—
Sinners wept and sinners wailed—
But Noah'd done barred the door.

Even people who know little about the Bible
are familiar with the story of Noah and the Ark.

NARRATOR   *God looked at the world*
             and saw that it was evil . . .
             people were all living evil lives.

GOD   *[to Noah]*
             I have decided to put an end
             to all mankind. . . .
             Build a boat. . . . Go into the boat
             with your whole family . . .
             you are the only one in the world
             who does what is right. . . .

NARRATOR   *Rain fell on the earth*
             for forty days and nights. . . .

             The water . . .
             became so deep
             that it covered the highest mountains.
                          GENESIS 6:12–14; 7:1, 12–19

Is this a factual story,
a symbolic story, or a combination of both?
By a combination of both,
we mean a symbolic story based on an actual flood.

37

Following his discovery,
Woolley made digs
in other parts of Mesopotamia
to determine the extent of the clay deposit.

The Bible as History
WERNER KELLER

Gradually, by a variety of tests,
the limits of the Flood waters could be established.
According to Woolley, the disaster
engulfed an area northwest of the Persian Gulf
400 miles long and 100 miles wide.
Looking at the map today,
we could call it a "local occurrence,"
but for the inhabitants of the river plains
it was, in those days, their whole world. . . .

A vast catastrophic inundation,
resembling the Biblical Flood . . .
had not only taken place but was, moreover,
an event within the compass of history.

Later archaeologists are not so sure
that the tests prove adequately that the deposits
were as widespread as Woolley estimates.

The question returns. Did the biblical writer
intend his flood story to be a factual report?

The literal readers say "Yes!" Moreover,
they insist that the flood was worldwide.

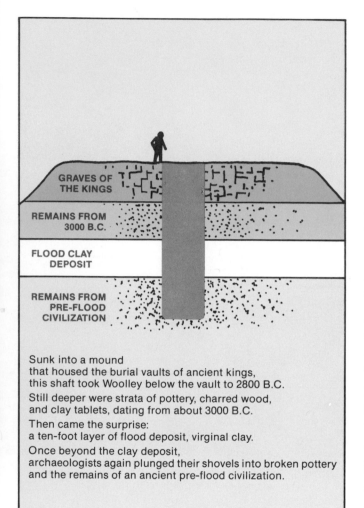

GRAVES OF THE KINGS

REMAINS FROM 3000 B.C.

FLOOD CLAY DEPOSIT

REMAINS FROM PRE-FLOOD CIVILIZATION

Sunk into a mound
that housed the burial vaults of ancient kings,
this shaft took Woolley below the vault to 2800 B.C.

Still deeper were strata of pottery, charred wood,
and clay tablets, dating from about 3000 B.C.

Then came the surprise:
a ten-foot layer of flood deposit, virginal clay.

Once beyond the clay deposit,
archaeologists again plunged their shovels into broken pottery
and the remains of an ancient pre-flood civilization.

LITERALIST VIEW

In his excavations in 1929, British archaeologist
Sir Leonard Woolley startled the world
with the news that he had discovered evidence
of a great flood that occurred about 4000 B.C.

Coinciding with the date of the biblical flood,
it was a layer of clay deposit about ten feet thick.

Is the Bible Really the Word of God?
WATCH TOWER BIBLE AND TRACT SOCIETY

If the Flood did not cover all the earth,
why bring animals and birds into the ark
to preserve all the different kinds?
Animals elsewhere could have survived.
And the birds could have easily escaped
by flying to another area.

Literalists continue to sponsor expeditions
to Mount Ararat in Turkey, hoping to find
some evidence of the 450-foot ark.
Since 1961 over 30 forays have been attempted.
Recently, however, Turkish officials have said
"no" to further expeditions, because Ararat lies
in a politically touchy area on the Russian border.

Interest in the ark mounted in recent decades
because of two episodes in particular.
One was a U.S. Skylab photo taken in 1974
showing something "foreign" on the mountain.
The other was an L-shaped timber found in 1955
in an icy crevice 13,500 feet up the mountain.
The timber has been tested for dating.
A recent report sums up the results.

Science News
EDITORS

Perhaps the last hope that the battered remains
of Noah's Ark exist on Mount Ararat
near the Turkish-Soviet border has been washed
away by a new wave of scientific evidence.
Recent tests at the University of California at
Los Angeles, La Jolla and Riverside all conclude
that a piece of timber found at the Ararat site
is only about 1,200 years old —
some 2,700 years younger
than the first known account of the Ark.

Using carbon-14 dating, UCLA archaeologist
Rainer Berger confirmed earlier findings
"that the timber came from a tree
that was chopped down around A.D. 700."
In other tests, R. E. Taylor of Riverside
and Hans Seuss of La Jolla got similar results.

One theory is that the timber could be
the remnant of a shrine built by early monks
to celebrate the biblical account.
Meanwhile, interest in the ark continues
among literalist biblical interpreters.

CONTEXTUALIST VIEW

Contextualists see the flood story
as another link in the chain of symbolic sin stories.
A few feel that the story is totally symbolic,
designed to teach an important religious truth.

The majority, however,
feel the story is "factual-symbolic."
It is factual to the extent
that it is based on an ancient flood tradition.
It is symbolic in the sense that the writer
uses this tradition as a vehicle
to get across an important religious teaching.
Here's how one modern interpreter puts it.

Searching the Scriptures
JOHN J. DOUGHERTY

Evidence of a flood has been found in excavations
at Ur and at Kish. It is not surprising
that there were floods in Mesopotamia,
the name meaning "the land between the rivers,"
the Tigris and Euphrates.
Archaeology . . .
does not supply evidence for a universal flood.

When all the relevant data are assembled
and weighed, the conclusion would seem to follow
that a popular tradition is common . . .
and that the inspired author used the popular
tradition to teach men a moral lesson.

The genre of Genesis 6-9 is therefore
didactic rather than historical,
and it is bootless to ponder such questions
as whether the flood covered the whole earth
or destroyed all men.

Regardless of how you interpret the flood story,
its main point remains the same.
The biblical writer wishes to teach
that sin leads people down a one-way street:
destruction of themselves and the world.
God, alone, can save them.

This clay tablet from Nineveh
is part of a series
on which was found "The Epic of Gilgamesh."

Gilgamesh Epic

Archaeologists have found other flood stories
similar to the one in the Bible.
One such story
forms part of "The Epic of Gilgamesh,"
thought by many experts
to be the oldest recorded story.

Gilgamesh is a young king of Uruk.
He is plunged into deep sadness
when his closest friend, Enkidu, dies.
The sadness stems not only from the loss,
but also from the realization
that he too must die some day.

Then Gilgamesh learns of an ancestor
who lives in the "land of the immortals."
Of all human beings, he alone has cheated death.
But the land lies beyond the Bitter River—
outside the limits to the human world.

Gilgamesh sets out to find his relative.
After unbelievable ordeals,
the youth reaches the Bitter River
and crosses it into the land of the immortals.
There he finds his relative.

"I am Gilgamesh; you are my ancestor.
I have come far to seek your help.
I am told that you know the secret of life and death."

The old ancestor then tells his story.
He survived a great flood that covered the earth.
Because he survived,
the gods granted him immortality.
But no man can achieve this gift on his own.

But the old man tells Gilgamesh of a magic plant
that grows at the bottom of the Bitter River.
If man could ever find it and eat it,
he would never die.

The youth starts back across the river.
Reaching midstream,
he strips and dives into the deep waters.

When he surfaces,
he holds the magic plant in his hand.

Now, Gilgamesh begins the long journey home.
One day he stops to bathe in a lake.
While he does,
a snake steals the magic plant.
Deeply saddened, Gilgamesh resumes his journey.

When the youth arrives home, he can find no rest.
His heart is troubled,
and he decides to set off on another journey—
this time to try to discover where Enkidu
resides in death.

Friendly gods direct him to the hidden
"gate to the underworld," inside which the youth
finds his friend and learns the fate of the dead.

Fearful, Gilgamesh starts to run away.
Then he stops. After several minutes of thought,
he walks over to his friend,
looks at him, and lies down beside him in death.

11

Still Falls the Rain

The chain of biblical sin stories
climaxes with the Tower of Babel incident.
This event takes place after Noah's descendants
have repopulated the earth. They say:

*"Now, let's build a city with a tower
that reaches the sky,
so that we can make a name for ourselves."*

GENESIS 11:4

But the project stops before it can be completed.
God confuses the speech of the people,
and they are forced to stop work.
The biblical writer ends his story saying:

*And from there he scattered them
all over the earth.*

GENESIS 11:9

FINAL ALIENATION

Again, archaeologists have illuminated this story.
The biblical writer has in mind a ziggurat.
The top of this pyramidlike structure
was intended as a meeting place for gods and people.

The writer uses the ziggurat as a pride-symbol
of people's desire "to be like the gods."
Recall the snake's promise to Eve.

Some think that the original purpose of the story
was to explain the origin of nations and languages.
But within the context of a sin-story sequence,
the biblical writer gives the story a deeper meaning.
Its purpose is to show that sin alienates not only

person from self	(Adam's nakedness),
person from God	(Adam's hiding),
person from nature	(curse),
person from person	(Cain's violence), but also
nation from nation	(Babel story).

When we finish reading the chain of sin stories
of Genesis 3-11, we get this bleak impression.
People, individually and collectively,
are trapped in a giant whirlpool of sin.
Every person born, regardless of how noble,
is doomed to be caught
in its all-engulfing, destructive power.

This biblical picture is strikingly similar
to a newspaperwoman's impression
after her visit to a Nazi concentration camp.

Still Falls the Rain

You wouldn't expect
the dean of American psychiatry
to get up and start talking about sin.
But that's what Dr. Karl Menninger does
in his book *Whatever Became of Sin?*

Sin Comes Back on the Scene
GEORGE HIGGINS

Dr. Menninger
is deeply troubled about what he calls
"sin as collective irresponsibility."
He is bothered not only by individuals
who refuse to acknowledge personal sin,
but also by groups—even whole nations—
who refuse to admit "collective sins."

Discrimination,
war, polluting the environment,
ignoring the poor in ghettoes,
exploiting migrant workers—
these are some of the things that scare him.
He says that in "group sins,"
no single individual
considers himself responsible or guilty.

I kept thinking of that statement
as I was watching the CBS two-hour special
"The Autobiography of Miss Jane Pittman." . . .

A few days after the Jane Pittman show,
CBS scored again with a dramatic presentation,
written by playwright Tennessee Williams,
on the dreadful plight of migrant workers. . . .

Once again we were led
to think about "sin as collective irresponsibility"
and about our own personal involvement,
however indirect or marginal.

"When I surveyed Dachau," she said,
"my soul trembled within me."

What made her tremble was not just the memory
of the crimes that took place there.
Rather, it was the terrifying fact that
good prisoners helped commit these crimes.
Read her own words:

The Lesson of Dachau
DOROTHY THOMPSON

Does the world realize
that some of the worst crimes in these camps
were committed by inmates?

Reduce a man to the lowest level . . .
you can make him . . .
the executioner of his fellow victims . . .
the scientific experimenter on human bodies. . . .

The physicians who inoculated
concentration-camp victims with malaria . . .
were prisoners of the Nazis themselves. . . .
By assisting in the extermination
of their fellow prisoners,
they prolonged the lease on their own lives. . . .

They came into the camps because they believed . . .
in democracy, or communism, or because
they were patriots, loving Poland, or France. . . .

Under the pressure of life or death—
life for an extra week, or an extra day—
no beliefs of economic theories,
or physician's Hippocratic oaths,
or national affiliations were decisive.

Viktor Frankl, Europe's most noted psychiatrist,
and a prisoner of these camps himself,
makes one exception of Thompson's observations.

In *Man's Search for Meaning,*
he says that when a prisoner had a deep,
authentic faith, he was in touch with something
that enabled him to maintain his humanity.

Barbed-wire fence at Auschwitz.

The conclusion we draw from the sin stories
of Genesis 3-11 is this:
Given people as they are (vulnerable beings),
and given the world as it is (a corruptible power),
neither people nor the world can survive
unless God himself intervenes
in some drastic way to save them.

SITUATION TODAY

Four thousand years after Genesis,
a modern poet writes soberly:

Still Falls the Rain
EDITH SITWELL

Still falls the Rain—
Dark as the world of man, black as our loss—
Blind as the nineteen hundred and forty nails
Upon the Cross. . . .

Still falls the Rain
In the Field of Blood where the small hopes breed and
the human brain
Nurtures its greed, that worm with the brow of
Cain. . . .

It Can Work

The light-hearted film *Oh, God!*
contains this thought-provoking scene.

Oh, God!
AVERY CORMAN

GOD   *Looking back . . . I made a few mistakes.*
Giraffes. It was a good thought,
but it didn't really work out.
Avocados—on that I made the pit too big.
There are things that worked pretty good.
Photosynthesis is a big favorite of mine.
Spring is nice. . . .

AVERY   *But what about* Man? *. . .*
The future of the planet?

GOD   *It's a good question. . . . I don't get into that.*
Of course I hope you make it. I mean,
I'm a real fan. . . .

AVERY   *You're God. You can protect our future,*
alleviate suffering, work miracles! . . .
You have the power to intervene,
to help us in emergencies. . . .
So you've decided to just let us stumble
along and never do a thing to help? . . .

GOD   *Such a smart fella*
and you missed the point.
Now write this down, word for word. . . .
The thing is . . . God lives! . . .
If God was dead or never was,
then you should be plenty worried. . . .
But God is here
and He's giving you a guarantee.
I'm telling you that I set all this up for you
and made it so it can work.
Only the deal is you have *to work at it*
and you shouldn't look to me to do it for you. . . .
Tell them what I said. God says they got
everything they need—it's all built in,
and on that I give my word.

43

Mediterranean Sea

TANIS

Rosetta

EGYPT

GOSHEN

● PITHOM

Sphinx

● CAIRO

Lake Timsah

Great Pyramid

Nile River

Gulf of Suez

Tell el Amarna

THEBES ●

Karnak Temple

Aswan Dam
Elephantine Island

King Tut's Tomb
Merneptah Temple

Abu Simbel

Time Chart

2000 BC	**ziggurat built at Ur**
1750	**Hyksos overrun Egypt** **Hammurabi heads Babylonian empire** **Abraham leaves Ur**
1590	**Hittites invade Mesopotamia**
1567	**Egypt ousts Hyksos** **Joseph in Egypt**
1304	**Rameses II begins long reign**
1300	**Israelite Slavery**
1240	**Israelite Exodus**
1200	**Israelites at Promised Land** **Egypt declines in power**

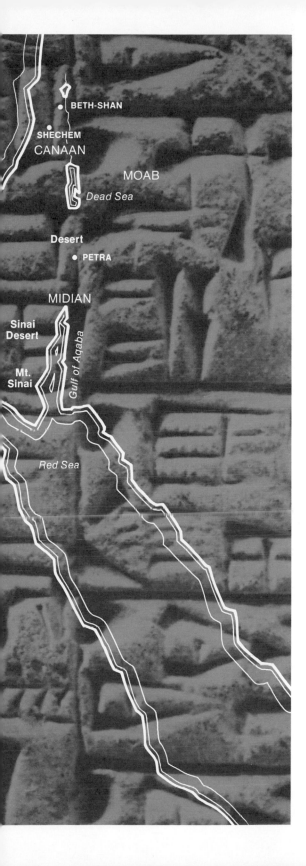

FOLK HISTORY
PEOPLEHOOD

Books

Genesis 12-50
Exodus
Leviticus
Numbers
Deuteronomy

12
The Sheik Who Said "Yes"

Adam's sin,
Cain's murder of Abel,
the declining ages of people,
the "supernatural beings" and the "human women,"
the flood, the Tower of Babel—
when we finish reading these sin stories,
we get the impression that sin is spreading
like a cancer. People are doomed.

It is against this bleak backdrop
that the biblical writer introduces Abram in
chapter 12 of the Book of Genesis.
This desert sheik
is destined to be the father of a new people
who will be the vehicle
of a dramatic intervention by God in the world.

With Abram's appearance, the Book of Genesis
makes a dramatic switch in content and style.
The content of the first 11 chapters
is biblical prehistory or protohistory:
the origin of the world, life, people, good, evil.
The literary style of these chapters
is highly stylized and charged with symbolism.

Beginning with chapter 12,
the writing style and content change.
The literary style carries with it
the flavor of actual historical happenings.
The content takes on a historical continuity.
It begins with Abram in his native city of Ur.

BEHISTUN
A trilingual inscription on rock cliffs here
provided the key to decoding cuneiform writing.
It opened new doors to a world
long buried beneath the sands of history.

UR
Art objects and clay tablets
found here have been deciphered and bring alive
the world into which Abraham was born.

MARI
Archaeologists unearthed a palace library
of thousands of clay tablets here. The tablets
add new brush strokes to the picture of everyday life
in Abraham's time.

NUZI
Clay tablets found here clarify practices described,
but not explained, in the Bible—
e.g., Hagar and Abraham (Genesis 16:1-3).

SUSA
An inscribed stone pillar, the Law Code of Hammurabi,
was discovered at this location.
It describes the rights of citizens who traded
in the same marketplaces as did Abraham.

Terah took his son Abram,
his grandson Lot . . .
his daughter-in-law Sarai, Abram's wife,
and . . . left the city of Ur in Babylon
to go to the land of Canaan.
They went as far as Haran
and settled there.
Terah died there.

GENESIS 11:31-32

EXCAVATED GRAVEYARD

Abram's world is no longer a faceless world
buried under the debris of history.
Archaeologists have exhumed the cities
of Abram's time and made them retell their stories
and well-kept secrets.

Terah means "moon."
Since Ur was the center of a moon cult,
his ancestors were probably moon worshipers.

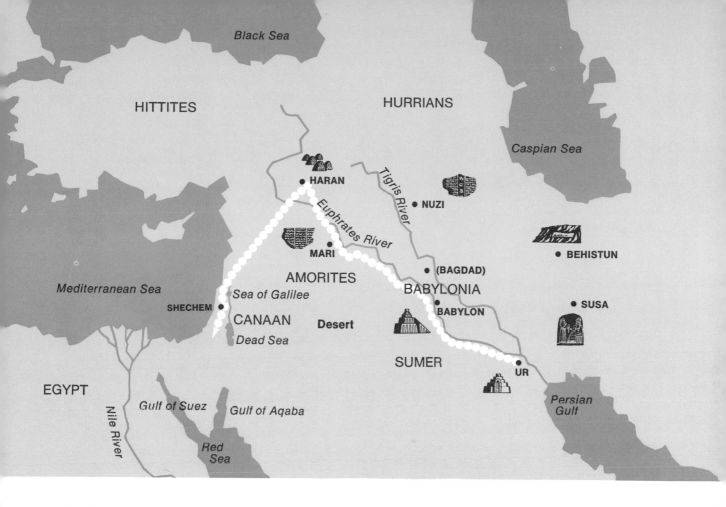

Black Sea

HITTITES

HURRIANS

Caspian Sea

Tigris River

HARAN

NUZI

Euphrates River

BEHISTUN

MARI

(BAGDAD)

AMORITES

BABYLONIA

Mediterranean Sea

Sea of Galilee

BABYLON

SUSA

SHECHEM

CANAAN

Desert

Dead Sea

SUMER

UR

EGYPT

Nile River

Gulf of Suez

Gulf of Aqaba

Persian Gulf

Red Sea

Archaeology shows
that Abram's moon-worshiping world of 2000 B.C.
bore similarities
to our moon-landing world of A.D. 2000.
It too was a period of radical change.
For one thing, Hurrians from the north
introduced new weapons of war—
the chariot and an improved fighting bow.

Second, seminomadic tribes, Amorites
("Westerners"), began to change their life-style.
They came in out of the desert
and began to settle in towns.
Abram's ancestors probably belonged to these
tribes before they settled in Ur.

Ur was once the capital of ancient Sumer,
where the first great civilization
was born over 5,000 years ago.
Today, Ur lies in an excavated graveyard

Once proudly called "Hill of Heaven,"
this crumbling mound of brick is all that remains
of the beautiful ziggurat that marks the spot
where Abraham began his history-making journey.
Desert storms, scavengers, and amateur archaeologists
have wrecked its upper levels, once crowned
with a temple to the moon god, Nanna-Sin.

47

Writing began in Mesopotamia
out of a need to keep records.
The earliest writing on clay tablets
followed columns that read
from top to bottom and right to left.
The symbols stood for
concrete objects (picture writing).

Cuneiform writing
developed from picture writing
as a kind of early shorthand.
At first
the cuneiform symbols
stood for abstract ideas
and then for human sounds.
This Assyrian tablet,
pre-dating Abraham,
is an example of early
cuneiform writing.

near the northern tip of the Persian Gulf.
The Bagdad railroad still stops there
for history-minded tourists.
Towering over the site, like a giant tombstone,
are the crumbling remains of an ancient ziggurat.
Atop this man-made mountain of masonry
once stood a temple dedicated to the moon god.

Archaeologists began digging at Ur around 1845.
Not until the 1920s, however, did Ur come alive
under the excavations of Sir Leonard Woolley,
the British archaeologist.

Among his discoveries
was a tomb chamber dating from 2500 B.C.
It contained 74 skeletons, still ornately clothed,
teams of oxen, still in harness,
tableware, and musical instruments.
Apparently, the whole group was buried alive
to join their nobleman master in death.

48

STRANGE WRITING

Also found were thousands of clay tablets.
As early as 1800, similar tablets were discovered
by adventure seekers in the Near East.

At first, no one could read the odd wedge-shaped
(cuneiform) writing on these tablets.
Tourists and museum visitors jokingly referred to it
as "bird tracks on wet sand."

The dramatic breakthrough in translating it
came when similar "bird tracks" were found,
cut into a rock cliff at Behistun in Persia.
Paralleling the cuneiform inscription were two
other inscriptions, both in different languages.
Apparently, the same text
was repeated in three different languages,
a practice not uncommon among ancient peoples.

Whereas pictorial writing
was done with a pointed stylus
drawn across soft clay,
cuneiform writing
was done with a triangular stylus
pressed into the clay.
The result was a series
of wedge-shaped impressions.

The above impressions were made by rolling cylinder stones
across soft clay. The stones, from which these impressions
were made, are shown at the right.
They pre date Abraham by over 1,000 years.

In 1835, Henry Rawlinson, a daring Englishman,
risked his life on the face of the 340-foot cliff
to make an exact copy of the three inscriptions.
Playing one against the other,
he broke the mysterious code 15 years later.
The inscription turned out to be
a report of the feats of Darius the Great,
the Persian king (521-486 B.C.).

At last the key to the wedge-shaped writing
was found.
Scholars began to read the tablets.
A library of Sumerian poetry, mythology,
and commercial documents leaped to life.
Suddenly, Ur and other Sumerian cities
burst into "living color."

There were even hundreds of clay tablets
which apparently had been used
by Sumerian schoolboys as copybooks.

The World of Abraham
SAMUEL NOAH KRAMER

We have found hundreds of their practice tablets,
ranging from the sorry scratches of beginners
to the elegant copybooks of young men
about to "graduate." One delightfully human tablet
tells of a boy's bad day:

"When I awoke early in the morning,
I faced my mother and said to her,
'Give me my lunch, I want to go to school.'
My mother gave me two rolls and I set out. . . .
In school the monitor in charge said to me,
'Why are you late?'
Afraid and with pounding heart, I entered
before my teacher and made a respectful curtsy."

It did no good. A marked boy all day,
he took canings for talking, for standing,

for poor stylusmanship.
We are quite sure of the rendering of caning,
since the sign consists of stick *and* flesh.

The clay tablets also tell us
that Sumerian mathematicians solved equations,
calculated square and cube roots,
and even the areas of circles and rectangles.
They also used our system
of the 360-degree circle and the 60-minute hour.
Abraham lived in this civilization.

MYSTERIOUS ENCOUNTER

Abram grew up in Sumer.
He walked along the streets of Ur
and bartered with its peddlers and merchants.

Eventually, however, Abram's father
moved his family up the Euphrates River to Haran.
At this city, which archaeologists have discovered,
Abram became the family head at his father's death.

At Haran, Abram underwent a religious experience
that rocked his own life and all history as well.
Here, for the first time in history,
a human being encountered the mysterious reality
that people now call God.

Abram's experience
was so profound and so unmistakable
that he responded to it without question.

The LORD said to Abram,
"Leave your country, your relatives,
and your father's home, and go to a land
that I am going to show you. . . ."

. . . Abram took his wife Sarai,
his nephew Lot,
and all the wealth and all the slaves
they had acquired in Haran,
and they started out for the land of Canaan.

When they arrived in Canaan,

Abram traveled through the land until
he came to . . . the holy place at Shechem.

GENESIS 12:1–6

This experience is referred to as Abram's *call.*
It begins a pattern that repeats itself over and over
again in biblical history: certain people
experience an inner summons
to leave all and to embark upon a mission
that God reveals to them only gradually.
Abram was the first of a long line of people
called by God.

STORY OF SINHUE

When Abram pitched his tents at Canaan,
it was sparsely settled and controlled by Egypt.
The pattern of life Abram settled down to in Canaan
is described not only in the Bible,
but also in old Egyptian documents.

One fascinating record is the "Story of Sinhue."
Written in Egyptian script, it tells of a nobleman
who fled from Egypt to the hills of Canaan
to save his life.

Hiding in tall bushes,
Sinhue passed the Egyptian frontier at night.
In the desert, he nearly died of thirst.
His throat became "hot with the taste of death,"
but he was found and saved by a Bedouin chief.
Eventually, Sinhue reached Canaan and freedom.

The Sinhue story confirms with striking accuracy
many of the biblical details
about daily life in Canaan. Sinhue says:

It was a good land. . . .
Figs grew and so did grapes.
Wine was more available than water.
We had plenty of honey and olives.
There was every kind of fruit tree.

13

A Mystery Unfolds

Arab boy in Jerusalem.
He and his ancestors claim descendancy
from Ishmael, Abraham's son by Hagar.

Abram settled down to his new life in Canaan.
What lay ahead for him was shrouded in mystery.
All he could do was to wait for further revelation
from the strange "new God" he had encountered
in Haran.

At this point in Abram's life, his wife, Sarai,
was childless.
Sarai had, however, a maid servant called Hagar.
One day Sarai approached Abram.

SARAI   *The LORD has kept me*
         from having children. Why don't you
         sleep with my slave girl?
         Perhaps she can have a child for me.

NARRATOR *Abram agreed. . . .*
         Hagar bore Abram a son,
         and he named him Ishmael.

GENESIS 16:2, 15

Clay tablets found at Nuzi in Iraq
help us to understand this puzzling passage.
Among the tablets was an old marriage contract
stating that a sterile wife had to provide her husband
with a substitute wife for childbearing.
Thus Sarai, who appeared to be sterile,
merely carried out her obligation to Abram.

Sometime after this event, Abram experienced
a second encounter with the unknown God.

GOD   *Do not be afraid, Abram.*
         I will shield you from danger
         and give you a great reward. . . .

         Look at the sky and try to count
         the stars; you will have
         as many descendants as that. . . .

ABRAM   *Sovereign LORD, how can I know*
         that it will be mine?

GOD   *Bring me a cow, a goat, and a ram,*
         each of them three years old,
         and a dove and a pigeon.

NARRATOR *Abram brought the animals . . .*
         cut them in half, and placed
         the halves opposite each other . . .
         but he did not cut up the birds.

51

*Vultures came down on the bodies,
but Abram drove them off.*

*When the sun was going down,
Abram fell into a deep sleep,
and fear . . . came over him. . . .*

*A flaming torch suddenly appeared
and passed between the pieces. . . .
The LORD made a covenant with Abram.*

GOD   *I promise to give your descendants
all this land.*

GENESIS 15:1–18

The meaning of this ancient rite is preserved
for us in the Bible.

*[They] made a covenant with me by walking
between the two halves of a bull. . . .
But they broke the covenant. . . .
So I will do to these people
what they did to the bull.*

JEREMIAH 34:18–19

The parties passing between the cut-up animal
signified that they would rather die a death
as violent as did the animal,
than break their agreement.

Abram's second experience puts into focus
the purpose for which God called him.
He is to be the father of a people,
who will receive a land, grow into a great nation,
and enjoy a unique relationship to God.

The unusual ceremony
that is depicted as sealing this promise to Abram
was known as cutting a covenant.

Unlike modern nations and peoples,
ancients rarely signed treaties or contracts.
Rather, they solemnized important agreements
by a symbolic covenant rite.

The two parties split an animal down the middle.
Laying the two sides opposite each other,
they walked between them.

THIRD EXPERIENCE

Sometime later, Abram encountered God again.

GOD   *I am the Almighty God.
Obey me
and always do what is right. . . .
Your name will no longer be Abram,
but Abraham,
because I am making you
the ancestor of many nations. . . .*

*You and your descendants
must all agree to circumcise
every male among you . . .
a physical sign to show that
my covenant with you
is everlasting. . . .*

Moving from place to place and setting up camp
under open skies, this modern Sinai Bedouin
lives much in the same fashion as did Abraham over
3,500 years ago.

*You must
no longer call your wife Sarai;
from now on
her name is Sarah.
I will bless her,
and I will give you a son by her. . . .
You will name him Isaac. . . .*

NARRATOR   *When God
finished speaking to Abraham,
he left him.*

GENESIS 17:1-22

Thus, by a series of progressive encounters,
God revealed himself to Abraham.

BIRTH OF ISAAC

*[Sarah] became pregnant
and bore a son to Abraham. . . .
Abraham named him Isaac,
and when Isaac was eight days old,
Abraham circumcised him. . . .
On the day that he was weaned,
Abraham gave a great feast.*

*One day Ishmael, whom Hagar
the Egyptian had borne to Abraham,
was playing with Sarah's son Isaac.
Sarah saw them and said to Abraham,
"Send this slave girl and her son away. . . ."
This troubled Abraham very much. . . .
But God said to Abraham,
"Don't be worried
about the boy and your slave Hagar.
Do whatever Sarah tells you,
because it is through Isaac
that you will have the descendants
I have promised.
I will also give many children
to the son of the slave girl,
so that they will become a nation.
He too is your son."*

GENESIS 21:2-13

Names and Naming

Names were important in ancient times.
They did more than arbitrarily identify a person.
They said something significant about the person.

A change in a person's name
indicated an important change in the person.
God's action in the lives of Abram and Sarai
changed them so radically
that their original names no longer identified
the new persons they had become.

Similarly, the power to name
also indicated something important.
It symbolized control
over the person or thing named.
Recall the beautiful scene
in the second creation story in Genesis
where God parades the animals and the birds
before Adam to be named.

*So he took some soil from the ground
and formed all the animals
and all the birds.
Then he brought them to the man
to see what he would name them;
and that is how they all got their names.
So the man named all the birds
and all the animals.*

GENESIS 2:19-20

Adam's naming of the animals and the birds
was symbolic.
It was the biblical writer's way of saying
that God intended Adam
to exercise dominion over them.

53

14
Trial By Fire

NARRATOR   *Some time later*
God tested Abraham. . . .

GOD   *Take your son,*
your only son, Isaac,
whom you love so much. . . .
Offer him as a sacrifice to me.

NARRATOR   *. . . Abraham cut some wood. . . .*
Abraham made Isaac carry the wood
for the sacrifice,
and he himself carried a knife
and live coals for starting the fire.

GENESIS 22:1-6

It is difficult for the modern mind to realize
that human sacrifice was not entirely unusual
in Abraham's time.
Here's how a modern novelist reconstructs
the atmosphere that surrounded the event.

The Source
JAMES A. MICHENER

The last child was a boy of nearly three . . .
he was old enough to understand . . .
and when they lifted him to the god
he screamed, trying to hold on to the stone fingers
and save himself,
but the priests pulled away his small, clutching hands,
and with a violent push
sent him tumbling into the flaming mouth.

As soon as the boy disappeared,
wailing in fiery smoke,

the mood of the temple changed.
The god Melak was forgotten;
his fires were allowed to die down
and his priests turned to other important matters.
Drums resumed their beat—
this time in livelier rhythms—and trumpets sounded.
The people of Makor,
satisfied that their new god would protect them . . .
gathered about the steps of the temple. . . .

[The people had adopted the new god]
partly because his demands upon them were severe,
as if this proved his power,
and partly because they had grown
somewhat contemptuous of their local gods
precisely because they were not demanding.
Melak, with his fiery celebrations,
had not been forced upon the town;
the town had sought him out
as the fulfillment of a felt need,
and the more demanding he became,
the more they respected him.

No recent logic in Makor was so persuasive as that
of the priests after the destruction of the town:
"You were content to give damaged sons to Melak
and in return he gave you damaged protection."
Equally acceptable
was the progression whereby Melak's appetite
had expanded from the blood of a pigeon
to the burning of a dead sheep
to the immolation of living children,
for with each extension of his appetite
he became more powerful and therefore
more pleasing to the people he tyrannized. . . .

Furthermore, the cult of human sacrifice
was of itself not abominable,
nor did it lead to the brutalization of society:
lives were lost
which could have been otherwise utilized,
but . . . excessive numbers were not killed,
nor did the rites in which they died
contaminate the mind.

In fact, there was something grave and stately
in the picture of a father willing to sacrifice
his first-born son as his ultimate gift
for the salvation of a community.

ABRAHAM OBEYS

Thus, the sacrifice of a son
was not a bizarre event in Abraham's time.
Still, it pained Abraham's heart
and confused his mind.
What about God's promise:
"It is through Isaac that you will have descendants"?
Nevertheless, Abraham obeyed.

NARRATOR   *When they came to the place*
which God had told him about,
Abraham built an altar. . . .

ANGEL   *Abraham, Abraham! . . .*
Don't hurt the boy. . . .
Now I know that you have obedient
reverence for God,
because you have not kept back
your only son from me.

GENESIS 22:9-12

New Testament writers
explained Abraham's trial by fire this way:

It was faith that made Abraham obey
when God called him. . . .
He left his own country
without knowing where he was going. . . .

It was faith that made Abraham
offer his son Isaac as a sacrifice
when God put Abraham to the test. . . .
God had said to him, "It is through Isaac
that you will have the descendants I promised."
Abraham reckoned that God was able
to raise Isaac from death—and, so to speak,
Abraham did receive Isaac back from death.

HEBREWS 11:8, 17-19

Upon reflection, Abraham and his descendants
regarded the Isaac episode as revelation
that God did not want human sacrifice.
It could never be an option in Hebrew worship.

DYNAMIC OF BIBLICAL FAITH

Abraham's test of faith underscores
several key points concerning biblical faith.

First, it is not something totally intellectual,
like finding the answer to a math problem.
The old priest in *The Exorcist* came close
to the idea of biblical faith when he said:

I think belief in God is not a matter of reason at all;
I think it finally is a matter of love,
accepting the possibility that God could love us.

Biblical faith is loving trust in God—
even in the face of intellectual difficulties.
For example, Abraham's human reason
told him that Isaac was the vehicle
by which God's promise to him would be carried out.
But then he was told to sacrifice Isaac.
Abraham had to make a choice.
Had he relied solely on reason,
he would have set aside his trust.
But he did not. He chose to trust,
even in the face of deep intellectual turmoil.

Second,
because biblical faith involved loving trust,
it also demanded personal risk.
An everyday example illustrates this point.
When two people marry, neither is absolutely sure
the other will remain faithful,
should major difficulties arise.
In other words, they have no intellectual certainty.

Biblical faith was something like this.
It always involved a knowledge gap
that loving trust alone could bridge.

I Believe

On a cellar wall in Cologne,
an unknown World War II fugitive from the Nazis
left a beautiful testimony of faith.

Workers found the inscription
while clearing away debris and rubble
from a bombed-out house
that once stood on the cellar walls.
The inscription read:

I believe in the sun
*   even when it is not shining.*
I believe in love
*   even when I do not feel it.*
I believe in God
*   even when he is silent.*

Third,
biblical faith is pictured as an ongoing process.
The biggest mistake a person could make
was to think that some day he would "get the faith"
and never have any more questions about it.

Psychology makes an interesting observation here.
Consider this statement by a young man.

One day,
I decided to make God the center of my life.
This decision gave me unbelievable peace and joy.
But two days later,
I did something that no believer would ever do.
I was totally discouraged and concluded
that I had not really committed myself to God at all.
I had only psyched myself into believing I had.

But then I realized something important.
I realized that when we commit ourselves to God,
we commit only that part of ourselves
which we are aware of at the moment.
That's all any man can do.

Psychology tells us that the greater part of ourselves
lies below our consciousness.
It surfaces only gradually with each new experience.
This means that people constantly evolve
and change as persons.

Thus, faith-commitment is never achieved
by one decision on one occasion.
It is an ongoing process.

Finally, biblical faith involved periods of darkness.
It had a way of going in and out of focus.
Many modern believers report a similar experience.
There are times when their faith
seems to go behind a cloud, even seems lost.
They undergo a "dark night of the soul,"
a kind of "trial by fire" as Abraham experienced.

The agony this kind of experience can cause
has been graphically illustrated in a modern novel.

The Devil's Advocate
MORRIS WEST

How does one come back to belief? . . .
I tried to reason myself back to a first cause
and first motion, as a foundling might reason
himself back to the existence of his father.
He must have existed, all children have fathers.
But who was he?
What was his name? What did he look like?
Did he love me—
or had he forgotten me forever? . . .

I groped for Him and could not find Him.
I prayed to Him unknown and He did not answer.
I wept at night for the loss of Him.
Lost tears and fruitless grief.

Then, one day, He was there again. . . .
There are no words to record,
no stones scored with a fiery finger,
no thunders on Tabor.
I had a Father and He knew me
and the world was a house He had built for me. . . .
I had never understood till this moment
the meaning of the words "gift of faith."

Types and Figures

Alert readers note that Isaac resembles Jesus.
His father's only son, he carried the wood
of sacrifice on his shoulder, was to be sacrificed
on a hill, and was not defeated by death.

Are these resemblances coincidental?
Some say yes; others say no; many are not sure.
This much is certain.
New Testament writers occasionally drew parallels
between Old and New Testament events.
For example, Paul writes:

Just as all people die
because of their union with Adam,
in the same way all will be raised to life
because of their union with Christ. . . .
Just as we wear the likeness
of the man made of earth,
so we will wear the likeness
of the Man from heaven.

1 CORINTHIANS 15:22, 49

Jesus, himself, drew similar parallels to clarify
his mission of healing people
to save them from spiritual death. He said:

As Moses lifted up the bronze snake
on a pole in the desert,
in the same way the Son of Man
must be lifted up, so that everyone
who believes in him may have eternal life.

JOHN 3:14-15

Jesus had in mind Numbers 21:6-9,
where Israelites were dying from serpent bites.
God tells Moses to mount a serpent on a pole.
Those who look on it and believe will not die.

An Old Testament person or event
that points to a New Testament person or event
is called a "type" or "figure."
Early Christians used "types"
to try to show Jews that Jesus was the person
toward whom the Old Testament was pointing.

57

Sand and Stars

The book *Letters from the Desert,*
by Carlo Carretto,
is exactly what the title says it is:
a journal of reflections by a person
who went into the desert to learn to pray.
Like Abraham,
Carlo felt an "inner call" to leave behind
his old life and to set out on a new one.
He writes:

God's call is mysterious;
it comes in the darkness of faith.
It is so fine, so subtle,
that it is only with the deepest silence within us
that we can hear it. . . .

Three times in my life I have been aware
of this call.

The first one brought about my conversion
when I was eighteen years old. . . .

In Lent a mission came to the town.
I attended it but what I remember most of all
was how boring and outdated the sermons were.
It certainly wasn't the words
which shook my state of apathy and sin.
But when I knelt before an old missionary—
I remember how direct his look was
and how simple. . . .

From that day on I knew I was a Christian,
and was aware that a completely new life
had been opened up for me.

The second time, when I was twenty-three,
I was thinking of getting married.
It never occurred to me
that I should do anything else. . . .

I was praying in an empty church where . . .
I heard the same voice that I had heard
during my confession with the old missionary.
"Marriage is not for you.
You will offer your life to me. . . ."

Many years passed. . . .

Then, when I was forty-four years old,
there occurred the most serious call of my life:
the call to the contemplative life.
I experienced it deeply. . . .

"Leave everything
and come with me into the desert.
It is not your acts and deeds I want;
I want your prayer, your love.". . .

I went into the desert.

Without having read the constitutions
of the Little Brothers of Jesus
I entered their congregation. . . .

When I reached El Abiod Sidi Seik
for the novitiate, my novice master told me
with the perfect calm of a man who had lived
twenty years in the desert:
"Il faute faire une coupure, Carlo."
I knew what kind of cutting he was talking about. . . .

In my bag I had kept a thick notebook,
containing the addresses of my old friends. . . .

I took the address book,
which for me was the last tie with the past,
and burnt it behind a dune. . . .

I can still see the black ashes of the notebook
being swept away into the distance
by the winds of the Sahara.

But burning an address is not the same thing
as destroying a friendship,
for that I never intended to do; on the contrary,
I have never loved nor prayed so much
for my old friends as in the solitude of the desert.

What is a life of prayer in the desert like?
Here are some insights from Carlo's book.

The first nights spent here
made me send off for books on astronomy
and maps of the sky;

and for months afterwards I spent my free time
learning a little of what was passing
over my head up there in the universe. . . .

Kneeling on the sand
I sank my eyes for hours and hours
in those wonders,
writing down my discoveries in an exercise book
like a child. . . .

Finding one's way in the desert is much easier
by night than by day. . . .
In the years which I spent in the open desert
I never once got lost, thanks to the stars.

Many times,
when searching for a Tuareg camp . . .
I lost my way
because the sun was too high in the sky.
But I waited for night and found the road again,
guided by the stars.

Elsewhere, Carlo writes:

Night came, and I could not sleep.
I left the cave and walked under the stars
above the vast desert. . . .

How dear they were to me, those stars;
how close to them the desert had brought me.
Through spending my nights in the open,
I had come to know them by their names,
then to study them,
and to get to know them one by one.
Now I could distinguish their colour, their size,
their position, their beauty.
I knew my way around them, and from them
I could calculate the time without a watch.

Summing up his reflections on the night,
Carlo writes:

"Go to a land
that I am going to show you."
Genesis 12:1

The friendly night is an image of faith. . . .

Faith is a gift of God but it needs effort
on our part if it is to bear fruit. . . .

David developed his faith by accepting to fight
against Goliath.
Gideon exercised himself in faith . . .
by going into battle
with a few soldiers against a stronger enemy.

Abraham became a giant in faith
by making the supreme act of obedience
which demanded of him the sacrifice of his son.

15

The Irreversible Word

NARRATOR   *Isaac was forty years old*
when he married Rebecca. . . .
Rebecca became pregnant . . .
and she had twin sons.
The first one was reddish . . .
so he was named Esau.
The second one was born holding
on tightly to the heel of Esau,
so he was named Jacob. . . .

The boys grew up,
and Esau became a skilled hunter,
a man who loved the outdoors,
but Jacob was a quiet man
who stayed at home.
Isaac preferred Esau,
because he enjoyed eating
the animals Esau killed,
but Rebecca preferred Jacob. . . .

Isaac was now old and . . . blind.
He sent for his older son Esau. . . .

ISAAC   *I am old and may die soon.*
Take your bow and arrows,
go out into the country,
and kill an animal for me.
Cook me some. . . .
After I have eaten it,
I will give you my final blessing
before I die.

NARRATOR   *. . . Rebecca was listening.*
So when Esau went out to hunt,
she said to Jacob,

REBECCA   *Go to the flock*
and pick out two fat young goats,
so that I can cook them. . . .
You can take it to him to eat,
and he will give you his blessing
before he dies. . . .

NARRATOR   *So he went to get them . . .*
and she cooked the kind of food
that his father liked. . . .

JACOB   *Father!*

ISAAC   *Which of my sons are you?*

JACOB   *I am your older son Esau. . . .*
Please sit up and eat . . .
so that you can give me
your blessing.

ISAAC   *How did you find it so quickly, son? . . .*
Are you really Esau?

JACOB   *I am.*

ISAAC   *Bring me some of the meat. . . .*
[Jacob obeys.]
Come closer and kiss me, son.

NARRATOR   *As he came up to kiss him,*
Isaac smelled his clothes—
so he gave him his blessing. . . .
As soon as Jacob left,
his brother Esau came in. . . .
He also cooked some tasty food. . . .

ESAU   *Please, father, sit up*
and eat some of the meat . . .
so that you can give me
your blessing.

ISAAC   *Who are you?*

ESAU   *Your older son Esau.*

NARRATOR	*Isaac began to tremble* *and shake all over.*
ISAAC	*Who was it, then, who killed* *an animal and brought it to me?* *I ate it just before you came.* *I gave him my final blessing,* *and so it is his forever.*
NARRATOR	*When Esau heard this,* *he cried out loudly and bitterly.*
ESAU	*Give me your blessing also. . . .*
ISAAC	*I have already made him* *master over you. . . .*
NARRATOR	*Esau hated Jacob,* *because his father had given Jacob* *the blessing.*
ESAU	*The time to mourn* *my father's death is near;* *then I will kill Jacob.*
NARRATOR	*When Rebecca heard* *about Esau's plan,* *she sent for Jacob.*
REBECCA	*Listen. . . .* *Go at once to my brother Laban* *in Haran.*

GENESIS 25:20–28; 27:1-43

HUMAN WORD

This episode highlights two key biblical ideas.
First, it shows how God dealt with biblical persons.
He did not dangle them from invisible puppet strings.
Nor did he program their actions.
Rather, he gave them autonomy
and worked through their free acts.

Second, Isaac's inability to withdraw his blessing
illustrates the biblical person's attitude
toward the spoken word.

Hebrews lived in a nonliterary culture.
The spoken word was important.
In business, it took the place of written contracts.
When a man gave his word,
nothing could excuse him from keeping it.

This was even more true with blessings or curses.
Once uttered, they could not be reversed.
Like an arrow shot from a bow,
they could not be stopped.

GOD'S WORD

God's word was even more powerful.
When God spoke,
nothing could keep his word from taking effect.
The creation story illustrates this.
God said, "Let there be light," and there *was* light.

We also see it in the lives of the prophets.
When God revealed his word to them,
they had to speak it. They could not hold it in.
Jeremiah says:

Your message is like a fire
burning deep within me.
I try my best to hold it in,
but can no longer keep it back.

JEREMIAH 20:9

The prophet Isaiah writes:

"My word
is like the snow and the rain
that come down from the sky. . . .
They make the crops grow
and provide seed for planting
and food to eat.
So also will be the word that I speak—
it will not fail to do . . .
everything I send it to do."

ISAIAH 55:10-11

New Testament writers portrayed God's word
as taking human form in Jesus.

61

The Word became a human being
and, full of grace and truth, lived among us.
We saw his glory,
the glory which he received
as the Father's only Son.

JOHN 1:14

God's word and its power were present in Jesus.
John described Jesus' miracles as works of power;
Luke described power going out from Jesus
to cure sick people (Luke 8:46).

After Pentecost, Jesus' power continued to reside
in those who preached in his name.
Peter said to the crowd, after he cured a cripple:

"Why are you surprised at this,
and why do you stare at us?
Do you think that it was by means
of our own power or godliness
that we made this man walk?
The God of Abraham, Isaac, and Jacob,
the God of our ancestors, has given
divine glory to his Servant Jesus. . . .
It was the power of his name
that gave strength to this lame man.
What you see and know was done by faith
in his name; it was faith in Jesus
that has made him well, as you can all see."

ACTS 3:12-16

Today, Christians still believe
that power goes out from Jesus' words in the Bible.
Consider this report
from a young man caught up in a life of evil.

The Confessions of Saint Augustine
SAINT AUGUSTINE

I threw myself on the ground
under a nearby fig tree and began to weep bitterly.
I cried out to God in words like this:
"And you, Lord! How long? How long will you
keep on being angry with me—forever?
How long will it be—tomorrow and tomorrow?

Why not now? Why not at this very hour
put an end to my evil life?"

I was crying out like this
when, suddenly, I heard the voice of a little boy
or a little girl—I couldn't tell which.
In sing-song fashion, the voice said:
"Take and read! Take and read!"

Immediately, my whole mood changed.
I asked myself if children at play
normally used such words.
I couldn't remember them ever doing so before.

I stood up. For the voice now seemed like
a divine command to open the Bible and read
the first passage that my eyes would fall upon. . . .
I got a Bible, opened it, and read:

"Let us conduct ourselves properly,
as people who live in the light of day—
no orgies or drunkenness, no immorality
or indecency, no fighting or jealousy.
But take up the weapons of the Lord Jesus
Christ and stop paying attention to your
sinful nature and satisfying its desires."
(Romans 13:13-14)

Then I stopped. There was no need to go on.
My heart suddenly became flooded with light,
vanishing the dark doubts
and leaving me with a profound peace.

Ballads and Stories

After Jacob fled from Esau,
he went in the direction of Haran.

NARRATOR *At sunset he came to a holy place*
and camped there.

He lay down to sleep,
resting his head on a stone.
He dreamed that he saw a stairway
reaching from earth to heaven,
with angels going up
and coming down on it.
And there was the LORD
standing beside him.

GOD *I am the LORD,*
the God of Abraham and Isaac.
I will give to you
and to your descendants
this land on which you are lying.
They will be as numerous
as the specks of dust on the earth.
They will extend their territory
in all directions,
and through you and your descendants
I will bless all the nations.

GENESIS 28:11-14

Jacob settled in Haran.
Later, he returned to the site of his dream.
Again, he experienced God's presence.

GOD *Your name is Jacob,*
but from now on it will be Israel. . . .
Nations will be descended from you,
and you will be
the ancestor of kings. . . .

NARRATOR *Then God left him.*
There,
where God had spoken to him,
Jacob set up a memorial stone
and consecrated it

by pouring wine and olive oil on it.
He named the place Bethel.

GENESIS 35:10-15

The colorful stories of Abraham, Isaac, and Jacob
are referred to as patriarchal narratives.
That is,
they deal with the origin of the people of Israel.
Since the stories were passed on by word of mouth,
they took the form of folk history.

Folk history is not scientific history.
Rather, it is expressed in popular form:
short stories that could be easily remembered,
folk ballads that could be sung for entertainment
and instruction.

As a result, these narratives carry the authentic
flavor of the desert, the smell of the tents,
and the atmosphere of the tribal campfire.
They are very human documents about real people.

The ability to preserve history in folk story
has been confirmed by nonbiblical sources,
especially archaeology.

Origin Stories

A part of the folk history of any people
consists in dealing with such questions as

how a group got its name,
how it developed its customs,
why it celebrates certain holidays.

For example, a Hebrew boy might ask:
Why are we called Israel?
Why do our grandfathers pilgrimage to Bethel?
Why are we 12 tribes, rather than 10?

Modern scholars place some of the stories
of Abraham, Isaac, and Jacob in this category.
The biblical writer's purpose seems to have been
to communicate background about his people,
rather than to teach specific revealed truths.

63

16

The Dreamer

Jacob settled in Canaan and had 12 sons.
Of these sons, Jacob loved Joseph best.
This favoritism led to problems.

NARRATOR   *When his brothers saw*
that their father loved Joseph
more than he loved them,
they hated their brother. . . .

One time Joseph had a dream,
and when he told his brothers
about it, they hated him even more.

JOSEPH   *Listen to the dream I had.*
We were all in the field
tying up sheaves of wheat. . . .
Yours formed a circle around mine
and bowed down to it. . . .

NARRATOR   *So they hated him even more. . . .*
[One day they plotted his death.]

BROTHERS   *Here comes that dreamer. . . .*
Let's kill him. . . . Then we will see
what becomes of his dreams. . . .

NARRATOR   *When Joseph came . . .*
they ripped off his long robe. . . .
Then they took him and threw him
into the well, which was dry.

While they were eating,
they suddenly saw a group
of Ishmaelites traveling. . . .

JUDAH   *What will we gain by killing*

our brother . . . ?
Let's sell him to these Ishmaelites. . . .

NARRATOR   *His brothers agreed.*

GENESIS 37:4–8, 19–27

Now the Ishmaelites
had taken Joseph to Egypt
and sold him to Potiphar,
one of the king's officers. . . .
Because of Joseph the LORD blessed
the household of the Egyptian.

GENESIS 39:1, 5

[One night the king of Egypt
had two disturbing dreams.]
In the morning he was worried,
so he sent for all the magicians
and wise men of Egypt . . .
but no one could explain them. . . .

The king sent for Joseph
[and told the dreams to him]. . . .

JOSEPH   *The two dreams*
mean the same thing;
God has told you
what he is going to do. . . .
There will be seven years
of great plenty in all the land. . . .
After that, there will be
seven years of famine. . . .

NARRATOR   *[Joseph] left the king's court*
and traveled all over the land.
During the seven years of plenty
[Joseph stored up grain]. . . .

The seven years of plenty . . .
came to an end,
and the seven years of famine
began. . . . So Joseph opened
all the storehouses. . . .
People came to Egypt
from all over the world to buy grain. . . .

The sons of Jacob came. . . .
When Joseph saw his brothers,
he recognized them,
but . . . they did not recognize him.
He remembered the dreams he
had dreamed about them.

GENESIS 41:8–42:9

JOSEPH   *Please come closer. . . .*
I am your brother Joseph,
whom you sold into Egypt.
Now do not be upset
or blame yourselves
because you sold me here.
It was really God
who sent me ahead of you
to save people's lives. . . .

God sent me ahead of you
to rescue you in this amazing way
and to make sure that you
and your descendants survive.
So it was not really you
who sent me here, but God. . . .

Now hurry back to my father
and tell him
that this is what his son Joseph
says:
"God has made me ruler
of all Egypt;
come to me without delay.
You can live in the region of Goshen."

GENESIS 45:4–10

NARRATOR   *The Israelites lived in Egypt*
in the region of Goshen,
where they became rich
and had many children.

GENESIS 47:27

ANCIENT EGYPT

When Joseph arrived in Egypt, we can imagine
that he stared in awe at the great pyramids.
They were already 1,000 years old in his time.

Standing in the shadow of the Pyramid of Cheops,
Joseph possibly studied it in disbelief.
Its base covered 13 acres of land, and its stone peak
pierced the sky 480 feet above the hot sand.
Over two million blocks made up its bulk,
each block weighing about two and one-half tons.

Human slaves, without the aid of machinery,
had shaped these blocks, transported them
from distant quarries, and hoisted them into place.
When Joseph saw the pyramids,
they were still veneered with polished, white stone
that reflected the rising sun like great mirrors.

Called "Joseph barns" by medieval pilgrims,
the pyramids were tombs of Egyptian kings.

Hieroglyphics

The breakthrough in deciphering hieroglyphics
came about by accident.

Some of Napoleon's engineers were digging
near the Rosetta branch of the Nile in 1799.
A worker's shovel struck a huge stone slab.
The face of the slab was covered with writing
in three different languages: hieroglyphics,
demotic (hieroglyphic script), and Greek.

When news of the Rosetta Stone reached France,
a schoolboy named Champollion
was fascinated by the discovery.

Listening wide-eyed to speculations about it,
he resolved to be the one
who would solve the mystery of hieroglyphics.

Learning Greek, Hebrew, Coptic, Syriac,
and Arabic, he undertook, in his twenties,
the task of trying to translate the Rosetta Stone.

Finally, in 1822, after years of tedious work,
Champollion broke the code.
The stone turned out to be a priestly decree
honoring Ptolemy V (196 B.C.).

Champollion died at the early age of 42,
but he left behind him the results of his studies.

Now, whole grammars of hieroglyphics
have been compiled.
With these tools,
libraries of Egyptian writings have come alive.
They shed new light on certain biblical stories.

Carved into the walls of the Pyramid of Unis
are these words:

O king . . .
you have not departed dead;
you have departed living!
You sit upon the throne of Osiris,
with scepter in hand, commanding those who live.

Perhaps the Great Sphinx also amazed Joseph.
This gigantic image, which still fascinates tourists,
was also over 1,000 years old in Joseph's day.

In 1926, archaeologists discovered that its
seven-story human head, jutting from the sand,
was attached to the body of a lion
that covered the length of a football field.
The desert sand had drifted over it and buried it.

Similarly, centuries of desert storms
have dimmed the contours of its headdress.
The cobra, coiled about its forehead—
the symbol of kingship—has all but disappeared.

No doubt Joseph also puzzled over the hieroglyphics
that blanketed the walls of Egyptian temples.
Only recently have scholars learned to read
these "sacred writings."

Legend says that while a prince rested in the shade
of the Sphinx, it spoke to him. It promised
him the throne of Egypt if he would remove
the sand that covered its base.
He did, and went on to become King Thutmose IV.

NEW INSIGHT

Joseph's rise to power in Egypt
was once surrounded with fairy-tale glamour.
How could a Hebrew slave rise so quickly
to a kcy position in Egyptian government?

We now know from Egyptian records
that around Joseph's time
Egypt fell under the heel of the Hyksos.

These invaders from the north
overran the country with horse-drawn chariots
at a time when these were not yet a part
of the Egyptian arsenal.

This makes Joseph's rise to prominence
more understandable. He rose in a period
of military and political upheaval.

Similarly, other details of the Joseph story
are supported by Egyptian records.

THE ROSETTA STONE
Champollion worked 14 years
on this trilingual inscription
found near Rosetta.
The vital clue came when he identified
Ptolemy's name among
the hieroglyphic characters (top)
and decided that the markings
should be read phonetically,
rather than pictorially
or abstractly.

Beautiful Inscriptions

Chiseled into stone, these hieroglyphic symbols
were concerned with beauty as well as practicality.
The symbols were often brilliantly painted
or coated in gold.

Thriving between 3100 B.C. and A.D. 400,
the writing flowed either horizontally or vertically.
A living creature usually pointed the direction
where one should begin reading.
Some recognizable symbols in the photo are:

sandal strap
(approximating the sound *ankh*),

milk jug (approximating the sound *me*),

bolt (approximating the sound *s*).

A papyrus, dating from 1300 B.C.,
gives detailed instructions for interpreting dreams.
Dream interpretation seems to have been
a highly respected art in Joseph's time.

Egyptian records also tell of massive famines.
One such record contains this communication
from King Zoser to a governor in Elephantine.

My heart is heavy over the great failure
of the Nile floods for the past seven years.
There is little fruit;
vegetables are in short supply;
there is a scarcity of food in general.

Everybody robs his neighbor. . . .
The storehouses have been opened,
but everything in them has been consumed.

NEW APPEAL

When we think back upon the Joseph story,
two significant points emerge.

First, God did not always act in biblical times
in superspectacular ways.
Rather, he often acted within the framework
of ordinary events and human circumstances.

Second, God did not always act through holy people.
The biblical writer makes this painfully clear.
He does not gloss over Jacob's lie to Isaac,
nor does he excuse the criminal actions
of Joseph's brothers.
He merely reports what happened, without endorsing
the actions or holding them up for imitation.

The biblical figures were everyday people.
But in spite of their defects and weaknesses,
they also had islands of honor and nobility
in their lives.
God used these to advance his work in history.
It is this kind of perspective
that is giving the Bible new appeal and credibility
among modern readers.

This solid gold mask fitted over the head and shoulders
of the mummified 18-year-old king.
The vulture and cobra headdress symbolized royalty;
the beard, divinity.

17

Go Down, Moses

Few pharaohs in Egypt's history rival Rameses II.
His mummified head is still a feature exhibit
in a Cairo museum.
As recent as 1965, Rameses was still grabbing
newspaper headlines.
The newly constructed Aswan Dam had doomed
to a watery grave the 3,000-year-old temple
he built at Abu Simbel on the Nile.

UNESCO engineers came to the rescue.
In a masterpiece of engineering, they dismantled
the temple (with its four six-story statues)
and hoisted it up a 212-foot cliff to dry ground.

It was this same Rameses II
who played such a key role in Israel's history.

*Joseph, his brothers,
and all the rest of that generation died. . . .*

*Then, a new king,
who knew nothing about Joseph,
came to power in Egypt.
He said to his people,
"These Israelites are so numerous and strong
that they are a threat to us. . . ."
So the Egyptians put slave drivers over them
to crush their spirits with hard labor.
The Israelites built the cities of Pithom
and Rameses to serve as supply centers
for the king.*

EXODUS 1:6-11

"Yes, Wonderful Things!"

Forty years before Rameses II,
the boy-king, Tutankhamen, ruled Egypt.
His royal grave was the only one missed
by tomb robbers of the 12th century.
While tunneling for another tomb,
the thieves carelessly heaped debris over it.
It was finally discovered in 1922
by British archaeologist Howard Carter.

On November 26, Carter peered into the tomb
through a tiny hole. He described what he saw:

*As my eyes grew accustomed to the light
details of the room began to emerge slowly
from the mist,
strange animals, statues, and gold. . . .
I was struck dumb with amazement,
and when Lord Carnarvon,
unable to stand the suspense any longer,
inquired anxiously, "Can you see anything?"
it was all I could do to get out the words,
"Yes, wonderful things."*

69

HEBREW SLAVERY

Modern archaeologists have unearthed
an ancient stone carving of Rameses II
that confirms the biblical report of city building.
It reads:

He built the city of Rameses
with Asiatic Semitic slaves.

In 1927, archaeologists began digging at Tanis.
Today, this Egyptian site has been identified,
almost beyond doubt,
as the ancient city of Rameses.
Visitors to the University Museum
can get an idea how the city was built.
There an ancient Egyptian tomb painting
shows slaves at work in Egyptian brickyards.

The plight of half-naked Hebrew slaves,
working under the hot desert skies,
has been vividly recreated by a modern novelist.

Moses
SHOLEM ASCH

Their bodies
showed the ribs and backbone starkly.
In the blazing sunlight the black-scorched skin,
wetted by the sweat of anguish and labor,
glistened like copper.

Their faces were dumb and careworn,
the lips thin, close-locked, parched. . . .
They did their work in dull silence;
their motion and footsteps maintained
a heavy rhythm under the threat of whips.

MOSES

Into this situation
stepped the remarkable figure of Moses.
He seems to combine rare extremes in personality.
Perhaps this is why artists find him fascinating.
How do you portray a man who, at times,

was so timid as to fear leading people,
yet, at times, was so bold as to talk back to God?

When Moses was called to lead the people,
he declined: "LORD, don't send me. . . .
I am a poor speaker" (Exodus 4:10).
Later, when God's patience wears thin with
Moses because of the people, Moses snaps:

"Why are you displeased with me? . . .
I didn't create them."

NUMBERS 11:11–12

BIRTH OF MOSES

Born at a time when Hebrew male babies were
exterminated systematically by Egyptian authorities,
Moses was saved by the ingenuity of his mother
(Exodus 2:1-10).
The story bears a similarity to the legendary birth
of Sargon of Akkad, who lived long before Moses.

Sargon's mother put him in a watertight basket
and set him afloat on the Euphrates River.
He was rescued by a peasant
and became king through the aid of a goddess.

The Greek historian Herodotus reports
similar legends surrounding Near Eastern heroes.
A remarkable escape from death in infancy
seems to have been a folk-history device
to show that a leader was approved by the gods.

Whether the rescue of Moses is factual or symbolic,
the author seeks to authenticate Moses'
divine mission to lead the people.

ADULTHOOD OF MOSES

In his twenties, Moses got into serious trouble.
He struck and killed an Egyptain foreman
for maltreating a Hebrew slave.
Fearful, he fled to Midian,
where he took up employment as a shepherd.

70

CALL OF MOSES

One day, while grazing his sheep in Midian,
he noticed a nearby bush on fire.
There wasn't anything alarming about it.
Occasionally a dried sagebrush caught fire
in the hot sun, blazed a moment, and died out.
But this time the fire didn't go out.
Moses decided to go over and find out why not.

GOD *Do not come any closer.*
Take off your sandals,
because you are standing
on holy ground.
I am the God of your ancestors,
the God of Abraham,
Isaac, and Jacob. . . .

I have seen how cruelly
my people are being treated
in Egypt. . . .
I am sending you to the king
of Egypt so that you can lead
my people out of his country.

MOSES *I am nobody.*
How can I go to the king
and bring the Israelites
out of Egypt?

GOD *I will be with you. . . .*

MOSES *When I go to the Israelites*
and say to them,
"The God of your ancestors
sent me to you," they will ask me,
"What is his name?"
So what can I tell them?

GOD *I am who I am.*
You must tell them:
"The one who is called I AM
has sent me to you." . . .
This is my name forever.

EXODUS 3:5–15

Yahweh

The expression "I am who I am"
introduces the Hebrew proper name for God.
Designated by the four letters YHWH,
it is usually translated "LORD" in English Bibles.
The original meaning of YHWH is uncertain,
but a number of scholars suggest the translation,
"I am who I am," that is,
"I cannot be named or defined."

Latter-day Jews
never pronounced the sacred name YHWH.
Thus, its original pronunciation became lost.
After some study, medieval scholars decided
to pronounce it Jehovah.

Today, no scholar holds this to be the original
Hebrew pronunciation,
even though some sects still use it.
Modern scholars,
with the newer resources at their disposal,
now believe YHWH was pronounced Yahweh.

Commenting on the burning bush,
one biblical expert makes this observation:

Understanding the Old Testament
BERNHARD W. ANDERSON

It should be read
with religious imagination and empathy,
as one would read a piece of poetry;
for it communicates a dimension of meaning
that cannot be cramped
into the limits of precise prose. . . .

Whatever Moses saw with his naked eye
was transformed into a religious "sign"
of the divine presence.
Moses' vision awakened the realization
that he was truly standing on holy ground.

He, indeed, encountered
the "unnameable" and the "undefinable."

Story in Stone

Egypt's history began around 3000 B.C.,
when Menes, the first pharaoh,
united its upper and lower "kingdoms."

Around 2600, its "Old Kingdom" period began,
and pharaohs, like Djoser,
ushered in the great age of pyramid building.

Around 2200, a north-south split occurred.
It healed around 2000,
and Egypt began its "Middle Kingdom" period.
This lasted till the Hyksos invasion in 1786.

In 1567 Ahmose I threw out the Hyksos
and launched Egypt's "New Kingdom" period.
During this great era, pharaohs like Rameses II
built monuments that boggle our imaginations.

In 1100 B.C., Egypt's day in the sun ended,
and desert sands buried its ancient glory.

Rameses II,
Egypt's greatest builder.

This temple of Amun
would swallow up St. Patrick's Cathedral in New York.
Taking 2,000 years to build, its columns
are ringed with the boasts of the pharaohs who built it.
The temple is part of a 60-acre complex at Luxor.

Close-up view before engineers began moving the
temple. The stone figure, nestled between the two feet
(center of photo), is about the size of a man.
This gives us an idea of the size of these giant figures.

72

Carved into the sandstone cliffs on the Nile at Abu Simbel,
this temple of Rameses II extended deep into the rock.
In 1965, engineers saved it from the waters of the Aswan Dam
by cutting it into 30-ton blocks and hoisting it to the dry ground.

View from inside, looking out.
Huge columns and walls,
blanketed with reliefs and inscriptions,
give the temple an atmosphere of awe.

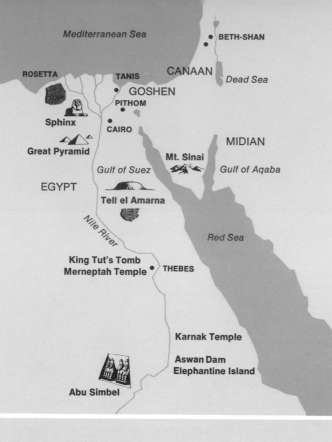

ROSETTA
Here engineers of Napoleon's army dug up
the stone slab that was the key to hieroglyphics.
A new library was opened
to fill in details concerning Hebrew life in Egypt.

TANIS
Here archaeologists found the city of Rameses.
Along with Pithom,
it was built with Hebrew slave labor.

BETH-SHAN
A stone pillar found here portrays Rameses.
Part of the inscription reads:
"He built up [the city of] Rameses
with Asiatic Semitic [Hebrew] slaves."

TELL EL AMARNA
Over 300 clay tablets found here turned out to be
14th century B.C. diplomatic correspondence.
The *Tell el Amarna Letters*
throw light on the Promised Land,
prior to Israel's invasion of it.

THEBES
It was here that Merneptah, the son of Rameses II,
left an Egyptian reference to Israel.
His hieroglyphic inscription boasts prematurely:
"Israel is laid waste."

18
The Night That Was Different

Moses returned to Egypt from Midian.
He reported his God-experience to the people
and they believed him.
Then Moses confronted Pharaoh.

MOSES   *The LORD,*
the God of Israel, says,
"Let my people go,
so that they can hold a festival
in the desert to honor me."

PHARAOH   *Who is the LORD?*
Why should I listen to him
and let Israel go?
I do not know the LORD;
and I will not let Israel go.

EXODUS 5:1–2

Nine times Moses made his demands.
Nine times Pharaoh shouted, "No!"
After each confrontation, a plague struck Egypt:

the Nile changed to blood,
frogs carpeted the land,
gnats swarmed as thick as dust,
flies buzzed everywhere,
boils infected man and beast,
animals toppled over sick,
hail splintered trees and plants,
locusts devoured what the hail missed,
darkness blanketed the land.

After all of this, Pharaoh still remained obstinate.

FINAL PLAGUE

Then the LORD said to Moses,
"I will send only one more punishment
on the king of Egypt and his people.
After that he will let you leave.
In fact, he will drive all of you out. . . ."
Moses then said to the king,
"The LORD says, 'At about midnight
I will go through Egypt,
and every first-born son in Egypt will die.'"

EXODUS 11.1-5

Then God instructed Moses
to prepare the Israelites for the tenth plague.
They must kill a lamb and smear its blood
on the outer door frame of each Israelite house.
Once this is done, they must stay indoors.

When the LORD goes through Egypt
to kill the Egyptians, he will see the blood
on the beams and the doorposts
and will not let the Angel of Death
enter your houses and kill you.

EXODUS 12:23

Moreover, the Israelites, dressed for departure,
with sandals on their feet and staff in hand,
must eat the lamb. God concludes:

"You must celebrate this day as a religious
festival . . . for all time to come. . . .

"When your children ask you,
'What does this ritual mean?'
you will answer,
'It is the sacrifice of Passover
to honor the LORD,
because he passed over
the houses of the Israelites in Egypt.
He killed the Egyptians, but spared us.'". . .

At midnight
the LORD killed all the first-born sons
in Egypt. . . .
There was loud crying throughout Egypt,
because there was not one home
in which there was not a dead son. . . .
That same night
the king sent for Moses and Aaron and said,
"Get out, you and your Israelites! . . .
Take your sheep, goats, and cattle, and leave."

EXODUS 12:14, 26-32

THE PLAGUES REVISITED

Few biblical events
have caused more discussion than the plagues.
The Old Testament does not call them "miracles,"
but "signs" (*'ot* in Hebrew).
Here are two observations concerning them.

Everyday Life in Bible Times
NATIONAL GEOGRAPHIC SOCIETY

Extraordinary as they seem,
these plagues have natural counterparts today.
Silt and microbes
sometimes pollute and redden the Nile in flood.
"The River,"
laments a text ancient in Moses' day, "is blood.
If one drinks of it,
one rejects it as human and thirsts for water."

Floodlands breed gnats and mosquitoes;
even ancients took refuge under netting.

Frogs breed when the river peaks;
hordes hop ashore from freak floods. . . .

As frog swarms die, vermin breed on the carcasses.
Pests such as the screwworm fly
inflame skin of man and beast,
sometimes killing animals.

Though hailstorms rarely hit Egypt,
locusts menace it still.
Some African swarms blanket 2,000 square miles,
stripping the land, fouling the air with excrement,
triggering epidemics as locust bodies rot.
Modern Egypt has tried traps, poisons,
even flamethrowers, but swarms still threaten
devastation about once a decade.
And the khamsin still howls—
the hot desert sandstorm that darkens spring days.

This Karnak carving shows Egyptian slaves carrying a boat. Most ancient countries had slaves. A fourth century B.C. census from Attica (Greece) lists 400,000 slaves, half of the total population.

Interestingly, the Sumerian word for "slave" is *foreigner,* suggesting the source of most slaves. Laws distinguished between native and foreign slaves. Slaves were usually owned by private individuals.

Biblical Eighth Plague Hits Again
DAVID N. NICHOL

London—*Today, more than 3,200 years later,*
this biblical eighth plague . . .
is on the march again. . . .

Restless swarms of locusts
have been extensively reported.
One recently seen in Ethiopia
covered eighty square miles.
A single swarm spotted over Africa's
Somali Republic in 1958 was measured
from the air.
It covered 400 square miles.

With an estimated density of 100,000,000
to 200,000,000 insects to the square mile
this one swarm
represented a minimum of 40 billion locusts. . . .

Though each locust weighs only about two grams,
it eats its own weight every day.
Small as this figure may be, the daily food
requirement for a swarm of 40 billion locusts . . .

amounts to about 90,000 tons.
This would be enough to feed 400,000 people
for a year on the sparse Middle Eastern diet. . . .

A single swarm may travel as far as 3,000 miles,
leaving its wake of destruction,
before it settles to begin a new breeding process.

THE POINT?

What conclusions can we draw from these reports?
Were the plagues natural events or not?
Some say yes. Others say no.

Some hold that only the timing was miraculous.
Others say that the last plague had to be miraculous,
because it bypassed the Hebrew firstborn.

All scholars agree, however,
that speculation about the plagues
risks missing the biblical writer's point:
The plagues were signs
that Yahweh was active in Israel's deliverance.

Freedom Celebration

Today, Jews still celebrate the Passover,
which commemorates their freedom.
It is highlighted by a meal called the seder,
which means "service."
Taking place in the evening,
it begins with the youngest present asking:
"Why does this night differ from all other nights?"

Thus, 3,000 years later,
Yahweh's command to the Israelites
on the eve of the tenth plague is still carried out.
Orthodox Jews still retain the original spirit
of the Passover, or Pesah.
Reform Jews, however, have broadened its meaning.
Here is one statement of the expanded spirit.

The New Haggadah
MORDECAI KAPLAN, EUGENE KOHN,
AND IRA EISENSTEIN, EDITORS

We have dedicated this festival tonight
to the dream and hope of freedom,
the dream and hope that have filled the hearts of men
from the time our Israelite ancestors
went forth out of Egypt....

But the freedom we strive for
means more than broken chains.
It means liberation from all those enslavements
that warp the spirit and blight the mind,
that destroy the soul
even when they leave the flesh alive.
For men can be enslaved in more ways than one.

Men can be enslaved to themselves....
When laziness or cowardice keeps them
from doing what they know to be the right,
when ignorance blinds them ... they are slaves.

Men can be enslaved by poverty and inequality.
When the fear of need drives them to dishonesty
and violence, to defending the guilty
and accusing the innocent—they are slaves....

Men can be enslaved by intolerance. When Jews
are forced to give up their Jewish way of life,
to abandon their Torah, to neglect
their sacred festivals, to leave off rebuilding
their ancient homeland—they are slaves.

Pesah calls upon us to put an end to all slavery!
Pesah cries out in the name of God,
"Let my people go."
Pesah summons us to freedom.

77

19
The Exodus

The Israelites left Egypt.
The Lord led them with a "pillar of cloud"
by day and a "pillar of fire" by night
(Exodus 13:21).
Meanwhile, Pharaoh regretted letting them go.
He pursued them
and caught up with them at the Red Sea.

Moses held out his hand over the sea,
and the LORD drove the sea back
with a strong east wind.
It blew all night
and turned the sea into dry land.
The water was divided, and the Israelites
went through the sea on dry ground,
with walls of water on both sides.
The Egyptians pursued them. . . .
The LORD . . . made the wheels
of their chariots get stuck,
so that they moved with great difficulty. . . .

The LORD said to Moses,
"Hold out your hand over the sea. . . ."
So Moses held out his hand over the sea,
and at daybreak the water returned
to its normal level . . .
and covered the chariots, the drivers,
and all the Egyptian army. . . .

On that day
the LORD saved the people of Israel . . .
and they had faith in the LORD
and in his servant Moses.

EXODUS 14:21–31

COLUMN OF FIRE

Those who believe that Yahweh used
ordinary events (but in an extraordinary manner)
to deal with Israel
ponder the mention of the columns of fire and clouds.
Could these guiding phenomena have been a volcano
that steered the people
through the desert toward Mount Sinai?

Most scholars, however, have found no evidence
of active volcanoes at this time in the Sinai desert.
They prefer to interpret the columns
as expressions of Israel's experience
of divine guidance during their ventures.

SEA CROSSING

The Bible says 600,000 people crossed the sea.
Most scholars think this figure is intended
in a symbolic sense, not a mathematical sense.
It merely designates a number beyond counting.

The Bible calls the crossing zone *yam suph.*
Early translators interpreted this to mean Red Sea,
but most modern scholars now believe Reed Sea
would be the more accurate description.
This would suggest that the area was a marshland,
typical of lake environs.
The biblical account seems to support this inference
when it says of the Egyptians:
"[The LORD] made the wheels of their chariots
get stuck" (Exodus 14:25).

Whether the onrushing wall of water
was an actual tidelike phenomenon
or a poetic flourish is debated.

WHAT WAS IT LIKE?

What would it be like to relive Israel's flight?
What lay between them and Mount Sinai?
These questions prompted a modern reporter
to retrace the route probably taken by Moses
and the Israelites. His account follows:

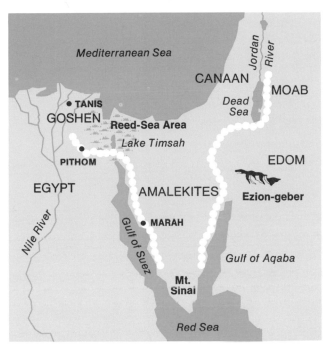

The general route followed by Moses
and the Israelites to Mount Sinai.
Sometime after the Sinai experience,
they proceeded to Moab,
where they encamped before entering the Promised Land

To Sinai and the Promised Land
JOHN PUTNAM

Two-thirty A.M.
A knock at the door and a lusty shout,
"Rise . . . we're on our way to Sinai!"
I roll out of a sagging bed . . .
and slip into sweater and slacks.

Doors slam and the murmur of voices builds
as we gather in the dining room
to gulp down bread and eggs.

We pile suitcases and food cartons
atop Suez taxis—old American cars
strengthened for desert work. . . .
We slide through dark, silent streets
to the Suez Canal and cross,

three cars at a time,
on a rattling, wheezing ferry.

Listening
to the parting of ink-black waters at the bow,
I think of those who have journeyed to Sinai
before us: Stone Age hunters,
prisoners bound for Pharaoh's mines . . .
and the children of Israel. . . .

The ferry bumped,
and we stepped ashore on Sinai's fabled sands. . . .
We rolled south along the coastal road. . . .
Our cars left the road
and soon trailed plumes of desert dust.
Here began the Biblical "wilderness of Sin."

On each side rose jagged peaks. . . .
Tumbleweed-like bushes clung to dust.
Dr. Raymond McLain broke the awesome silence:
"As a boy, I pictured the 'wilderness'
as a dark forest, like those I knew in Kentucky.
How different, and even more forceful,
is this wilderness of rock."

Little wonder that here the children of Israel
murmured against Moses, "for ye have brought us
forth into this wilderness, to kill this whole
assembly with hunger"(Exodus 16:3).

Semites knew this land before the Hebrews fled
this way. In these mountains
lay Pharaoh's turquoise mines. . . .
The walls of one mine bear Canaanite characters
carved by Semitic slaves.
These famous proto-Sinaitic inscriptions,
among the oldest writing in our alphabet,
date from the 15th century B.C.
From these crude pictographic symbols—
altered by Phoenicians, Greeks, and Romans—
developed the letters in which this story is written. . . .

Our caravan moved on, past rock-cut cubicles
where Christian hermits once lived
and Bedouin now bury their dead.
We stopped before a stand of willowy tamarisks.

Clouds

A popular "Peanuts" cartoon
shows Charlie Brown, Linus, and Lucy
lying on a hillside studying the sky.
Lucy says: "You can see lots of things in clouds
if you use your imagination. What do you see?"
Linus answers: "Well, those clouds there
look like a map of British Honduras.
And those over there look like Thomas Eakins,
the artist.
And that group there reminds me of the stoning
of Stephen."
Lucy is impressed: "Excellent, Linus!
What do you see, Charlie Brown?"
"Well, I was going to say I saw a ducky
and a horsie, but I changed my mind."

Clouds reminded Hebrews of God's presence
among them. For example, they recalled
God's guidance in their flight from Egypt,
when God preceded them with a cloud.
They also reminded them of God's instructions
to Moses at the foot of Mount Sinai:

"I will come to you in a thick cloud,
so that the people will hear me speaking
with you and will believe you from now on."

EXODUS 19:9

After the Sinai event, the people built
a portable shrine to house the two stone tablets
containing God's covenant agreement with them.
When it was finished, a cloud "covered it"
(Numbers 9:15).

Finally, when Solomon built the temple
in Jerusalem, a cloud descended upon it
(1 Kings 8:10).

Other biblical references to clouds
as signs of God's presence include
Exodus 34:5, Isaiah 19:1, Ezekiel 1:4,
Daniel 7:13, Matthew 17:5, Acts 1:9,
1 Thessalonians 4:17, Revelation 14:14.

"Manna trees!" shouted Otto.
"In spring insects puncture their bark,
drink the sap, and exude a clear liquid
which solidifies as a sugary globule.
This may well be the flaky substance,
fine 'as hoar frost on the ground,' which sustained
the Hebrews when they faced starvation."

Stark mountains rose before us,
only to fall away as we twisted and turned onward.
We rounded a final corner and there . . .
Mount Sinai. . . .

We . . . mounted Bedouin saddles
of wood and cloth. . . .

Halfway up we dismounted
and climbed rough steps, resting often.
Bare mountains seemed to surge around us
like storm-tossed waves. . . .
At last, we gathered at the small chapel
that marks the top and listened
to a reading of the covenant struck here
by God and His Chosen People:

"I am the Lord thy God,
which have brought thee out of the land of Egypt,
out of the house of bondage.
Thou shalt have no other gods before me. . . ."

In this awesome setting
the words of each commandment in Exodus 20
rang like hammer blows on an anvil. . . .

A few weeks later,
chatting on a hotel terrace by the Sea of Galilee,
I mentioned my trek to an Israeli acquaintance.
His eyes lit up.
He had been there too, briefly, in 1956
when Israeli paratroopers fluttered down on Sinai.
"I'm not a religious man," he mused.
"But there were archaeologists with us.
We watched them work,
and we read the Torah, and we studied the land.
And you know, it fit . . . it all fit."

Desert Days

Striking "signs" accompanied Israel's journey
from Egypt to Mount Sinai.
Seeing God's hand in this, the psalmist wrote:

He divided the sea and took them through. . . .
By day he led them with a cloud
and all night long with the light of a fire.
He split rocks open in the desert
and gave them water from the depths. . . .
And . . . he sent down birds,
as many as the grains of sand on the shore.

PSALM 78:13–15, 27

Exodus 17 describes Moses
getting water from a rock by striking it with a rod.
Some people read the episode skeptically,
until British Major C. S. Jarvis reported
seeing water gush from a limestone rock,
when a sergeant of the Sinai Camel Corps
accidentally perforated "the smooth hard crust"
with his shovel.

Similarly,
the "rain of quail" upon the camp of Israel
was once winked at by some sophisticated readers.
Once again, however, history and a knowledge
of the desert shed new light on the episode.

Geographical Twins a World Apart
DAVIS S. BOYER

Every year great migrations of quail
wing their way across the Mediterranean
and Red Seas en route between Europe and Africa.
Even today Bedouin of the Sinai peninsula
catch the exhausted birds
after their long flight over water.

A similar incident is recounted
in the histories of the Mormon pioneers.
The last refugees to leave Nauvoo, Illinois,
crossed the Mississippi River in late September
of 1846. Sick and without shelter,
they subsisted for ten days on parched corn.

Then says the History of Brigham Young,
"The Lord sent flocks of quail,
which lit . . . upon the ground within their reach,
which the saints, and even the sick
caught with their hands until they were satisfied."

The quail "in immense quantities had attempted
to cross the river," another Mormon writer added,
"but it being beyond their strength,
had dropped . . . on the bank."

What conclusion should we draw from all this?
Were the desert episodes truly miraculous,
or merely linked to natural causes?

You will find Bible readers on both sides.
One thing—the most important thing—is clear.
As Israelites recalled the chain of striking events
that marked their difficult days in the desert,
they were convinced beyond a shadow of doubt
that the guiding hand of God
was at work in their lives.

This is all that mattered to them.
In the end, it is all that matters to us, as well.

The mountains of the Sinai jut from the desert
floor like great stone altars.
They speak of
protection, danger, challenge, and mystery.

20
The Mountain Encounter

The historian shakes his head.
How did it happen?
How did a band of ex-slaves,
with no organization, no education, no apparent
way to survive, change the tide of history?
For this is exactly what Moses and the Hebrews did.

The historian shakes his head:
"How do you explain such a phenomenon?"

The biblical writer's own explanation is simple.
At the foot of a mountain in the Sinai desert,
the Israelite community encountered Yahweh.
That experience utterly transformed them.

Here's a modern journalist's firsthand report
of a visit
to the famous spot where it all happened.

Which Mountain Did Moses Climb?
GORDON GASKILL

I've seen many deserts,
but none like the gaunt tortured wasteland
sliding away under the wings of our small plane.
Somewhere down there, around 1250 B.C.,
Moses and his people made the most famous
Long March in all history. . . .
On the shore of the Gulf of Suez,
we piled into a jeep and set off. . . .

At last, 5,000 feet above sea level,
we wound up in a narrow chasm-like valley
and stopped by the walls of an ancient monastery,
St. Catherine's.
I know of no other spot
that so justifies the phrase "out of this world." . . .
Close by the southern wall of St. Catherine's,
the mountain rears up so steeply that it keeps the
monastery in shadow part of the day.
The climb to the top takes two or three hours. . . .

At the very top is a small flat area. . . .
Here, it is said, Moses lived 40 days and nights
communing with God. . . .
A Muslim mosque and tiny Christian chapel
mark the spot. The view in all directions
is stupendous: over great gulfs and deserts,
and rearing peaks of granite
that cast ever-longer purple shadows
as the sun sinks over Africa.

Next morning,
we arose so early the sky was still black.
Soon the bell of the monastery began pealing out
its morning call as it has for centuries,
33 strokes, one for each year of Jesus' life.

Around us,
people of three great faiths were waking up, too.
Christian pilgrims began making coffee.

A party of Jewish hikers
began crawling from sleeping bags,
to climb to the summit
while the morning was still fresh and cool.
Our Muslim driver began touching his head
to the ground in the first Muslim prayer of the day,
bowing toward holy Mecca. . . .

As we drove away,
the valleys and desert were still in shadow,
but the sun was rising fast out of Arabia,
and I saw its first rays strike the top
of Mount Moses to bathe it in flaming gold. . . .

Was it up there that it really happened?
Or was it on the peak . . . farther north?
Or was it one of the many other peaks
other scholars have suggested? . . .
No matter how plausibly professors argue,
the Mount Moses now fading away behind us
would remain, for most people,
the place it really happened

BIBLICAL STORY

Here is the biblical story of what happened
at Mount Sinai.

NARRATOR   *The people of Israel . . .
on the first day of the third month
after they had left Egypt . . .
set up camp
at the foot of Mount Sinai,
and Moses went up the mountain
to meet with God. . . .*

GOD   *You saw . . .
how I carried you
as an eagle carries her young
on her wings,
and brought you here to me.
Now, if you will obey me
and keep my covenant . . .
you will be my chosen people,
a people dedicated to me alone,
and you will serve me as priests.*

NARRATOR   *So Moses went down*
            and called the leaders
            of the people together
            and told them everything
            that the LORD had commanded him.

PEOPLE   *We will do everything*
            that the LORD has said. . . .

NARRATOR   *On the morning of the third day*
            there was thunder and lightning,
            a thick cloud
            appeared on the mountain,
            and a very loud trumpet blast
            was heard.
            All the people in the camp
            trembled with fear. . . .
            The LORD came down
            on the top of Mount Sinai
            and called Moses
            to the top of the mountain. . . .

GOD   *I am the LORD your God*
            who brought you out of Egypt,
            where you were slaves.

            Worship no god but me. . . .

            Do not use my name
            for evil purposes. . . .

            Observe the Sabbath
            and keep it holy. . . .

            Respect your father
            and your mother. . . .

            Do not commit murder.

            Do not commit adultery.

            Do not steal.

            Do not accuse anyone falsely.

            Do not desire
            another man's house;
            do not desire his wife . . .
            or anything else that he owns.

            EXODUS 19:1–20; 20:1–17

Moses wrote down
everything that the Lord commanded.
Early the next morning,
he built an altar at the foot of the mountain.
After sacrificing some cattle,
he read from the book of the covenant.
Then he poured
half of the animal blood on the altar
and half on the people.

MOSES   *This is the blood*
            that seals the covenant
            which the LORD made with you
            when he gave all these commands. . . .

NARRATOR   *The dazzling light*
            of the LORD's presence
            came down on the mountain.

            EXODUS 24:8, 16

84

IDENTITY AND DESTINY

This dramatic covenant experience
transformed the Israelites
from a band of ex-slaves into a chosen people.
It gave them an identity and a destiny.
Here's how one modern Jew expresses it.

Jewish Existence and Survival
WILL HERBERG

Israel is not a "natural" nation;
it is, indeed, not a nation at all
like the nations of the world.
It is a supernatural community, called into being
by God to serve his eternal purposes in history.

It is a community
created by God's special act of covenant,
first with Abraham . . .
and then, supremely, with Israel collectively
at Sinai. . . .
Apart from the covenant, Israel is as nothing
and Jewish existence a mere delusion.
The covenant is at the very heart of the Jewish
self-understanding of its own reality.

Israel experienced God at a specific point in time
and at a particular place on the globe.
This gives the religion of Israel its uniqueness.

Apart from Christianity and Islam,
which both owe their origin, in part, to Israel,
no other religion came about as did Israel's.
Other religions sprang from nature;
Israel's sprang from history.

Consistent with the conception of her origin,
Israel saw Yahweh's law not as something negative.
Rather, Israel saw it as something deeply positive.
The commandments were concrete signs

Modern Jews
celebrate the fall festival of Simchat Torah
(Rejoicing in the law).
The faces reflect the psalmist's words:
"How I love your law! . . ." (Psalm 119:97)

of God's personal love for his people.
Only in this light can modern readers appreciate
the psalmist when he prays:

How I love your law!
I think about it all day long.

PSALM 119:97

Israel saw God's law as freeing them
"from" their own ignorance and passion
and freeing them
"for" a life of love and service.

Israel's law is spelled out in the Book of
Deuteronomy with remarkable detail and clarity.
In Moses' own words,
it is not mysterious and remote.

It is not up in the sky.
You do not have to ask,
"Who will go up and bring it down for us,
so that we can hear it and obey it?"
Nor is it on the other side of the ocean.
You do not have to ask,
"Who will go across the ocean and bring it
to us, so that we may hear it and obey it?"
No, it is here with you.
You know it and can quote it, so now obey it.

DEUTERONOMY 30:12-14

Israel's law is totally uncompromising toward evil.
The law cannot tolerate it.
This is mirrored in numerous laws,
such as the following:

If one man tries to harm another
by falsely accusing him of a crime . . .
and if the man has made a false accusation
against a fellow Israelite,
he is to receive the punishment
the accused man would have received.
In this way you will get rid of this evil.

DEUTERONOMY 19:16-19

But Israel's laws also showed
deep sensitivity and humanity.

85

After a priest had admonished Israelite soldiers
to trust in Yahweh, an officer was instructed
to make this announcement before battle:

"Is there any man here
who has lost his nerve and is afraid?
If so, he is to go home. Otherwise,
he will destroy the morale of the others."

DEUTERONOMY 20:8

On several occasions,
the Bible reports that large numbers of soldiers
stepped from the ranks and did return home.

Showing similar sensitivity to human nature,
we find this law:

"When a man is newly married,
he is not to be drafted into military service
or any other public duty . . .
so that he can stay at home
and make his wife happy."

DEUTERONOMY 24:5

Finally, we find laws such as the following:

"Do not deprive foreigners and orphans
of their rights."

DEUTERONOMY 24:17

"When you have picked your olives once,
do not go back and get those that are left;
they are for the foreigners, orphans,
and widows."

DEUTERONOMY 24:20

COVENANT FORMAT

The external format of the Sinai covenant
(like God's covenant with Abraham)
took a pattern familiar to ancient peoples.
It closely paralleled pacts made between
powerful kings and lesser kings in Mesopotamia.

In these pacts (suzerainty treaties),
the greater king (suzerain) pledged certain favors
to lesser kings (vassals) who, in turn,

pledged special allegiance to the greater king.
Likewise, the blood ceremony,
by which Moses sealed a covenant,
was not an unfamiliar practice in ancient times.
A fourth-century B.C. historian has preserved
a description of the "blood ceremony"
used by Scythians.

Histories, IV
HERODOTUS

When Scythians
swear an oath or make a solemn compact,
they fill a large earthenware bowl with wine
and drop into it a little of the blood
of the two parties to the oath. . . .

Then they dip into the bowl a sword . . .
and speak a number of prayers;
lastly, the two contracting parties
and their chief followers
drink a mixture of wine and blood.

Ancient blood rites such as this
help us to understand
the symbolic action of Moses at Mount Sinai.
When Moses sprinkled half the blood on the altar
(symbol of God) and half on the people,
he was showing that a real life bond now existed
between God and Israel.

FINAL NOTE

Some students of the Bible are surprised to learn
that some religious groups
number the Ten Commandments differently.
For example, Jews regard the words
"I am the LORD your God" as the first commandment.
Most Christians treat this statement
as an introduction to the sentence that follows,
"You shall not have other gods besides me."

Jews treat the sentence
"You shall not have other gods besides me"
as the first part of the second commandment

This Jewish elder plays a *shofar*
at the conclusion of Yom Kippur.
Made from a hollow ram's horn,
it is shaped by plunging it into boiling water.
Often the horn was engraved
and a mouthpiece attached.
The shofar gives off a piercing, nonmusical sound.

which includes, for them, the words
"you shall not carve idols."

In a similar way, other variations arise.
The important thing, however,
is not the numbering of the commandments,
but the commandments themselves.

Life and Worship

The covenant experience
introduced a new life-style into Israel.
The Ten Commandments
provided the guidelines for it.
Likewise, Israel's covenant experience
introduced a new worship style among its people.
We find it described in the Book of Leviticus.
This book derived its name from the tribe of Levi.
The Levites were set apart by Moses
to serve as the priestly ministers of the people.

Indicative of Israel's new worship style
is the Day of Atonement, Yom Kippur.
This day was set aside annually to seek forgiveness
from God for the sins of the past year.
It was the only day of the year
when Aaron (or the reigning high priest)
entered the Holy of Holies, the inner sanctuary
that housed the Ark, containing the two tablets
upon which the covenant terms were inscribed.

Standing alone, behind the sanctuary curtain,
the high priest sprinkled blood
to atone for the sins of the entire community.
After this comes the "scapegoat" ceremony:

*When Aaron has finished performing the ritual
to purify the Most Holy Place . . .
he shall put both of his hands
on the goat's head
and confess over it all the evils, sins,
and rebellions of the people of Israel,
and so transfer them to the goat's head.
Then the goat is to be driven off. . . .
The goat will carry all their sins away
with him into some uninhabited land.*

LEVITICUS 16:20-22

Although this rite was externally dramatic,
the important thing was not the rite,
but the internal spirit that accompanied it.
A spirit of internal repentance and restitution
was essential.

87

21
On Eagle's Wings

An Arab saying reads:

When Allah finished making the desert
he had two lumps of clay left.
With one he made the camel;
with the other he made the palm tree.

Without the camel and the palm tree,
humans could not survive the desert.
Even with them, the desert tends to exclude people.
One of the most hostile features of the desert
is the unpredictable sandstorm.
It blows up suddenly and, just as suddenly,
vanishes into nowhere. One Sahara sandstorm
wiped out a caravan of 2,000 men and 1,800 camels.

On other occasions,
the desert is visited by rare rainstorms.
These storms leave in their wake
a lovely array of instant flowers
that spring up, bloom, and die overnight.

For all its delicate beauty, however,
the desert is a forbidding place for people.
More than any other land surface,
it jostles human pride.
It speaks to people of their human limitations.

INTO THE DESERT

Moses and the people stayed at Mount Sinai
for about a year.
Then they broke camp and set out into the desert,
in search of the land Yahweh promised them.

The desert into which the Hebrew caravans went
was made up of three regions:
stretches of sand, where nothing grew;
expanses of rock, with an occasional spring;
and patches of semiarid land, with just enough
growth to nourish sheep and goats.

This vast wilderness of sand and rock
became the stage for the 40-year-long drama
of Israelite history that now began.
The fourth book of the Bible, the Book of Numbers,
narrates it with disarming candor and honesty.

Once the Israelites penetrated the desert,
discouragement set in.
The honeymoon days of Mount Sinai quickly faded.
Any desert traveler who has experienced
the blazing heat of the Sinai can understand the
Israelite reaction. The sun beats down torridly,
and the oven-hot winds of the khamsin
take their toll on even the hardiest nomad.

This does not excuse the Israelite reaction,
but it does help us appreciate why the people
began to hanker for the green fields of the Nile delta.

"Make the tent you live in larger;
lengthen its ropes and strengthen the pegs!"
(Isaiah 54:2)
Hebrews probably lived in tents like this one,
which belongs to a modern Bedouin
of the Negeb Desert.

88

Soon, discouragement gave way to outright protest and dissatisfaction.

"In Egypt
we used to eat all the fish we wanted,
and it cost us nothing. . . .
But now our strength is gone.
There is nothing at all to eat—nothing
but this manna day after day!"

NUMBERS 11:5–6

The situation went from bad to worse,
and the people singled out Moses as their target.

"Why have you
brought us out into this wilderness?
Just so that we can die here
with our animals? . . .
There is not even any water to drink!"

NUMBERS 20:4–5

Soon, threats of rebellion were hurled at Moses.
A band of rebels confronted him to his face.

"You have gone too far! . . .
Isn't it enough
that you have brought us
out of the fertile land of Egypt
to kill us here in the wilderness?
Do you also have to lord it over us?
You certainly have not brought us
into a fertile land or given us fields
and vineyards as our possession,
and now you are trying to deceive us.
We will not come!"

NUMBERS 16:3, 13–14

Moses stood his ground.
Shortly after the confrontation,
the dissenters met with a violent death.

Rebellion was not the only problem Moses faced.
He and his people had to contend with threats
from without as well.

Foreign kings, on occasion,
refused the Israelites passage through their lands.

An oasis blooms out of rock and sand
near modern Jericho.

END OF AN ERA

Eventually, the end arrived.
After 40 years of wandering,
the Israelites emerged from the desert.
They found themselves
standing on the high plateaus of Moab.
Stretching out before them and below them
lay a luxurious valley as far as the eye could see.
It was the Promised Land.

Moses gave orders to pitch camp.
Then he called the people together for instructions
before entering the land.
The Book of Deuteronomy records the gist and spirit
of his series of instructions.
Moses explained how Israel's desert experience
was a means of testing their loyalty to Yahweh.

Remember how the LORD your God led you . . .
through the desert these past forty years,

The Biblical Way of Life

The image of a mother eagle
teaching her young ones to fly
was vividly described recently by a modern observer.

The Biblical Way of Life
BARNABAS AHERN

I shall never forget the day
that I stood on the barren plain at Petra
with its walls of blood-red rock.
Glancing up,
I saw a large bird soar out from a mountain crag.
Something dropped from its back
like a pellet of lead.
In a moment the pellet unfolded,
and I saw a little bird stretching its wings to fly.

Before long, however, the uprush of wind
proved too strong and the little bird,
once more a stone in the sky, began to drop.
In an instant the mother bird swooped down
and caught it on her back
to bear it aloft for a second trial.

This time
the young bird sustained itself longer in flight;
but once more it crumpled before the wind
and began to drop.
But the ever-present mother saved it again
for a third testing.
As before, the pellet dropped, the wings opened,
but this time the young bird flew off.

90

sending hardships to test you,
so that he might know
what you intended to do
and whether you would obey his commands.
He made you go hungry,
and then he gave you manna to eat,
food that you and your ancestors
had never eaten before.
He did this to teach you
that man must not depend on bread alone
to sustain him,
but on everything that the LORD says.

DEUTERONOMY 8:2–3

Then Moses
recited the words of this song:

"Listen closely to what I say. . . .
Your God is faithful and true;
he does what is right and fair. . . .
He is your father, your Creator,
he made you into a nation.

"Think of the past, of the time long ago; . . .
ask the old men to tell of the past. . . .

"He found them wandering through the desert,
a desolate, wind-swept wilderness.
He protected them and cared for them,
as he would protect himself.
Like an eagle teaching its young to fly,
catching them safely on its spreading wings,
the LORD kept Israel from falling."

DEUTERONOMY 32:1–11

DESERT EXPERIENCE

Like Moses' own desert experience,
Israel's desert experience
made the people aware of God in a new way.
The desert served as a schoolroom,
where they learned their infidelity and weakness
and God's fidelity and power.

Yahweh had revealed himself to be
a God of loving-kindness,
not a selfish tyrant or a blind force in nature.
Yahweh made a covenant and kept it,
even when Israel failed to do so.
Like an eagle, he rescued the people
when they faltered and failed.

DEATH OF MOSES

The Book of Deuteronomy ends
with Moses' death.

So Moses, the LORD's servant,
died there in the land of Moab. . . .
The LORD buried him in a valley in Moab,
opposite the town of Bethpeor,
but to this day no one knows
the exact place of his burial. . . .

The people of Israel
mourned for him for thirty days
in the plains of Moab.

DEUTERONOMY 34:5–8

It is, indeed, an irony of history
that great leaders who fight valiantly for a cause
often die without enjoying the results of it.
Moses was no exception.

CONCLUSION

The death of Moses
is the concluding entry in the Jewish Torah,
the first five books of the Bible.
These books are Genesis, Exodus, Leviticus,
Numbers, and Deuteronomy.
Sometimes called the Book of Moses,
the Torah is the foundation
upon which the rest of the Old Testament is built.

Modern Desert Experience

Inspired by Israel's experience,
many people today still "go out to the desert"
to try to deepen their awareness of God.
In most cases, it amounts to little more
than a temporary "retreat" from life.
Nevertheless,
it serves the same purpose as the desert of old.

Carl Sandburg expressed the value of the desert
when he said:

A man must get away now and then
to experience loneliness.
Only those who learn how to live with loneliness
can come to know themselves and life.

I go out there and walk and look at the trees
and sky.
I listen to the sounds of loneliness.
I sit on a rock or a stump and say to myself,
"Who are you, Sandburg?
Where have you been,
and where are you going?"

John the Baptist began his career in the desert
(Matthew 3:1).
Jesus entered the desert before his ministry
(Matthew 4:1).
Jesus returned to the desert to pray
(Matthew 14:13, 23).
Jesus led his followers into the desert to teach them
(Matthew 15:33).

22
Library of Books

What the Jews Believe
PHILIP S. BERNSTEIN

*When the synagogue of which this writer is now
minister burned down, an Irish policeman
dashed to the ark and seized the Torah.
He handed it to the rabbi
who was rushing up to the building.
"Here," he said, "I have saved your crucifix."
Well, the Jews have no crucifix,
but the policeman had the right idea:
the scrolls are the most sacred symbol of Judaism.*

As we have seen, the five scrolls of the Torah
developed piecemeal over many centuries.
For a long time, they were passed on orally.
Around campfires, flickering under desert skies,
Hebrew bards recited the Torah narratives.
There are reports of Jewish bards
who could recite the entire Torah by heart.

Eventually, scribes recorded these narratives.
They wrote to the same impulse
that moved Isaiah the prophet.

*God told me to write down in a book
what the people are like,
so that there would be a permanent record.*

ISAIAH 30:8

The Torah, like the Old Testament in general,
evolved not as a single scroll or book,
but as a library of literature
put together by many writers over many centuries.

This explains why the Torah sometimes
contains an idea or comment that developed
long after the historical period with which it deals.
Here some explanation is needed.

FIRST-PERSON HISTORY

Modern people think of history
in the third person.
Israelites thought of it in the first person.
For example, for the Israelites
the Exodus was not something that happened
to *them*.
Rather, it happens to *us*.
We are all there in the person of our ancestors.
Thus, *we* too are freed by it.

Israelites regarded the past as alive.
For each bore within himself the results of the past.
Therefore, he returned "in memory" to the past,
relived it, and made it his own.
Thus, the biblical writer did not hesitate
to add the experiences of later Israelites
to the original story.

All of this annoys the modern historian,
who wishes the biblical writer
would have described the biblical event
precisely the way it happened.

But the biblical writer
had a totally different purpose in mind.
He wanted to do much more than inform readers
about what happened centuries ago.
He wanted his readers to relive the events
and to experience their deeper meaning personally.

Thus, a Black slave singing "Go Down, Moses"
probably had a better grasp
of the deeper meaning of the Exodus event
that the biblical writer sought to communicate
than a biblical scholar sitting at his desk
trying to do a "literary X ray" of the text
to study it objectively.

Ancient Stories

Another "library of literature"
that was passed on orally for centuries
is *Grimm's Fairy Tales.*
It includes such famous literary creations as
Snow White, Cinderella, and Sleeping Beauty.

The Grimm brothers lived in Germany
when such tales were popular among peasants.

Happily Ever After . . .
GEORGE KENT

The stories
were part of a great oral tradition
in existence long before men knew how to write.
Some had been collected and published,
but many others had never been written down,
and only a few aged peasants here and there
remembered them.

When they died, the tales,
some of them dating back thousands of years,
would die with them.

To avoid this situation, the Grimm brothers
tracked down old peasants who knew the stories.
One excellent source was a tailor's wife.

Not only did she tell her stories well, but she
told them each time in exactly the same words.
If she went too fast and was asked to repeat,
she would tell them slowly, without change.

Eventually, the brothers collected 86 stories.
Then, in 1812, a few days after Christmas,
the first of 20,000 editions of the *Fairy Tales*
came off the presses. It was an immediate hit.

Thus it happened that the tales passed
from the oral to the written medium,
much as the Torah did in early biblical times.

DEAD SEA SCROLLS

People ask,
"Do we have the original biblical manuscripts?"
The answer is no.

Remarkably, the oldest copies we have
were discovered between 1947 and 1956.
One of the experts involved with the discoveries
from the start tells how it happened.

The Qumran Story
ROLAND DE VAUX

During the summer of 1947, a young Bedouin . . .
was tending his goats on the shore of the Dead Sea.
One of the goats disappeared.
Trekking up a mountainside in search of it,
Muhammad saw a hole in the spongy, rocky surface.
He threw a stone and heard something break.
Afraid, he ran away.

The next day
Muhammad returned with his cousin. . . .
Climbing through the hole and dropping to the
floor of the cave, they first groped in darkness;
but as their eyes grew accustomed,
they made out some jars with lids against the wall.
They opened one; it was empty.
They opened another one; it too was empty.
They opened still another
and from this one they took some hides that were
rolled up and inscribed and wrapped in linen.
The linen smelled so bad,
that they left it behind and took only the scrolls.

These young men were making
the first discovery of the Dead Sea Scrolls;
it was the beginning of a great adventure.

The discovery turned out to be the start
of the biggest biblical bonanza of all time.

Soon, other caves were found and searched.
Eventually, 11 caves yielded over 600 scrolls
and thousands of fragments from scrolls.
About one-third of these were biblical writings.

The scrolls were apparently hidden in the caves
by Essenes (Jewish "monks"),
who transported them from their Qumran library
when Roman armies invaded the area in A.D. 70.

The scrolls are important for two reasons.
First, they are nearly 1,000 years older
than the oldest manuscripts we previously had.
This brings us amazingly closer
to the original documents.

Second, the nonbiblical scrolls
not only fill a gap of missing Jewish history
between 200 B.C. and A.D. 50,
but also provide important new background data
to help clarify biblical writings from this period.

DATING THE SCROLLS

A fascinating chapter in the Dead Sea Scroll story
was trying to find out how old they were.
Here's how one newspaper reported the event.

Geiger Counters Prove Age of Biblical Scrolls
CATHOLIC UNIVERSE BULLETIN

New York—(NC)—*Pope Pius XII's statement
that "true science" discovers God
in an ever-increasing degree
has been graphically illustrated here.*

*Geiger counters have been used
by nuclear scientists to verify the age
of ancient Hebrew scrolls of the Book of Isaiah. . . .*

Popular Science *monthly, published here,
told the story. . . .*

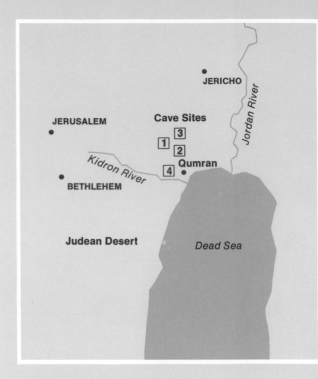

CAVE 1
Found in 1947, this cave yielded a large number of scrolls
(three in their original containers).
Among the discoveries was the Isaiah Scroll.

CAVE 2
Discovered in February 1952 by a Bedouin,
this cave contained a number of important fragments
from the lost Hebrew text of the Book of Sirach.

CAVE 3
Discovered in March 1952,
this cave yielded two badly oxidized copper scrolls.
The scrolls were written in Hebrew and listed sites
where treasures were supposedly buried in Palestine.

CAVE 4
This cave was searched
by archaeologists in September 1952.
Fragments of over 400 manuscripts were found.
Also found were manuscripts concerning
the beliefs and practices of the Qumran community.

Seven other caves were found.
The last cave was found in 1956.
It ranks with caves 1 and 4 as major discoveries.
From it came the famous "Temple Scroll,"
containing 66 columns of religious rules,
festive sacrifice descriptions,
and laws for the king and his army.

Two of the jars from Cave 1.
They served as containers for some of the scrolls.
Ancients frequently used jars like these
to protect important documents.

Hanging by ropes, work crews searched 200 caves
in the Dead Sea area. Eleven caves yielded
treasures of scrolls, coins, and pottery.
Cave 4 (front center section of this cloverleaf)
housed the richest find: over 400 different manuscripts.

Portion of a biblical scroll found at Qumran. Stitch marks on the right side show where the first leaf of the scroll was sewn to a prior leaf. Stitching was done with thread made from animal gut. Hebrew writing on the scroll reads from right to left.

DEAD SEA SCROLLS

Too brittle to be unrolled, these oxidized copper scrolls
were found in Cave 3. They were coated with plastic,
cut with a tiny electric saw,
and pieced together for reading.

Scholars sifted and strained the dirt of cave floors
for precious scroll fragments.
They were then cleaned and pieced together
like a jigsaw puzzle.
This fragment
is inscribed in Hebrew
and dates from
the first century A.D.

*Some language scholars said the scrolls were
written in the Middle Ages. But the Geiger counters
dated them back to the time of Christ,
as archaeologists had asserted.*

*Willard F. Libby, University of Chicago radio
chemist, burned fragments of the linen wrappings
around the scrolls to pure carbon.
Then, he measured their radioactivity.*

*He concluded that the flax from which the linen
had been made was alive and breathing 1,917 years
ago. . . . Libby noted, however, that there must be
allowance for error of a century or two either way.*

Popular Science *commented:*

*"When the atom bomb first mushroomed
its message of death and destruction into the sky . . .
there were many who speculated
on the future uses of atomic energy.
But few if any put Bible study on their list.*

*"Now . . .
we find the seeming miracle has come to pass.
Science is revealed as the handmaid of religion. . . .
Cosmic rays that bombarded the earth when Christ
was born have left behind a coded message
for nuclear physicists to decipher.*

*"It was strangely fitting that nuclear scientists,
turning from war to peacetime research,
should undertake the task of determining the age
of an ancient transcript of the Book of Isaiah,
usually considered
the greatest of the Old Testament prophets.*

*"For it was Isaiah who, 25 centuries ago,
envisioned a time when the weapons of war
would be reconverted forever into the tools of peace:*

*"'They shall beat their swords into plowshares,
and their spears into pruning-hooks;
nation shall not lift up sword against nation,
neither shall they learn war any more.'"*

BIBLICAL SCROLLS

Ancient scrolls were usually made of papyrus,
a paperlike product made from marsh reeds
that grew along the Nile in Egypt.
Sheets the size of typing paper
were glued or sewed together
in rolled-up lengths of about 30 feet.

Scribes wrote on the scrolls
in six- or seven-inch columns
that read from right to left.
Writing was done with a reed,
whose point was shredded to form a tiny brush.

In time, animal hide was substituted for papyrus.
This led to a more durable, leather material,
called parchment. By the fourth century after Christ,
parchment replaced both papyrus and animal hide.
This continued until the tenth century,
when paper became the common writing material.
The difficulty and awkwardness of rolling scrolls
led to the first book (codex) around A.D. 200.

When writing on scrolls,
biblical writers did not divide their writings
into chapters and verses—as we now find in the Bible.
Credit for dividing books into chapters
goes to thirteenth-century scholars.
Sixteenth-century scholars took the final step
and numbered the verses for easy reference.

In Jesus' time,
strict precautions surrounded the copying of scrolls.
Duplicates were made for each synagogue
by scribes who followed the strictest instructions.

Looking like green bamboo with tassles on top,
papyrus grew along the banks of the Nile.
The infant Moses was found among papyrus reeds
(Exodus 2:3-5).
Egyptians used the stalks not only for writing materials,
but also for fabrics, rope, blankets, and even boats.
Stalks grew to heights of 20-25 feet.

It is the duty of the scribe to prepare himself
by silent meditation for that holy task.
He must have before him a copy of the Pentateuch
[Torah] which has been corrected and verified.

The scribe must refer to it continuously
and never write a word from his own memory
or without first pronouncing it aloud.

Special care must be taken
in writing the divine names. Before each of these
the scribe must pronounce the formula:
"I intend to write the Holy Name."
If he forgets one single time,
the scroll is unfit to be read in public.
It must be entirely rewritten.

MINIATURE SCROLLS

The Book of Deuteronomy says of the Torah:

"Never forget these commands. . . .
Tie them on your arms

and wear them on your foreheads. . . .
Write them on the doorposts
of your houses and on your gates."

DEUTERONOMY 6:6-9

Orthodox Jewish males over 13 years
still wear *tefillin,* or *phylacteries,* at weekday prayer.
These miniature leather boxes contain tiny scrolls
of four biblical passages: Exodus 13:1-10, 13:11-16,
Deuteronomy 6:4-9, 11:13-20.

One box is attached to the left arm (near the heart),
as a sign
that the wearer subjugates his heart to God.

The other is attached to the forehead,
as a sign that he subjugates his mind to God.

Matthew 23:5 reports that Jesus had strong words
for some Pharisees who made a show of these boxes:
"They do everything
so that people will see them."

Many Jews attach a small box, called a *mezuzah,*
to the right doorposts of their houses.
This box contains the Shema and other verses
from Deuteronomy 11:13-20.
It proclaims that the house is Jewish,
and it reminds them that the house
is the temple of God, not too unlike the temple.

The Shema is the first lesson in faith
that the small Jewish child learns.
It is also the last prayer
heard from the lips of a dying Jew.
Recited twice daily by devout Jews, it reads:

"Israel, remember this!
The Lord—and the Lord alone—
is our God.
Love the Lord your God
with all your heart, with all your soul,
and with all your strength."

DEUTERONOMY 6:4-5

Biblical Translations

The word *Bible*
comes from the Greek, meaning "book."
The word *testament* comes from the Greek,
meaning "last will and testament" or "covenant."

Thus, for believers, the expression *Old Testament*
refers to God's original covenant with Israel,
mediated by Moses.
The expression *New Testament* refers to God's
final covenant with all people, mediated by Christ.

The Old Testament was translated from Hebrew
into Greek by Jewish scholars around 200 B.C.
It was badly needed, because many Jews living
in Greek-speaking nations no longer knew Hebrew.

The translation was called the *Septuagint* (seventy)
after the number of Alexandrian (Egyptian) Jewish
scholars reputedly involved in the task.

The Septuagint contains a number of writings
that modern Jews omit from their canon
of biblical writings. These include:

Judith	Sirach
Tobit	Baruch
1 and 2 Maccabees	Esther (longer version)
Wisdom	Daniel 3:24-90;13-14

Modern Jews follow ancient Palestinian Jews who,
unlike their Greek-speaking brothers in Alexandria,
gave lesser weight to writings in Greek.
Catholics follow the Septuagint version;
most Protestants do not.

Jerome made the first official Latin translation
of the Bible around A.D. 400.
It was called the *Vulgate* (common use) version.
The first complete English translation
was made in the 14th century.

Time Chart

1200 BC	Joshua invades Canaan
	Judges rule Israel
1175	Philistines enter Canaan
1020	Samuel anoints Saul
1000	David becomes king
960	Solomon succeeds David
922	Solomon dies
	North-South split

Mediterranean Sea

MEGIDDO

SHECHEM

CANAANITES

BETHEL

AI

GIBEON

PHILISTINES

(JERUSALEM)

LACHISH

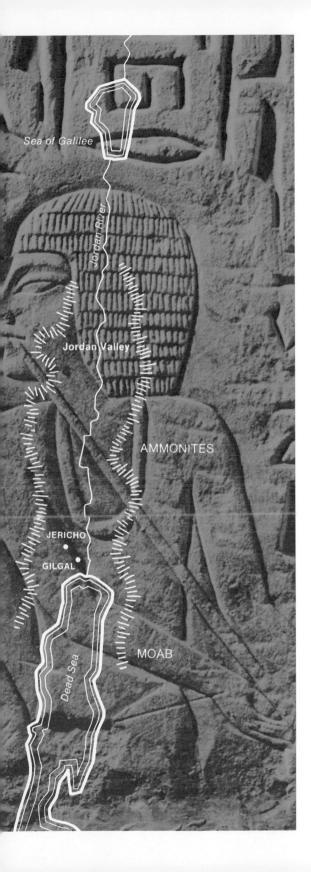

PEOPLEHOOD
NATIONHOOD

Books

Joshua	1 Chronicles
Judges	2 Chronicles
Ruth	Psalms
1 Samuel	Proverbs
2 Samuel	Song of Songs
1 Kings 1-11	

23
Stage of History

"Moses is dead!"
When the reality of these words began to sink in,
some Israelites had second thoughts
about entering the promised land of Canaan.

Their fears were ill-founded, however.
Excavated records testify
to the growing weakness of Canaanite city-states
about this time.

PROMISE FULFILLED

Joshua took command of the Israelites.
Appointed by Moses before he died, Joshua fired
the desert-hardened Hebrews with his own faith.

When preparations were complete,
horns sounded everywhere.
As the great wave of Israelites thundered downhill
to cross the Jordan,
the entire valley echoed with shouts.
Yahweh's ancient promise was being fulfilled.

TO ABRAHAM   *I am going to give you*
and your descendants
all the land that you see,
and it will be yours forever.

GENESIS 13:15

TO ISAAC   *I am going to give*
all this territory to you. . . .
I will keep the promise
I made to your father Abraham.

GENESIS 26:3

Over 300 inscribed clay tablets (like these)
were unearthed at Amarna in Egypt.
Called the *Tell el Amarna Letters,*
some were letters from Canaanite city-states
asking Pharaoh Akhenaton to help repel
marauding bands of *Habiru.*
The Pharaoh had his own problems and could not comply.
The letters testify that the situation in Canaan
was deteriorating in the years prior to Israel's actual
invasion of it.

TO JACOB   *I am the LORD, the God*
of Abraham and Isaac.
I will give to you and to
your descendants this land
on which you are lying.

GENESIS 28:13

TO ISRAELITES   *I will make you*
my own people, and . . .
bring you to the land that
I solemnly promised to give to
Abraham, Isaac, and Jacob.

EXODUS 6:7–8

TWIN EVENTS

The first Israelites to ford the Jordan
were the priests carrying the Ark of the Covenant.

As soon as the priests stepped into the river,
the water stopped flowing and piled up. . . .
The flow downstream to the Dead Sea
was completely cut off.

JOSHUA 3:15–16

The entire mass of Israelites
crossed over without accident or loss of life.
The shouts of the people mounted;
Yahweh was with them, as he had been
when they crossed the Reed (Red) Sea.

The stoppage of the Jordan River,
matching the stoppage of the Reed Sea,
points up the connection between the two events.
They were opposite sides of the same coin.
The Reed Sea crossing
marked Israel's *exit* from a land of slavery;
the Jordan crossing
marked Israel's *entry* into a land of freedom.

The stoppage of the Jordan River
has been much discussed. Some ask:
"Could the event have been connected
with an earthquake that blocked the Jordan?"
The question is not out of line
because the Jordan lies along an earth fault,
which has caused many earthquakes in history.

The most recent major earthquake
occurred in 1927, killing over 500 people.
A landslide from this earthquake
blocked the Jordan for 24 hours.
Similar earthquakes occurred in 1906 and 1924.

Besides records of modern earthquakes,
the prophets Amos and Zechariah
refer to them also in their writings.

You will flee
as your ancestors did
when the earthquake struck
in the time of King Uzziah of Judah.

ZECHARIAH 14:5

Some experts think an earthquake
lies behind the story of the sudden destruction
of Sodom and Gomorrah.

Suddenly the LORD rained burning sulfur
on the cities of Sodom and Gomorrah. . . .
Abraham . . .
looked down at Sodom and Gomorrah . . .
and saw smoke rising from the land,
like smoke from a huge furnace.

GENESIS 19:24-28

Coal and petroleum deposits, still found in this area,
could have ignited and produced this description.

Once again, God's action in Israel's history
could have occurred within the context
of ordinary events and circumstances.
Only the "timing" needs to have been extraordinary.

CELEBRATION

When the Israelites were safe on the other side,
they pitched camp at a site called Gilgal.
To celebrate the event, Joshua took the 12 rocks
from the river, on which the priests stood.
Erecting a monument, he said to the people:

"In the future, when your children ask you
what these stones mean,
you will tell them about the time
when Israel crossed the Jordan on dry ground.
Tell them that the LORD your God
dried up the water of the Jordan for you
until you had crossed,
just as he dried up the Red Sea for us.
Because of this everyone on earth will know
how great the LORD's power is,
and you will honor the LORD your God forever."

JOSHUA 4:21-24

In later years, the Hebrew psalmist composed
this song to commemorate the crossings:

The Red Sea looked and ran away;
the Jordan River stopped flowing.
The mountains skipped like goats;
the hills jumped around like lambs.

What happened, Sea, to make you run away?
And you, O Jordan, why did you stop flowing?
You mountains, why did you skip like goats?
You hills, why did you jump around like lambs?

PSALM 114:3-6

Once settled at Gilgal, the people gathered
to celebrate the feast of the Passover (Joshua 5:10-12).

The Jordan, Palestine's largest river,
coils over 200 water miles in length.
Its average width is about 90 feet;
its depth rarely exceeds 10 feet.

Palestine runs from above the Sea of Galilee
to below the Dead Sea (about 150 miles in length).
It is bound on the west by the Mediterranean Sea
and on the east by the hill country and desert.
The western hills rise 2,500 feet above sea level;
the eastern hills soar to nearly 3,000 feet.
The valley itself goes from 700 feet below sea level
in Galilee to about 1,300 feet below sea level
in the Dead Sea area.

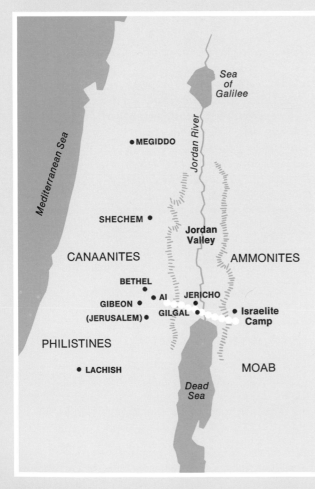

The Land

The land itself was a spectacular site.
To eyes used to the sandy dunes of the Sinai desert,
it was indeed a "rich and fertile land"
(Deuteronomy 26:9).

About the size of Vermont,
the land lies in the same latitude as Georgia.
The heart of the land
is a ten-mile-wide valley, running north and south.
The floor of the valley slopes southward,
dropping to about 1,300 feet below sea level.

Walling in both sides of the valley are barren hills.
Looking like piles of unfinished creation,
the hills accentuate its depth.

Though the Sea of Galilee looks peaceful here,
six-foot waves crash along the shoreline
when winds swoop down from the surrounding hills.
Archaeological evidence suggests
the sea was once entirely circled by dwellings.

From these Mediterranean waters,
ancient fishermen caught sea creatures
and extracted their famous purple dyes from them.
Now snorkel divers explore the same waters
along Israel's "Sunshine Coast."

Salt-encrusted driftwood sparkles in the sun.
Lying 1,300 feet below sea level,
and 1,200 feet deep in spots,
the Dead Sea has no outlet.
Arabs claim that in ancient times
no bird could survive flight
across the acrid-smelling waters.

The Bible as History
WERNER KELLER

Over the western ridge of hills
sprawls the Mediterranean Sea,
with its exciting cliffs and elegant white beaches.

At the north end of the valley is the Sea of Galilee,
a fisherman's paradise even to this day.
Sixty-five airline miles south is the Dead Sea.
The two seas are linked by the Jordan River.
To an airplane pilot, the river looks like a giant
snake coiling downhill through dark green foliage.

The Dead Sea is the lowest body of water on earth;
its salt content is six times that of the ocean.
Not even the poorest swimmer can sink in it.
An ancient tale
is still told about the water's buoyancy.

During the siege of Jerusalem in A.D. 70,
it is said that the Roman army commander Titus
sentenced certain slaves to death....
He had them bound together by chains
and thrown into the sea
at the foot of the mountains of Moab.
But the condemned men did not drown.
No matter how often they were thrown into the sea
they always drifted back to the shore like corks.
This inexplicable occurrence
made such a deep impression upon Titus
that he pardoned the unfortunate offenders.

105

24

The Walls Came Tumbling Down

All the Amorite kings . . .
and all the Canaanite kings . . .
heard that the LORD had dried up the Jordan
until the people of Israel had crossed it.
They became afraid and lost their courage.

JOSHUA 5:1

Joshua's first target was Jericho.
Next he stormed the cities of Ai and Gibeon.
They fell before his armies.
The battles are reported in the Book of Joshua.

Though listed in some Bibles as a "historical" book,
Joshua is not historical
in our modern sense of the word.

First of all, like the Torah, the Book of Joshua
deals with an early period in Israel's history.
Many of its battle legends
were handed down orally for generations.
Only later were they committed to writing.

Second, the battle accounts were simplified,
and the time-lapse between them telescoped.
This is a characteristic of oral communication.
But there was also a deeper reason.
The editor wanted to make sure
that the point of the book was not lost:
Yahweh, not Joshua's armies, was responsible
for the takeover of the Promised Land.

To stress this point, the Hebrew psalmist
composed this song to eulogize the event:

O God . . .
Your people did not conquer the land
with their swords;
they did not win it by their own power;
it was by your power and your strength. . . .
We will always praise you.

PSALM 44:1, 3, 8

Yahweh is the real hero of the Book of Joshua.
He guided his people to victory
and gave them the land.

ANCIENT GRAVEYARDS

Archaeologists have excavated
many of the sites recorded in the Book of Joshua.
The location of such sites is rather easy to spot.
They normally assume the appearance of a lone hill
standing in an otherwise flat area.

Called "tells," these hills house the remains
of a long-destroyed city.
Wind, rain, and the centuries have camouflaged
the sites with a "skin" of earth and grass,
giving them a hill-like appearance.

The systematic excavation of tells began in 1890.
Instead of digging haphazardly into tells
for buried treasures, archaeologists
sliced into them, as one cuts into a cake.
This method revealed at one glance
all the strata that made up the mound or tell.
Other methods were to cut steps into the tell
or to sink pits into various points of it.

To understand how the layers of a tell developed,
we must recall that when an ancient city
was destroyed by fire, war, or famine,
the wreckage was not carted away.
New settlers merely leveled the old city,
often made of adobe huts, and built on the debris.
Often the walls of the destroyed city
were merely built higher for the new city.
Thus, the walls contained the tell as it grew.

Some tells have 10 or 12 strata,
meaning that 10 or 12 cities are stacked there
in pancake fashion. The University of Chicago
uncovered 20 strata in the 13-acre tell
at Megiddo (1 Kings 9:15).
The site has witnessed so many historic battles
that the author of the Book of Revelation
made it the symbolic site for the final battle
on earth between the forces of good and evil.
The book refers to the site as Armageddon,
that is, *har* (Mount) Megiddo (Revelation 16:16).

BROKEN POTTERY

The first thing archaeologists look for in a tell
is pieces of broken pottery.
Called the "alphabet of archaeology,"
pottery does not decay, takes many shapes,
and contains many decorations. It breaks easily.
Since ancient housewives wanted to keep up with
the times, they bought pottery of newer designs
when old pottery broke.

There were also improvements
in methods of firing clay as time went on.

All of this is studied by archaeologists.
Thus, when a piece of pottery is found in a tell,
archaeologists can date it
with remarkable accuracy.
The shape, style, design, and firing method
place it in a definite period of history.

Pottery was also used as a kind of writing tablet.
This was a practical way of using broken pottery
in a day when writing materials were scarce.
An inscribed piece of pottery
is especially valuable to archaeologists.

PUZZLES

The book of Joshua says
that Joshua captured the city of Lachish (10:32).

Describing his excavations at this site in 1965,
one archaeologist gives this report:

> The World of David and Solomon
> ───────────────────────────
> G. ERNEST WRIGHT

I found great piles of smashed pottery
that we could readily date
to the time of Joshua. . . .
Other tells fill out a picture
of a series of city-state capitals destroyed,
strongly supporting the account of the campaigns
in Joshua 10.

But archaeologists have also run into problems.
For example, the Bible reports:

Joshua burned Ai and left it in ruins.
It is still like that today.

JOSHUA 8:28

How could this be? Excavations indicate
that Ai was abandoned long before Joshua's time.
In fact, the Hebrew word *Ai* means "ruin."
G. Ernest Wright offers this explanation:

Our dig at Bethel, only two miles away,
yielded a vital clue.
Stripping away the swaths of rubble,
we worked our way past 1200 B.C.
Suddenly, we encountered signs of a raging fire—
piles of charcoal debris, some five feet deep,
in the remains of well-built homes.
Undoubtedly, Hebrew scribes
had accurately recorded the burning, but tradition
shifted the incident to the "ruin" nearby.

A second archaeological problem is Jericho.
The Book of Joshua reports Yahweh as saying:

"I am putting into your hands Jericho,
with its king and all its brave soldiers.
You and your soldiers are to march
around the city once a day for six days.
Seven priests, each carrying a trumpet,
are to go in front of the Covenant Box.
On the seventh day you and your soldiers

are to march around the city seven times
while the priests blow the trumpets.
Then they are to sound one long note.
As soon as you hear it,
all the men are to give a loud shout,
and the city walls will collapse."

JOSHUA 6:2–5

So it happened. Archaeological excavations
show that the walls of Jericho did collapse
at one period in their long history.
But the collapsed walls
date from a period other than Joshua's.
Perhaps they are the wreckage of an earthquake.

The Jericho problem is compounded by the fact
that archaeologists can find no evidence of life
in Jericho dating from Joshua's period.
Commenting on its absence, G. Ernest Wright says:
"Perhaps the centuries
have eroded all signs of Joshua's victory."

This would not be surprising,
for the site at Jericho dates from about 5000 B.C.
It is the oldest city on earth.
Archaeologists estimate
that, prior to Joshua's attack on the city,
its walls had been repaired or rebuilt 16 times.

THE BAN

They killed everyone in the city,
men and women, young and old.
They also killed the cattle.

JOSHUA 6:21

This kind of mass killing, called the ban,
was common among ancient peoples.
Although this practice shocks us,
we should recall the saturation bombings
and the mass executions of Jews in World War II.
These modern atrocities do not justify
the ancient ban, but they do sober our outrage.

108

Digging Up Yesterday

What would it be like
to spend a summer in Israel as a volunteer,
helping archaeologists excavate a tell?
Here's a report of a typical day,
which begins before sunrise.

From a Volunteer's Viewpoint . . .
CHARLOTTE D. LOFGREEN

The music,
coming over a loudspeaker at maximum volume,
is a mixture of Israeli and John Philip Sousa . . .
as you trudge in the dark
to rows of sinks to brush your teeth.
Nourishment is bread and milk or coffee. . . .
The work groups
slowly place one foot in front of the other,
up the hill until their area is reached.
A bucket, trowel, pick,
and sundry equipment is placed in your hand.
An area inspector advises you on filling buckets,
hauling buckets, and emptying buckets. . . .

Buckets of pottery may be found in a single day;
a new wall, bones, charred logs, cult objects,
and home utensils are the most common finds.
Everything must be photographed. . . .
It is exciting to discover a missing piece
in the puzzle of man's history.
A small ostracon (a piece of pottery with writing
on it) may give an important message. . . .

The afternoon brings a welcome rest or study time.
Since this tell
has been designated as an educational dig,
half of the camp is taking classes. . . .

By late afternoon,
most volunteers are ready to wash pottery
and learn the secrets it can reveal.
Piece by piece, each find is catalogued. . . .
The student feels satisfied
when at last, he can identify the correct age,
type, burnishing, and culture of his piece.

Tell site at Beer-Sheva.

Volunteers from many nations
work in their area squares,
surrounded by well-trimmed catwalks.

An inscription on the rim of a stone bowl.
The inscription is in Old Hebrew script.

IMAGE OF GOD

More to the point, however,
is an appreciation
of Israel's incomplete understanding of God
in this early stage of her history.
This understanding was a highly primitive one;
it would take centuries of revelation
under the prophets to develop and mature.

For the present,
Israel thought of Yahweh as a nationalistic God.
As other nations had special "protector-gods,"
so Israel had Yahweh.
And any enemy of Israel
was automatically an enemy of Yahweh.

Moreover, at this point in her history,
Israel had no idea of an afterlife.
This revelation would come much later.
Therefore, Israel assumed
that Yahweh executed judgment
upon wicked people (enemies) in *this* life.
Thus, to chastise an enemy
was to act as the instrument of Yahweh's justice—
a noble occupation.

The portrait of Yahweh in the Book of Judges
was a highly primitive rendering.
Yahweh was a God of battles and victories.
He ordered wars,
took Israel's side, and destroyed Israel's enemies.

Only with the passage of time
would this portrait be filled out in full color
and refined drastically by the prophets.

25
Charismatic Leaders

The Book of Joshua ends on a deeply religious note.
Joshua assembles the people
to renew the covenant with Yahweh.

Joshua said to all the people,
"This is what the LORD . . . has to say. . . .
'I brought your ancestors out of Egypt. . . .

"'You lived in the desert a long time. . . .
I gave you a land that you had never worked
and cities that you had not built . . .
and olives from trees that you did not plant.'

"Now then," Joshua continued,
"honor the LORD and serve him. . . ."

The people then said to Joshua,
"We will serve the LORD our God.
We will obey his commands."

So Joshua
made a covenant for the people that day,
and there at Shechem he gave them laws
and rules to follow. . . .
Then Joshua sent the people away,
and everyone returned
to his own part of the land.

After that, the LORD's servant
Joshua son of Nun died.

JOSHUA 24:2–29

What happens when a leader dies
and there is no one to take his place?

This problem faced Israel after Joshua's death.
It came into sharp focus when Israelites of Joshua's
generation died and a new generation arose.

They stopped worshiping the LORD . . .
and they began to worship other gods. . . .

And so the LORD became furious with Israel
and let raiders attack and rob them. . . .

Then the LORD gave the Israelites leaders
who saved them from the raiders. . . .
But when the leader died,
the people would return to the old ways.

JUDGES 2:12–19

BACKTRACK

Whereas the Book of Joshua
shows Israel totally committed to Yahweh,
the Book of Judges paints a different picture.
Israel is depicted as constantly backtracking
on her commitment.

The book is a back-and-forth replay
of the same fourfold theme:
sin, punishment, repentance, and forgiveness.
Like a drama in four acts, the same play repeats
itself over and over during the Era of the Judges.

Act I   Israel sins
Act II   Yahweh punishes
Act III   Israel repents
Act IV   Yahweh forgives

Typical of this cycle is the story
of Israel's struggle against the Ammonites.

Act I
Once again
the Israelites sinned against the LORD. . . .

Act II
So the LORD became angry with the Israelites,
and let the . . . Ammonites conquer them.

For eighteen years they oppressed
and persecuted all the Israelites. . . .

Act III
But the people of Israel said to the LORD,
"We have sinned. Do whatever you like,
but please, save us. . . ."
So they got rid of their foreign gods. . . .

Act IV
It was some time later
that the Ammonites went to war against Israel.
When this happened,
the leaders of Gilead went to . . . Jephthah. . . .
They told him, "Come and lead us. . . ."

Then the spirit of the LORD
came upon Jephthah . . .
and the LORD gave him victory.

JUDGES 10:6–16; 11:4–6, 29–32

The impression the Book of Judges conveys is this:
Israel prospers or suffers in direct proportion
to her loyalty to Yahweh and his convenant.

JUDGES

Jephthah's leadership role against the Ammonites
introduces us
to the role of the "judges" in Israelite history.
It also illustrates
how these leaders rose to power in Israel.

Israelite judges were not black-robed men
who sat in courtrooms and decided legal cases.
Rather, they were military champions
who surfaced at critical periods
to defend Israel against her enemies.
We might compare them to Joan of Arc
in French history.
She appeared with the right kind of leadership
at the right moment in history.

Because judges were believed to be endowed
by God with special gifts of wisdom and courage,

scholars refer to them
as charismatic or "gifted" leaders.

The judges were not always holy people.
On the contrary, they were products of their time.
Yahweh acted through them,
in spite of their personal shortcomings.
Such a person was Samson.

Belonging to the tribe of Dan in the north,
he is said to have owed his legendary strength
to a vow never to cut his hair.
A mistress, Delilah,
entered his life, coaxed the secret from him,
and betrayed him to the Philistines.
Imprisoned, blinded, and ridiculed, Samson later
avenged himself when his hair grew back.

NARRATOR   *The Philistine kings*
           met together to celebrate
           and offer a great sacrifice
           to their god Dagon. . . .

KINGS   *Call Samson. . . .*

NARRATOR   *When they brought Samson . . .*
           they made him entertain them
           and made him stand between
           the columns. . . .

SAMSON   *God, give me my strength*
           just this one time more. . . .

NARRATOR   *Samson took hold of the two*
           middle columns
           holding up the building.

SAMSON   *Let me die with the Philistines!*

NARRATOR   *He pushed with all his might,*
           and the building fell down
           on the five kings and everyone.
                              JUDGES 16:23–30

Once again the fourfold theme
of the Book of Judges is dramatized:
sin, punishment, repentance, and forgiveness.

BOOK OF RUTH

Rounding out the 200-year Era of the Judges
is the Book of Ruth.
This brief book opens in the midst of a great famine
that struck Israel.

The book's heroine, Naomi,
sets out with her husband and two sons to Moab.
There her husband dies.
Her two sons marry Moabite women (non-Jews).
Soon, tragedy strikes; both sons die.

Naomi decides to return home.
Ruth, wife of one of her dead sons,
decides to go with Naomi. She says:

"Wherever you go, I will go;
wherever you live, I will live.
Your people will be my people,
and your God will be my God.
Wherever you die, I will die,
and that is where I will be buried."
                              RUTH 1:16–17

The two women arrive back at harvest time.
While gathering grain in a field,
Ruth meets Boaz, the wealthy owner of the field.
When Boaz learns that he is a relative
of Ruth's dead husband, he decides to marry her.
Thus, he honors the ancient custom
that a kinsman is responsible for a widow's care.
In time, Ruth bears him a son.

[They] named the boy Obed. . . .
Obed became the father of Jesse,
who was the father of David.
                              RUTH 4:17

Though written at a later period of Jewish history,
the Book of Ruth
follows the Book of Judges in the Bible.
It acts as a *bridge book* between
the Era of the Judges and the Era of the Kings.
It does this by having its setting

in the last days of the Era of the Judges
and by presenting the genealogy
that leads to David, Israel's greatest king.

In addition, the book challenges
overnationalistic Jews to widen their vision
about God's concern for non-Jewish peoples.
It does this by presenting Ruth, a non-Jew,
as a direct ancestor of David.

New Testament writers used
the line of descendancy in the Book of Ruth
to indicate Jesus' descendancy from David.

*This is the list of the ancestors
of Jesus Christ, a descendant of David. . . .
Boaz . . . , Obed (his mother was Ruth),
Jesse, and King David.*

MATTHEW 1:1–6

Ruth is presented as the direct ancestor of David,
portrayed here by Michelangelo.

Brink of Disaster

Israel was like a ship without a rudder
when the Era of the Judges ended.
The Book of Judges says:
"There was no king in Israel at that time.
Everyone did whatever he pleased" (21:25).
Into this leadership vacuum stepped Samuel.

Although the details of Samuel's life
are wrapped in obscurity,
his role in history is as bright as the noonday sun.
For this reason alone, he deserves to have
two books of the Bible bear his name.

Some scholars label Samuel
the last judge and the first prophet (1 Samuel 3:20).
But Samuel does not fit the description
of either a judge or a prophet
in the strict biblical sense.
Perhaps the best way to describe him
is to call him a *bridge person* between
the Era of the Judges and the Era of the Kings.
For he is the one who announces
and anoints Saul as Israel's first king.

DOUBLE THREAT

When Samuel stepped into the spotlight,
Israel was in serious danger
both from within and from without.

The danger from within was caused by
a drift of the people away from the covenant.
Worse yet, it was aggravated by a growing tendency
by some Jews to blend into their worship of Yahweh
certain features of the Canaanite worship of Baal.

Bowl with typical Philistine decoration.

Today, archaeologists can easily trace
Philistine growth and expansion
by the unique design of their pottery.
It bore a striking resemblance
to the geometric markings found on pottery
in the Aegean sector of the Mediterranean.
The Philistines probably came from this area.

But the Philistines were artists in another way.
They began to mine and process iron ore
south of Palestine (1 Samuel 13:19-22).
This new material gave them a definite superiority
in fighting weapons, namely, spears and swords.
Israel's armies found themselves
on the losing end of an arms race.

Finally, a major military showdown
shaped up between Israel and the Philistines.
The bloody battle took place near modern Tel Aviv.
When the dust of battle cleared,
tradition says, 30,000 Israelites lay dead.

More tragic yet was the destruction of Shiloh,
Israel's religious capital.
The Ark of the Covenant was kidnapped
and paraded off in triumph by the Philistines.

The people cried out in horror and disbelief:
"God's glory has left Israel . . .
God's Covenant Box has been captured"
(1 Samuel 4:22).

For seven nightmarish months,
the Ark remained in enemy hands.
Finally it was recovered.
Samuel used the occasion to admonish the people.

*"If you are going to turn
to the LORD with all your hearts . . .
he will rescue you
from the power of the Philistines."*

1 SAMUEL 7:3

This gave rise to further danger and disunity.
During the Era of the Judges,
the 12 tribes of Israel divided themselves
into territorial states.
The terrain of Palestine,
carved up by ravines and mountainous areas,
made communication between tribes difficult.
The only real source of unity, therefore,
was their common worship of Yahweh,
symbolized by a central sanctuary at Shiloh,
where the Ark of the Covenant was housed.
When worship distortions set in,
their real source of tribal unity began to crumble.

As if this was not enough,
external threats to Israel began to develop.
Canaanite strongholds still pockmarked Palestine.
Now they grew more bold and began to harass
the tribes.
An even worse threat was the Philistines,
who now occupied a large part
of the coastal region along the Mediterranean Sea.

The people answered:
"We have sinned against the LORD" (1 Samuel 7:6).

FIRST KING

To reverse the downhill skid in Israel,
Samuel reluctantly decided
that the nation must have a king.
He realized the dangers of human kingship,
but it seemed to be Yahweh's will.
The man selected was a military hero, Saul.

Then Samuel took a jar of olive oil
and poured it on Saul's head,
kissed him, and said,
"The LORD anoints you
as ruler of his people Israel.
You will rule his people
and protect them from all their enemies. . . ."

After Saul became king of Israel,
he fought all his enemies everywhere. . . .
Wherever he fought he was victorious.
He fought heroically. . . .
He saved the Israelites from all attacks.

1 SAMUEL 10:1; 14:47–48

But success has a way of turning a man's head.
Soon Saul began to follow his own mind;
he grew insensitive to the spirit of Yahweh.

The LORD said to Samuel,
"I am sorry that I made Saul king;
he has turned away from me
and disobeyed my commands."

1 SAMUEL 15:10–11

Thus Saul became one of the great tragic figures
of Old Testament history.

As the star of Saul dipped below the horizon,
the star of another young man began to rise.

27
Man of Destiny

In Palestine brooks,
you can still spot water-smooth stones,
like the fabled disk David used against Goliath.
Alert tourists quickly pocket them
and bring them home as souvenir paperweights.
Fingering one of these flat stones helps to bridge
the 3,000-year gap that separates David from us.

As a youth, David was a shepherd.
While his flocks munched grass on the hillside,
David practiced the sheepherders' time-honored
defense against unwelcome intruders: the slingshot.

Little did he realize that this skill would catapult
him into the limelight of Israelite history.
The moment came when Philistine armies
invaded Israel and set up camp for an assault.
A sporting Philistine warrior of monstrous size
issued a pre-battle challenge to duel any Israelite.

Fingering one of these stones helps to bridge
the 3,000-year gap that separates David from us.

115

Young David, not an Israelite warrior at the time,
figured the odds
and surprised everyone by calling the challenge.

The slow-moving Goliath was no match
for the agile youth and his deadly sling.
David's shepherding days were over
and his career as a warrior was launched.

With natural battle instincts, and a flashing
personality to match, the young warrior
soon captured the imagination of everyone.
Even Saul was eclipsed in the public eye by David.
The First Book of Samuel reports:

Women from every town in Israel
came out to meet King Saul. . . .
In their celebration the women sang,
"Saul has killed thousands,
but David tens of thousands."
Saul did not like this,
and he became very angry.
He said, "For David they claim tens of thousands,
but only thousands for me.
They will be making him king next!"
And so he was jealous
and suspicious of David from that day on.

1 SAMUEL 18:6-9

MANHUNT

Saul's jealousy mounted until, one day,
David was forced to flee for fear of his life.
Shortly afterward,
men from Ziph reported to Saul
that David was hiding on Mount Hachilah.

At once, Saul set out with a small army
to track down David.
When Saul got to Mount Hachilah,
he pitched camp.

Upon learning that Saul and his troops
were camped nearby,
David decided upon a daring move.

NARRATOR   *That night David and Abishai*
            entered Saul's camp
            and found Saul sleeping
            in the center of the camp
            with his spear stuck in the ground
            near his head.
            Abner and the troops
            were sleeping around him.

ABISHAI   *God has put your enemy*
            in your power tonight.
            Now let me plunge his own spear
            through him and pin him
            to the ground with just one blow—
            I won't have to strike twice!

DAVID   *You must not harm him!*
            The LORD will certainly punish
            whoever harms his chosen king. . . .
            The LORD himself will kill Saul,
            either when his time comes
            to die a natural death
            or when he dies in battle.
            The LORD forbid that I should
            try to harm the one whom
            the LORD has made king!
            Let's take his spear
            and his water jar, and go.

NARRATOR   *So David took the spear*
            and the water jar
            from right beside Saul's head. . . .

            [Then David crossed a ravine,
            opposite Saul's camp.
            Shouting at the top of his voice,
            he woke the entire camp
            and taunted them.]

DAVID   *Look! Where is the king's spear?*
            Where is the water jar
            that was right by his head?

1 SAMUEL 26:7-12, 16

116

Was It Here?

David taunted Saul
across a ravine like this canyon at Ein Avdat.
Some think this is the actual spot of the taunt.

The water shown here is from a spring.
It is one of the few major water sources
of the Negeb Desert.

Water was *sold* on Jerusalem street corners.
Water was even more precious outside of towns.
Thus the Israelites assure the Edomites:

*"If we or our animals drink any of your water,
we will pay for it."*

NUMBERS 20:19

Living water—water from a spring or stream—
was preferred to still water from pools.
Sheep, however, preferred still water.
This explains the psalmist's words:

*The LORD is my shepherd . . .
and leads me to quiet pools of fresh water.*

PSALM 23:1–2

Against this backdrop, it is easy to see
how water became a popular biblical symbol
for life and salvation (John 4:10-11; 7:37-39).

FRIENDSHIP

In spite of Saul's jealousy of David,
a deep friendship developed between Saul's son,
Jonathan, and David.

*Jonathan swore eternal friendship with David
because of his deep affection for him.*

1 SAMUEL 18:3

When Jonathan was killed in battle,
David wept over his fallen body.

*"I grieve for you, my brother Jonathan;
how dear you were to me!
How wonderful was your love for me,
better even than the love of women."*

2 SAMUEL 1:26

SAUL'S DEATH

Saul's resentment of David ended
only with Saul's death in battle.
The death of Saul came at Mount Gilboa.
Seeing his three sons killed before his eyes,
Saul fell, grief-stricken, on his own sword.

After Saul's death,
the men of Judah anointed David king.

*The Philistines were told
that David had been made king of Israel,
so their army set out to capture him.*

2 SAMUEL 5:17

A dramatic battle followed,
and David routed the Philistines.
He crushed the power of the "sea people" forever.

117

Dominating Jerusalem
is the octagonal Dome of the Rock,
a mosque built by Arabs
in the seventh century A.D.
It was nearly destroyed by fire in 1448,
started by children who had climbed
inside the dome with candles
to hunt for pigeon eggs.
The dome
was heavily damaged by mortar fire
in the 1948 Arab-Israeli War.
Beneath the dome
lies a 40-by-60-foot rock,
said to be the site where Abraham
led Isaac to be sacrificed.
David chose this spot for the temple.

ERA OF DAVID

Under the magic of David's leadership,
Israel began her "years of lightning."
With remarkable insight, David made Jerusalem
the center of government and worship.
Today, it still ranks
among the great symbol cities of all time.

A modern novelist has recaptured
the love Israelites had for Jerusalem.
He describes an old woman's pilgrimage to the city.

The Source
JAMES A. MICHENER

Like many Hebrews of her generation
she longed for Jerusalem
as bees long for spring to open the flowers
or as lions trapped in the valley hunger for the hills.

It was the golden city, the site of the temple,
the focus of worship, the target of longing. . . .

It was a distance of more than ninety miles
over difficult and wearing terrain,
to be finished in the hot time of autumn,
so that the journey occupied eight days.
Mother and son left the zigzag gate at dawn,
a tall pair dressed in the cheapest clothes,
shod in heavy sandals and carrying staves.
On their backs they carried a little food,
in their purses a few pieces of silver. . . .

Leading his gaunt mother,
who had no idea as to where the city lay,
Rimmon started south through the olive grove. . . .

[Other Israelites were also headed for Jerusalem.]
Those who could afford to do so
led animals for sacrifice at the temple altars,
and one could hear
the lowing of cattle and the cry of sheep.

118

Jewish pilgrims leave prayers
penciled on paper
in the cracks of the Western (Wailing) Wall.
"Hear my prayer, LORD God Almighty"
(Psalm 84:8).

Off to the side of the Dome of the Rock,
and at a lower level, is the Western (Wailing) Wall.
The stones encased in it are all that remains
of the Jerusalem temple destroyed by the Romans in A.D. 70.
Jews come from all over the world to worship here.

*Others carried chickens intended for their own
consumption and some women had white doves
captured in cages made of reeds:
these were for the temple.
A few farmers rode donkeys, but most came on foot
to worship at the central shrine of the Hebrews,
to see with their own eyes
the everlasting glory of Jerusalem. . . .*

*[Once in Jerusalem] many fell to their knees,
to think that they had lived to see this city,
but Gomer noticed that Rimmon stood apart,
staring at the extraordinary walls. . . .
Watching her son absorb the wonder of Jerusalem
she tried to guess
what divine need had brought him to this spot,
but she knew not. . . .*

*In the morning they rose early
and left the mount of olives, returning inside the city,
where they worshiped at the temple,*

*Gomer standing outside with the women
while her son went into the sacred place
to gaze at the holy of holies,
to which only a few priests were admitted.
Later he joined his mother to observe
the animal sacrifices during which perfect bulls
were led lowing to the altar,
and here as the solemn rite
was concluded, with incense penetrating the brain,
Rimmon caught an understanding
of man's eternal submission to Yahweh;
and as the sacrificial fires twisted upward
the significance of his faith was burned into his
consciousness.
This city he would remember forever,
and on the sixth day Gomer heard him whispering,*

*"O Jerusalem,
if I forget you let my eyes be blinded,
let my right hand lose its cunning."*

119

GREAT HOUR

After Jerusalem was set up as the nation's capital,
David ordered
the Ark of the Covenant to be brought to the city.

Amid shouts of joy and great festivity,
the Ark was solemnly escorted to Jerusalem
by the picked men of Israel (2 Samuel 6:1-15).
As the men approached the city gates,
the excitement of the people broke into singing.

Fling wide the gates,
open the ancient doors,
and the great king will come in.
Who is this great king?...

Who is this great king?
The triumphant LORD—
he is the great king!

PSALM 24:7-10

Once inside the city,
the Ark was placed in the tent built for it.
David himself made offerings before the Lord.
When he finished, he blessed the people,
and they left for their homes (2 Samuel 6:12-19).

The psalmist commemorated the event in song.

Of Zion it will be said
that all nations belong there
and that the Almighty will make her strong.
The LORD will write a list of the peoples
and include them all as citizens of Jerusalem.
They dance and sing,
"In Zion is the source of all our blessings."

PSALM 87:5-7

This stone portrayal
of the portable shrine,
which carried the Ark of the Covenant
from place to place,
was found in excavations
at Capernaum.
It dates from about Jesus' time.

FROM DAVID'S LINE

Life in Jerusalem settled down to normal.
Then one day David was strolling through his palace
with Nathan the prophet.
Suddenly, he stopped and turned to Nathan.

DAVID   *Here I am*
          living in a house built of cedar,
          but God's Covenant Box
          is kept in a tent!

NATHAN   *Do whatever you have in mind,*
          because the LORD is with you.

NARRATOR *But that night*
          the LORD said to Nathan,

LORD   *Go and tell my servant David*
          that I say to him,
          "You are not the one to build
          a temple for me to live in. ...

          I will make one of your sons king
          and will keep his kingdom strong.
          He will be the one
          to build a temple for me,

and I will make sure
that his dynasty continues forever.
I will be his father,
and he will be my son. . . ."

NARRATOR   *Nathan told David everything
that God had revealed to him.*

*Then King David went into the Tent
of the LORD's presence,
sat down and prayed.*

DAVID   *Sovereign LORD, I am not worthy
of what you have already done. . . .
Yet now you are doing even more,
Sovereign LORD. . . .
How great you are. . . .
There is none like you. . . .
You have made Israel
your own people forever,
and you, LORD,
have become their God.*

*And now, LORD God,
fulfill for all time
the promise you made about me
and my descendants.*

2 SAMUEL 7:2–25

This prophecy of a messiah ("anointed one")
from the kingly line of David
became the cornerstone of Israel's faith.
The psalmist set it to music.

*"I have made my servant David king
by anointing him with holy oil. . . .
He will say to me,
'You are my father and my God. . . .'
I will make him my first-born son,
the greatest of all kings.
I will always keep my promise to him,
and my covenant with him will last forever.
His dynasty will be as permanent as the sky;
a descendant of his will always be king."*

PSALM 89:20–29

Medieval cathedral at Amiens, France.

Bible in Stone

Like David,
medieval Christians showed a special concern
for God's house.

For the many Christians
who could not own a personal Bible,
or who could not read,
the cathedral was a "Bible in stone."

On a Sunday afternoon,
you could walk around the cathedral
and "read" the fascinating stories
of the Old and New Testaments
in the life-sized statues of the cathedral's walls
and the beautifully colored stained glass
of the cathedral's windows.

121

This boy has just completed
his Bar Mitzvah ("Son of the Law").
This ceremony takes place when a boy
reaches his 13th birthday.

Modern Judaism

It is customary to think of modern Judaism
as being made up of three main groups:
Reform, Conservative, Orthodox.

A rabbi comments on the relationships
among these groups.

Judaism
STUART E. ROSENBERG

*All three groups hold more in common
than their divisions seem to indicate.
All stress belief in the unity of God
and proclaim their joint desire to bear witness,
as Jews, to the word of God,
as given to their ancestors at Sinai.
All are in agreement with most of the traditional
theological concepts, although each grouping gives
these their own shadings and interpretation. . . .
Modern Judaism, to be sure, like all of Gaul,
is divided into three parts.
Essentially, however, it is the noun "Judaism"
that is more important to all three groups
than the new-found adjectives, "Reform,"
"Orthodox," or "Conservative."*

Concerning "messianism," Rabbi Rosenberg says:

*Orthodox Jews still pray
for the coming of the Messiah, and believe
that the redemption of the world awaits his advent. . . .
All regard him as God's messenger,
endowed with the power and authority
to cleanse the world of its evil.
While Orthodox Jews believe in a personal Messiah,
it is a man, not a God-man, they mean.
He will serve as the "anointed one,"
the king of Israel, and will lead his people
as the "light of the nations."*

*The Messiah, they believe, will not come
until Israel is restored to its place
as the Messiah-people in the land of Israel,
where their moral example may serve
to remind the world of the teachings of the Lord. . . .*

*Conservative and Reform Jews, by and large,
do not accept the idea of a personal Messiah. . . .
Rather, they say, Judaism was essentially
concerned with the quality of human life that would
be experienced in "The Days of the Messiah."
Thus, they see Jewish messianism
as the provider of a distinctive Jewish theology:
it helps to project mankind forward to a Golden Age
yet to come. . . .*

*The age to come, "The Days of the Messiah,"
need not necessarily be regarded as being
outside history, but may even be possible
within the time of man. . . .
Jewish theology is inevitably earthbound
and leads to the conclusion that in the long run,
and in this world, God is going to be the winner,
because man, whom he created in his image,
can learn to repent of his evil ways and do good.
This life can be transformed when man
does God's will and welcomes him
into the events of history.*

This prophecy of a future messiah
gave new focus to the covenant.
At Sinai the covenant was set up in a general way
between Yahweh and the people.
Now it is linked specifically with the Davidic kings,
who represent the kingdom
and are responsible for its welfare.

28
Clay Feet

NEW TESTAMENT INTERPRETATION

New Testament writers
saw God's promise of a future messiah
from David's house fulfilled in Jesus. Luke writes:

NARRATOR *In the sixth month*
of Elizabeth's pregnancy
God sent the angel Gabriel to a
town in Galilee named Nazareth.
He had a message for a girl
promised in marriage
to a man named Joseph, who was
a descendant of King David.
The girl's name was Mary.

ANGEL *Peace be with you!*
The Lord is with you
and has greatly blessed you!

NARRATOR *Mary was deeply troubled. . . .*

ANGEL *Don't be afraid, Mary;*
God has been gracious to you.
You will . . . give birth to a son,
and you will name him Jesus.
He will be great and will be called
the Son of the Most High God.
The Lord God will make him
a king, as his ancestor David was,
and he will be the king of
the descendants of Jacob forever;
his kingdom will never end!

LUKE 1:26–33

Napoleon once said:

I have so inspired men
that they would die for me . . .
the lightning of my eye, my voice,
a word from me,
then the sacred fire was kindled in their hearts.
I do, indeed, possess the secret
of this magical power that lifts the soul.

David, too, possessed a strange, magical power
that could lift the souls of men.
Here's how one modern writer describes it.

Kingly Glory and Ordeal
ROBERT WALLACE

David's ability
to inspire love and loyalty was remarkable;
no other biblical figure,
until the appearance of Christ, approaches it.
During one battle in which he was severely pressed,
David expressed a longing
for a drink of cool water from a well in Bethlehem,
apparently several miles distant.
Without hesitation three of his men
broke through the enemy lines to gratify the whim.

On another occasion,
David and his soldiers had to flee for their safety.
A foreigner (Ittai), who had just joined David,
wanted to go with them.

DAVID   *Why are you going with us?...*
             You are a foreigner....
             You have lived here only a short
             time, so why should I make you
             wander around with me?...

ITTAI   *Your Majesty...*
             I will always go with you
             wherever you go,
             even if it means death.

                              2 SAMUEL 15:19–21

Another insight into David's character
is found in the Second Book of Samuel.
David, Abishai, and several of David's officers
were passing a certain place.

NARRATOR   *Shimei, son of Gera,*
             came out to meet him,
             cursing him as he came.
             Shimei started throwing stones....

SHIMEI   *Get out! Get out!*
             Murderer! Criminal!...

ABISHAI   *Why do you let this dog curse you?*
             Let me go over there
             and cut off his head!

DAVID   *...If he curses me because the LORD*
             told him to, who has the right
             to ask why he does it?...
             Let him do it.
             Perhaps the LORD
             will notice my misery
             and give me some blessings
             to take the place of his curse.

NARRATOR   *So David and his men*
             continued along the road.
             Shimei kept up with them,
             walking on the hillside;
             he was cursing and throwing
             stones and dirt at them
             as he went.

                              2 SAMUEL 16:5–13

NOT ALL SAINT

But there was another side to David.
For some reason, many people don't expect
the heroes of the Bible to have clay feet.
The Bible erases this false notion quickly—
often violently.

Unmatched as a warrior and king, David was like
every other man when it came to human weakness.
His court historian
leaves us a brutally honest report of the sin
that planted tragedy in David's personal life.

NARRATOR   *One day, late in the afternoon,*
             David got up from his nap
             and went to the palace roof.
             As he walked around up there,
             he saw a woman
             taking a bath in her house.
             She was very beautiful....
             She was Bathsheba...
             the wife of Uriah [a soldier]....

             David sent messengers
             to get her;
             they brought her to him
             and he made love to her....
             Then she went back home.
             Afterward she discovered
             that she was pregnant
             and sent a message
             to David to tell him.

             [When a cover-up plot fails,
             David sent a letter to Joab,
             Uriah's commanding officer.]

             "Put Uriah in the front line,
             where the fighting is heaviest,
             then retreat
             and let him be killed."...

             [Joab obeyed David's order.]

*When Bathsheba heard
that her husband had been killed,
she mourned for him.
When the time of mourning
was over, David had her brought
to the palace;
she became his wife
and bore him a son.*

2 SAMUEL 11:2-27

CONFRONTATION

Then followed a dramatic encounter
between Nathan, the prophet, and King David.

NATHAN
*There were two men
who lived in the same town;
one was rich and the other poor.
The rich man had many cattle . . .
while the poor man
had only one lamb. . . .
He took care of it,
and it grew up in his home
with his children. . . .
One day a visitor arrived
at the rich man's home.
The rich man didn't want
to kill one of his own animals
to fix a meal for him; instead,
he took the poor man's lamb
and prepared a meal
for his guest.*

DAVID
*I swear by the living LORD
that the man who did this
ought to die! . . .*

NATHAN
*You are that man. . . .
You had Uriah killed in battle . . .
and then you took his wife! . . .*

DAVID
I have sinned against the LORD.

NARRATOR
. . . Then Nathan went home.

2 SAMUEL 12:1-15

Sheep

A man's wealth, in biblical times,
was often measured by the size of his flocks.

Sheep furnished milk, cheese, and butter.
The ordinary Israelite ate mutton
only on major feasts and at major celebrations.

Sheep also furnished wool for clothing.
Here we should note that not all sheep were white.
Some were brown and some were black.

The care of sheep was demanding.
They had to be protected against wild beasts
and theft (Amos 3:12, John 10:10).
Sometimes the shepherd had to protect his flocks
with his naked hands (1 Samuel 17:34-35).

Finally, the sheep had to be protected
against the weather itself.
Commenting on the natural elements,
Laban says to Jacob in Genesis 31:40:

*Many times
I suffered from the heat during the day
and from the cold at night.*

Against this backdrop, we can see why
the shepherd became a popular biblical symbol.

125

TRAGEDY

Tragedy now descended upon David.
The son born of Bathsheba died.
Next, Absalom, David's son by a prior wife,
revolted against his father.
Although David instructed his commander, Joab,
to deal mercifully with Absalom, Joab slew him.
Moved deeply by these events, David repented.

Be merciful to me, O God. . . .
Wash away all my evil
and make me clean from my sin! . . .

Create a pure heart in me, O God,
and put a new and loyal spirit in me. . . .
Give me again the joy
that comes from your salvation. . . .

My sacrifice is a humble spirit, O God;
you will not reject
a humble and repentant heart.

PSALM 51:1–2, 10–17

DEATH OF DAVID

Finally, death came for David.
As it neared, David's eldest son, Adonijah,
sought to proclaim himself the new king.
The prophet Nathan undercut the move.
He informed Bathsheba, who prevailed upon David
to designate their second son, Solomon, as king.
David, then, gave Solomon these instructions:

"My time to die has come.
Be confident and determined,
and do what the LORD your God orders. . . .
Obey all his laws and commands . . .
so that wherever you go
you may prosper in everything you do."

1 KINGS 2:2–3

Then runners carried the news to all Israel:
"David is dead! Solomon is king!"

126

29

Israel's Soul Book

It began as a four-day climb up Mount Hood.
About 9,000 feet up, a blinding blizzard struck.
Sixteen-year-old Gary Schneider and two friends
tunnelled into a snowbank to wait out the storm.

For eleven days the storm continued to rage.
The boys' sleeping bags grew wet and lumpy;
their food supply dwindled to a meager ration
of two spoonfuls of pancake batter daily.
Their sole comfort was the Bible.

Ordeal on Mt. Hood
PHILIP YANCEY

They read aloud, taking turns, eight hours a day.
It was an eerie scene—three bodies propped up
on their elbows inside a five-foot square,
the Bible lit
by a spooky, reflected light from the tunnel.
Psalms seemed to fit best—
David wrote many of them
while trapped in situations not unlike theirs—
hungry, lonely, sometimes even in a cave. . . .
"Wait on the Lord," he said. "Trust him."
It was hard.

Finally, on the 16th day, the weather cleared,
and the three boys crawled from their snow cave.
Weakened badly by their ordeal,
they could take only a few steps at a time.
Later in the day, rescuers caught sight of them.
Their ordeal was over.

THE BOOK OF PSALMS

David is often credited
with writing the Book of Psalms.
Actually, he probably wrote only a handful of them.

Ancient peoples frequently credited authorship
to a great person who began or gave support
to an important literary project.
Started in David's time, the Book of Psalms
was not completed until about 400 B.C.
Thus, over 600 years elapsed before all 150 psalms
were collected together in the form they now have.

The arrangement in the Book of Psalms
is not the order in which they were written.
Nor are the psalms arranged
with any special theme or idea in mind.
Later editors did divide them into five booklets,
probably in imitation of the Torah.

The Book of Psalms played a key role
in the life and worship of the Israelites.

It is first of all a prayerbook.
It puts into prayer form
the history, beliefs, and feelings of the Israelites.

Thus, more than any other book of the Bible,
it allows us to glimpse the "soul" of the Israelite.
We see how he talks to God
in times of deep doubt, depression, and joy.

Second, the Book of Psalms is a song book.
The Israelites were an emotional people;
they expressed their total being in prayer.
"To sing is to pray twice," they believed.
Moreover, they knew that singing has a way
of touching the deepest part of people
and shaping their spirit as nothing else can.

"Give me the making of the songs of a nation,"
said one revolutionary,
"and I care not who makes its laws."
The Israelites would have agreed.

Children learned the lyrics and melodies
of the psalms just as children of slaves
in southern cotton fields
learned the Negro spirituals from their elders.

Perhaps even more than the books of the law,
the Book of Psalms helped to shape the spirit
of the common people of Israel.

To catch the spirit in which the psalms were sung,
let us imagine two settings.

The first is under the open skies at night.
Gathered around several campfires are Israelites,
relaxing after a day's work.
Suddenly, a colorfully dressed man rises.
A musical instrument is slung over his shoulder.
He strums it a few times and the crowd hushes.
Then, he strums it again and begins to sing.

This blind harpist from Karnak
dates back to Hebrew slave days in Egypt.
Equipped with eight strings and sound box below,
the harp was played with both hands.
Singers used the harp to accompany many of their psalms.

Listen, my people,
to my teaching, and pay attention to . . .
things that our fathers told us.
We will not keep them from our children:
we will tell the next generation about
the LORD's power and his great deeds. . . .

He gave laws to the people of Israel. . . .
He divided the sea and took them through. . . .
By day he led them with a cloud
and all night long with the light of a fire. . . .

They deliberately put God to the test
by demanding the food they wanted. . . .

He stirred up the south wind;
and to his people he sent down birds. . . .
So the people ate and were satisfied. . . .

He brought them to his holy land. . . .
But they rebelled against Almighty God. . . .
He was angry . . .
and let them be killed by their enemies. . . .

At last the LORD . . .
chose his servant David . . .
and made him king of Israel. . . .
David took care of them
with unselfish devotion and led them with skill.

PSALM 78:1-29, 54-72

These Tel Aviv dancers remind us
that psalms were not merely sung, but performed.

Children learned the psalms from their elders
and sang them at play and at worship.
"We will not keep . . . from our children . . .
the LORD's power and his great deeds."

Psalm 78:4

Sea of Galilee in the background.

Psalms as Poetry

A poetic dimension found in some psalms,
but lost in translation, was acrostic construction
Each successive line began
with one of the 22 letters of the Hebrew alphabet.
Here's an attempt to duplicate the idea
in translating the opening lines of Psalm 112.

A happy man is one who reveres the LORD,
believing and loving what the LORD commands.
Children of strength will flow from him;
descendants of his will all be blessed.
Enjoyment and prosperity will visit his house.

Another poetic dimension of many psalms
is their rhyme scheme.
Unlike English poets,
the Hebrew poet did not utilize sound rhyme,
but thought rhyme.
This means he relates two lines,
either by repeating, opposing, or completing
the thought of one line in a second line.

Repetition:

I am gripped by fear and trembling;
I am overcome with horror.

PSALM 55:5

He is like a puff of wind;
his days are like a passing shadow.

PSALM 144:4

Opposition:

The wicked man borrows and never pays back,
but the good man is generous with his gifts.

PSALM 37:21

Tears may flow in the night,
but joy comes in the morning.

PSALM 30:5

Completion:

If the LORD does not protect the city,
it does no good for the sentries to stand guard.

PSALM 127:1

It is better to trust in the LORD
than to depend on human leaders.

PSALM 118:9

Sometimes the psalmist relates several lines.
Here are two examples.

His words were smoother than cream,
but there was hatred in his heart;
his words were as soothing as oil,
but they cut like sharp swords.

PSALM 55:21

When my thoughts were bitter
and my feelings were hurt,
I was as stupid as an animal;
I did not understand you.

PSALM 73:21–22

In conclusion,
because the psalms are poetic pieces,
they do not yield their treasures readily.
They resist the hurried observer
and open themselves only to the prayerful reader.

129

These musicians, unearthed at Nineveh, date from the seventh century B.C. Cymbals and lyres similar to these were used in performing the psalms.

Praise him with harps and flutes.
Praise him with cymbals.
Praise him with loud cymbals.
Praise the LORD, all living creatures!

Praise the LORD!

PSALM 150

Other psalms were designed as a back-and-forth chant between the leader of song and the people. Drums and trumpets enhanced the dialogue.

LEADER	*Give thanks to the LORD . . . ;*
PEOPLE	*his love is eternal. . . .*
LEADER	*He made the sun and the moon;*
PEOPLE	*his love is eternal. . . .*
LEADER	*He divided the Red Sea;*
PEOPLE	*his love is eternal. . . .*
LEADER	*He freed us from our enemies;*
PEOPLE	*his love is eternal. . . .*

PSALM 136:1, 7, 13, 24

THEMES

Many attempts have been made to group psalms according to themes. One possible grouping is praise psalms, wisdom psalms, royal psalms, thanksgiving psalms, lament psalms.

PRAISE PSALMS

The psalms often begin with the word *Alleluia,* which means "Praise Yahweh!"

As in Psalm 150, the opening line was probably intoned by a soloist.
Then the people or the choir joined in.

O LORD, my God, how great you are! . . .
You spread out the heavens like a tent
and built your home on the waters above.
You use the clouds as your chariot
and ride on the wings of the wind. . . .

TEMPLE WORSHIP

A second setting in which the psalms were sung was in the temple on holidays and on the Sabbath. At these times
the psalms were not merely sung, but performed.

Psalm 150 gives us an insight into how elaborate these performances were.
We can read the psalm in 20 seconds.
Actually, it probably took closer to 20 minutes—or even two hours —to perform.

Apparently written as a grand finale to worship, it was intended to be sung, played, and danced. Thus it involved a leader of song, a chorus, musicians, dancers, and the entire congregation. The leader of song coordinated the whole, signaling when each group was to come in.

Praise the LORD!

Praise God in his Temple!
Praise his strength in heaven!
Praise him for the mighty things he has done.
Praise his supreme greatness.

Praise him with trumpets.
Praise him with harps and lyres.
Praise him with drums and dancing.

130

From the sky you send rain on the hills,
and the earth is filled with your blessings.
You make grass grow for the cattle
and plants for man to use. . . .

You created the moon to mark the months;
the sun knows the time to set.
You made the night, and in the darkness
all the wild animals come out. . . .
When the sun rises, they go back
and lie down in their dens. . . .

LORD, you have made so many things!
How wisely you made them all!

PSALM 104:1-24

WISDOM PSALMS

These psalms deal chiefly with human conduct
and how it affects a person's happiness.
They frequently begin with "Happy the man."
Wisdom psalms usually draw comparisons between
the wise and the foolish, the just and the unjust.

Happy are those
who reject the advance of evil men. . . .
Instead, they find joy in obeying the Law. . . .
They are like trees . . . beside a stream,
that bear fruit at the right time. . . .

But evil men are not like this at all;
they are like straw
that the wind blows away.
Sinners will be condemned by God
and kept apart from God's own people.

The righteous are guided . . . by the LORD,
but the evil are on the way to their doom.

PSALM 1:1-6

ROYAL PSALMS

Royal psalms concern the king.
Beginning with Yahweh's promise to David,
the king became more than a political figure.
He became a religious symbol as well.
Each new king was seen as a step toward

the "king of kings," the promised Messiah,
who would come from David's line.

Consequently, psalms were composed
to celebrate the coronation of each new king.
Psalm 101 sounds like the king's oath of office.

I will live a pure life in my house
and will never tolerate evil.
I hate the actions of those
who turn away from God;
I will have nothing to do with them. . . .
I will destroy the wicked in our land.

PSALM 101:2-8

The introduction to Psalm 20 reads like a toast
to a new king at his coronation banquet.

May the LORD
answer you when you are in trouble! . . .
May he send you help from his Temple. . . .
May he give you what you desire
and make all your plans succeed.

PSALM 20:1-4

Psalm 72 reads like the people's prayer to God
for the new king.

Teach the king
to judge with your righteousness, O God. . . .
May he help the needy. . . .
May his glory fill the whole world.

PSALM 72:1, 4, 19

THANKSGIVING PSALMS

These psalms are expressions of gratitude to Yahweh
for some benefit or blessing.

I praise you, LORD,
because you have saved me. . . .

You have changed my sadness
into a joyful dance;
you have taken away my sorrow
and surrounded me with joy. . . .

I will give you thanks forever.

PSALM 30:1, 11-12

131

The Psalmist Was Right

If the Lord does not build the house,
the work of the builders is useless;
if the Lord does not protect the city,
it does no good for the sentries to stand guard.

PSALM 127:1

The Psalms: Hymnbook of Humanity
JAMES DANIEL

In 1787 the Constitutional Convention
meeting at Philadelphia was near failure
because the 13 former colonies could not agree
on a form of effective national government.
When the deadlock appeared too great
for human power to break,
81-year-old Benjamin Franklin rose to his feet.
All his life, he said, he had been convinced
that the Psalms were right in saying,
"Except the Lord build the house,
they labor in vain to build it."
He moved that the delegates begin
the next day's meeting with a prayer
offered by a Philadelphia clergyman.
The motion carried. . . .
Congress still observes Franklin's precedent.

LAMENT PSALMS

Lament psalms are perhaps the most difficult
for modern people to understand.
In these "songs of woe,"
the poet pours out his heart to Yahweh,
often in extreme and contradictory language.

The psalmist's purpose
is not to give a literal description of his afflictions.
This is why these psalms are often more poetic.

Listen to my prayer, O Lord. . . .

I am beaten down like dry grass;
I have lost my desire for food. . . .
I am nothing but skin and bones.
I am like a wild bird in the desert,
like an owl in abandoned ruins. . . .
Ashes are my food,
and my tears are mixed with my drink.

PSALM 102:1–9

Lament psalms often deal with defeat
at the hands of an enemy
or injury at the hands of a wicked man.
In some of these psalms,
the violence voiced by the psalmist shocks us.
God is addressed as a bloodthirsty avenger.

Break the teeth of these fierce lions,
O God. . . .
May they be like a baby born dead
that never sees the light.

PSALM 58:6, 8

Again:

Babylon, you will be destroyed.
Happy is the man who pays you back
for what you have done to us—
who takes your babies
and smashes them against a rock.

PSALM 137:8–9

What can be said of these violent "prayers"?

The answer is not simple.
We must remember, however,
that the psalms were composed at a time
when Israel had no clear idea of life after death.
Reward and punishment in an afterlife
did not emerge fully until the second century B.C.,
and only then in vague terms.

Thus, the psalmist assumed
that God would punish the wicked
and reward the good in *this* life.
Seen in this light,
the psalmist's prayer for vengeance
was really a prayer for justice.

We must remember, too,
that Israel's first ideas of God were primitive.
Only with the passage of time and more revelation,
especially through the prophets,
did these ideas of God develop and mature.

Although the Book of Psalms was edited
after Israel's concept of God had passed beyond
the primitive expressions of earlier psalms,
the editor included them anyway.
There is an honesty here that is appealing.

The inclusion of these psalms
gives us a yardstick
to measure how Israel's idea of God
matured over the years.

There is a final feature about the lament psalms.
They almost always end with an act of faith.
Even though the psalmist cannot understand
why God allows wicked people to go unpunished,
he never doubts God.

But my trust is in you, O LORD;
you are my God.

PSALM 31:14

Song of Songs

Closely related to the Book of Psalms
is the tiny biblical book called the Song of Songs.
This book is short enough to be printed
on the front page of any daily newspaper.

Although the Song of Songs, which is a love poem,
is attributed to David's son Solomon,
it was set down in writing long after his death.
This need not rule out the possibility
that it derives its inspiration from Solomon.
Here is a sample of its poetic text.

Come then, my love;
my darling, come with me.
The winter is over; the rains have stopped;
in the countryside the flowers are in bloom.
This is the time for singing;
the song of doves is heard in the fields.
Figs are beginning to ripen. . . .
Come then, my love;
my darling, come with me.

SONG OF SONGS 2:10-13

The Song of Songs reads like a love song,
because it is a love song.
Some experts think that it was used
as part of the Israelite marriage ceremony.
The bride and groom saw their love as a covenant
with each other, similar to the covenant between
Yahweh and Israel.

Thus the poem has two levels of meaning.
On the surface it describes the love of two people.
At a deeper level, however, it symbolizes the love
between Yahweh and Israel.

Psalms and Life

The Israelites prayed the psalms
not just to have obstacles removed,
but also to receive strength to carry on.
They prayed not just to have doubts erased,
but also for courage to keep walking in the dark.

Today, people still derive
similar strength and courage from the psalms.

Sea Psalm

During World War II, Eddie Rickenbacker
and a crew of seven crashed into the Pacific.
All supplies were lost in the crash,
except for four small oranges.
After eight days it rained,
and the men were able to collect water to drink.
On another occasion,
a seagull landed on Rickenbacker's head.
He caught it for food which the men shared.

After 21 days, rescue came.
Seven of the eight men were still alive.
One of the things that kept them going was a prayer
session each day.

One of the most popular prayers they used
was the following psalm.

LORD, you have examined me
and you know me.
You know everything I do; from far away
you understand all my thoughts.

You see me, whether I am working or resting;
you know all my actions.
Even before I speak,
you already know what I will say.

You are all around me on every side;
you protect me with your power.
Your knowledge of me is too deep;
it is beyond my understanding.

"Where could I get away from your presence?"
Psalm 139:7

Where could I go to escape from you?
Where could I get away from your presence?

If I went up to heaven, you would be there;
if I lay down in the world of the dead,
you would be there.
If I flew away beyond the east
or lived in the farthest place in the west,
you would be there to lead me,
you would be there to help me. . . .

I praise you because you are to be feared;
all you do is strange and wonderful. . . .
O God, how difficult I find your thoughts;
how many of them there are!

PSALM 139:1–17

134

Prison Psalm

American Vietnam prisoners found similar strength
in the psalms.

Salvation
GEORGE W. CORNELL

Almost all of them say that faith
and the power of prayer sustained them. . . .
Chaplain Aronis details this conversation
with one of the returning PWs:

"Without God,
I would not have been able to survive,"
the ex-PW said.

"In other words, God really helped you?"

"No, not merely helped.
I mean it when I say I could not have made it
without God pulling me through." . . .

PWs told of setting up worship services. . . .
"The most frequently used verses of Scripture,"
he said, "was the 23rd Psalm."

The LORD is my shepherd;
I have everything I need.
He lets me rest in fields of green grass
and leads me to quiet pools of fresh water.
He gives me new strength.
He guides me in the right paths, as he promised.
Even if I go through the deepest darkness,
I will not be afraid, LORD, for you are with me.
Your shepherd's rod and staff protect me.

You prepare a banquet for me,
where all my enemies can see me;
you welcome me as an honored guest
and fill my cup to the brim.
I know that your goodness and love
will be with me all my life;
and your house will be my home
as long as I live.

PSALM 23

Passion Psalms

Jesus made frequent use of the psalms.
After the Last Supper,
he and his disciples prayed Psalms 115-119.

I will not be afraid. . . .
It is the LORD who helps me,
and I will see my enemies defeated. . . .

This is the day of the LORD's victory;
let us be happy, let us celebrate!

PSALM 118:6–7, 24

While hanging on the cross,
Jesus prayed Psalm 22.

My God, my God,
why have you abandoned me? . . .

I am no longer a man; I am a worm. . . .
All who see me make fun of me. . . .
"You relied on the LORD," they say.
"Why doesn't he save you? . . ."

My strength is gone,
gone like water spilled on the ground.
All my bones are out of joint;
my heart is like melted wax.
My throat is as dry as dust,
and my tongue
sticks to the roof of my mouth.
You have left me for dead in the dust. . . .

They tear at my hands and feet.
All my bones can be seen.
My enemies look at me and stare.
They gamble for my clothes
and divide them among themselves.

PSALM 22:1–18

Finally when death arrived,
Jesus prayed Psalm 31.

I place myself in your care.

PSALM 31:5

30
The King Who Failed

Solomon's Mines Found in Arabia
UNITED PRESS INTERNATIONAL

WASHINGTON (UPI)—*Geologists believe
King Solomon's lost gold mines have been found.*

*The U.S. Geological Survey
says it has discovered the fabled Ophir . . .
in Saudi Arabia. . . .*

*Dr. Robert Luce, a USGS geologist
who was a member of the study team of American
and Saudi geologists, said . . .*

*"Our investigations have now confirmed
that the old mine could have been as rich as
described in Biblical accounts and, indeed,
is a logical candidate to be the lost Ophir. . . .
We believe the legendary King Solomon's lost mines
are no longer lost."*

*The Bible reports that King Solomon . . .
and King Hiram brought 31 tons of gold
to Jerusalem from Ophir.
Although four books of the Bible mention Ophir,
its location is never pinpointed.*

This newspaper report recalls the prosperity
that surrounded the reign of Solomon.
Solomon had a kind of Midas touch.
If David united Israel, Solomon made it a power.

Clever in politics and shrewd in finance,
Solomon entered the arena of international trade.
Money poured in, and the economy ballooned.

With the increased income,
Solomon stockpiled Israel's arsenal,
purchasing an army of war horses and chariots.

*Solomon built up
a force of fourteen hundred chariots
and twelve thousand cavalry horses.
Some of them he kept in Jerusalem
and the rest
he stationed in various other cities.*

1 KINGS 10:26

Archaeological digs at Megiddo, Hazor, and Gezer
bear further evidence
of Solomon's national defense program.

WISDOM

But Solomon's real fame lay in his reputed wisdom.
It is this side of Solomon's portrait
that the First Book of Kings paints most vividly.

Standing guard over the centuries, these copper-
bearing rocks jut from the desert hills near
Ezion-geber. In the vicinity are copper mines worked
by Solomon's laborers and new mines being
worked by modern Israelis.

Just as David launched
the "psalm" literature of the Bible,
so Solomon launched its "wisdom" literature.

When Solomon was crowned king, around 960 B.C.,
he prayed to Yahweh for wisdom.

O LORD God,
you have let me succeed my father as king,
even though I am very young
and don't know how to rule. . . .
So give me the wisdom I need
to rule your people with justice
and to know the difference between
good and evil. . . .

The LORD was pleased
that Solomon had asked for this,
and so he said to him,
"Because you have asked for . . . wisdom . . .
instead of long life . . . or riches . . .
I will do what you have asked."

1 KINGS 3:7-12

Describing Solomon's wisdom, the Bible says:

God gave Solomon
unusual wisdom and insight. . . .
Solomon was wiser
than the wise men of the East. . . .
Kings all over the world . . .
sent people to listen to him.

1 KINGS 4:29-34

To dramatize Solomon's wisdom,
the biblical writer relates this narrative:

NARRATOR   *Two prostitutes came . . .*
            before King Solomon.

1ST WOMAN   *Your Majesty,*
            this woman and I
            live in the same house,
            and I gave birth to a baby. . . .
            Two days after my child

was born, she also gave birth. . . .
She accidentally
rolled over on her baby
and smothered it.
She got up during the night
[and exchanged babies]. . . .
When I woke up
and was going to nurse my baby,
I saw that it was dead.
I looked at it more closely
and saw that it was not my child.

2ND WOMAN   *No! The living child is mine,*
            and the dead one is yours!

NARRATOR   *And so they argued. . . .*

            [Solomon sent for a sword.]

SOLOMON   *Cut the living child in two*
            and give each woman half of it.

1ST WOMAN   *Please, Your Majesty,*
            don't kill the child!
            Give it to her!

SOLOMON   *Don't kill the child!*
            Give it to the first woman—
            she is its real mother.

1 KINGS 3:16-27

THE TEMPLE

Solomon's final achievement
was to fulfill his father's dream and build a temple
for Yahweh.

The stones with which the Temple was built
had been prepared at the quarry,
so that there was no noise
made by hammers, axes, or any other
iron tools as the Temple was being built.

1 KINGS 6:7

Jewish rabbis said that metal was not used
because it was the symbol of war.
The temple, on the contrary, was a symbol of peace.

The temple took over seven years to complete.

The inside walls
were covered with cedar panels. . . .
In the rear of the Temple an inner room
was built, where the LORD's Covenant Box
was to be placed. . . .
The whole interior of the Temple
was covered with gold.

1 KINGS 6:15–22

When the temple was finished,

the priests
carried the Covenant Box into the Temple
and put it in the Most Holy Place. . . .
There was nothing inside the Covenant Box
except the two stone tablets
which Moses had placed there at Mount Sinai,
when the LORD
made a covenant with the people of Israel.

1 KINGS 8:6–9

When the moment came to dedicate the temple,

Solomon went and stood in front of the altar,
where he raised his arms and prayed,
"LORD God of Israel. . . .
Not even all of heaven is large enough
to hold you, so how can this Temple
that I have built be large enough? . . .
Hear my prayers and the prayers of your
people when they face this place and pray."

1 KINGS 8:22–30

Jews regarded the temple as the palace of Yahweh.
To enter it was to appear before Yahweh's face.

DECLINE OF A KING

Solomon's career ended in tragedy.
Prosperity and fame took their toll.
The king's court gradually took on the pageantry
and glitter of a typical oriental court.
Solomon also adopted the oriental custom
of taking many wives—even foreign ones.

By the time he was old
they had led him into the worship
of foreign gods.
He was not faithful to the LORD his God,
as his father David had been. . . .

So the LORD was angry with Solomon
and said to him,
"Because you have deliberately broken
your covenant with me . . .
I will take the kingdom away from you
and give it to one of your officials. . . .
I will leave him one tribe
for the sake of my servant David
and for the sake of Jerusalem,
the city I have made my own."

1 KINGS 11:4, 10–13

Wearing a prayer shawl
and a phylactery about his forehead and arm,
this youth carries the Torah following a prayer service
before Jerusalem's Western Wall.

138

New Temple

In New Testament times,
Jesus showed deep regard for the temple.
He was presented in the temple (Luke 2:22).
He expelled merchants from it (John 2:16).
He taught in it daily (Matthew 26:55).
Yet Jesus placed himself above the temple.
Matthew 12:6 has Jesus say:

*"I tell you that there is something here
greater than the Temple."*

John 2:19-21 adds:

*"Tear down this Temple,
and in three days I will build it again."* . . .
*But the temple
Jesus was speaking about was his body.*

A dramatic incident occurred in the temple
at the moment of Jesus' death.

*Then the curtain hanging in the Temple
was torn in two from top to bottom.*

MATTHEW 27:51

From that point on,
the temple declined rapidly in Jewish history.
Then dawned the fateful day.
True to Jesus' prophecy,
Roman armies destroyed the temple in A.D. 70.
Today, all that remains of it is the Western Wall,
which once supported the temple terrace.

New Testament writers called Jesus' followers
the new temple.
Paul wrote to the Christians at Ephesus:

*You, too, are built upon the foundation
laid by the apostles and prophets,
the cornerstone being Christ Jesus himself.
He . . . holds the whole building together
and makes it grow into a sacred temple . . .
where God lives through his Spirit.*

EPHESIANS 2:20–22

To the Christians at Corinth he wrote:

*Surely you know that you are God's temple
and that God's Spirit lives in you!*

1 CORINTHIANS 3:16

Peter wrote:

*Come to the Lord. . . .
Come as living stones, and let yourselves
be used in building the spiritual temple,
where you will serve as holy priests
to offer spiritual and acceptable sacrifices
to God through Jesus Christ.*

1 PETER 2:4–5

Finally, Jesus said:

*"Where two or three come together in my name,
I am there with them."*

MATTHEW 18:20

139

31
Wisdom of Israel

RUSSIA   *Pray to God*
         but continue to row to the shore.

CHINA   *Fool me once, shame on you;*
         fool me twice, shame on me.

ITALY   *The same fire that burns the straw*
         purifies the gold.

GREECE   *When the fox cannot reach the grapes,*
         he says they are sour.

JAPAN   *At the first glass, we drink the wine;*
         at the second, wine drinks the wine;
         at the third, the wine drinks us.

SPAIN   *Who loses the right moment, loses all.*

IRELAND *Long sleep makes a bare back.*

Every nation has its proverbs.
Cervantes called a proverb
"a short sentence based on long experience."
Lord Russell called it
"the wisdom of many and the wit of one."

Many of Israel's wisdom sayings are recorded
in the Book of Proverbs,
one of the Wisdom Books of the Bible.
Solomon's name is often linked to this book.
This is not because he wrote it,
but because he was the ideal of Israelite wisdom.

God gave Solomon unusual wisdom and insight,
and knowledge too great to be measured.

1 KINGS 4:29

SEVEN BOOKS

Many Christian Bibles include the following
as Wisdom Books:

Job	Song of Songs
Psalms	Wisdom
Proverbs	Sirach
Ecclesiastes	

Here we should note that Jews and Christians divide
the Old Testament books into different categories.
Roughly, the two divisions match up this way:

Jews	*Christians*
Torah (Law)	Torah (Law)
Writings	Writings (Wisdom Books)
Prophets (Latter &	Prophets (Latter prophets)
Former)	History (Former prophets)

THREE AREAS

Judaism, like other religions,
may be viewed in terms of creed, cult, and code:

creed	what members believe,
cult	how members worship,
code	how members live out their belief in everyday life.

In ancient Israel,

priests	dealt mostly with creed and cult,
scribes	with code and style,
prophets	with all three—rebuking errant members and encouraging the weak.

Thus, priests were linked mainly to the *law*,
scribes with the *writings* or wisdom literature,
prophets with the *prophetic* literature.

Chinese commune workers near modern Canton.

Chinese Wisdom

About the same time that Israelite scribes
were compiling the Book of Proverbs,
a wise person named Confucius
was using the same method to teach in China.
For nearly a century and a half,
his sayings were passed on orally by his disciples.
Around 350 B.C., they were compiled in the
Analects of Confucius. Some examples are:

*To see the right
and not do it is want of courage.* (2:24)

*A scholar who loves comfort
is not worthy of the name.* (14:3)

*When a man of forty is hated,
it will be so to the end.* (17:26)

A heart set on love will do no wrong. (4:4)

The fault is to cling to a fault. (15:29)

SCRIBES

Scribes still operate today
in countries where illiteracy is high.

Before the invention of printing,
scribes also copied all books.
Historical records explain how a nobleman in Italy
employed 45 scribes for two years to copy
200 books of his private library.

Scribes were first used in Israel because even kings
and generals could not read or write.
Thus, a kind of secretary was needed for them.
Because the scribe's job
put him in touch with a wide range of knowledge,
he became highly informed in many matters.
Referring to the scribe, the Book of Sirach says:

*He memorizes the sayings of famous men
and is a skilled interpreter of parables. . . .
Great men call on him for his services,
and he is seen in the company of rulers.
He travels to foreign lands in his efforts
to learn about human good and evil.*

SIRACH 39:2–4

Around 500 B.C.,
scribes began to collect and write down
what they learned about good and evil.
Thus, the Book of Proverbs was born.

Missing his vital pen hand, this Egyptian scribe
did his writing from a squat position.
Scribes held the rank of a court officer
(1 Kings 4:3).

BIBLICAL WISDOM

The Book of Proverbs states its purpose
in a brief foreword.
It is to help everyone, especially the young,
learn what is right, just, and honest.

The book's 31 chapters consist of short,
easy-to-remember sayings about everything
from how to win friends and influence people
to reasons for staying sober.

The sayings are not all original with Israel.
Many were collected from foreign sources.
Hebrew scribes, then, adapted them
to fit Israel's faith and practical needs.

For example, one section of the Book of Proverbs
deals with instructions for young men
studying to be courtiers.
When Israel switched her government
from rule by judges to rule by kings,
a program was needed
to train young men to work around the king.

As a guide for this program,
Israel borrowed ideas from the Egyptians.
Here are some directives adapted from a program
of the Egyptian, Amen-em-ope.

*When you sit down to eat with an important man,
keep in mind who he is.*

PROVERBS 23:1

*Don't hesitate to rescue someone
who is about to be executed unjustly. . . .
[God] will reward you
according to what you do.*

PROVERBS 24:11-12

MEDITATION TRIGGERS

Other proverbs are designed to prod the Israelite
into meditating on the ordinary things of life.
Among these are the so-called numerical proverbs,
popular among Arabs.

*There are four things
that are too mysterious for me to understand:
an eagle flying in the sky,
a snake moving on a rock,
a ship finding its way over the sea,
and a man and a woman falling in love.*

PROVERBS 30:18-19

Again:

*There are four things
that the earth itself cannot tolerate:
a slave who becomes a king,
a fool who has all he wants to eat,
a hateful woman who gets married,
and a servant girl
who takes the place of her mistress.*

PROVERBS 30:21-23

What Is Meditation?

Some people ask:
"Are meditation and prayer the same thing?"

Although we sometimes treat them as such,
technically, they are different.
An example may help.
A young person described this experience:

It was my junior year in high school.
I was listening to some music.
I wasn't thinking about a thing.
I was just enjoying the sound.

Suddenly, I found myself
wondering about something I once read:
"Music is love in search of a word."

I liked the expression,
even though I never fully understood its meaning.
I still don't know if I do.

Anyway, it occurred to me
that praying to God was like that at times.
I sometimes feel that I want to pray to God,
but I can't seem to find the words to do it.
That's kind of like "love in search of a word."

Then something strange happened to me.
All of a sudden I was just filled with words;
and I began to express myself to God
as never before in my life.
I talked to him from the depths of my heart—
about my problems, my doubts, even my dreams.
For the first time, I think, I really prayed.

The young person's experience
is a perfect illustration of what prayer is.
It illustrates, also, three forms prayer can take:
contemplation, meditation, conversation.

The first part of the experience
was *enjoying* something (listening to music).
This corresponds to *contemplation*.

The second part was *exploring* an idea
("music is love in search of a word").
This corresponds to *meditation*.

The third part was *expressing* one's self
("I began to express myself to God").
This corresponds to *conversation*.

Prayer can involve each of these three forms.
Moreover, the three forms frequently occur together,
like three sides of the same triangle.

Contemplation is *enjoying* the presence of God.
Meditation is *exploring* something about God.
Conversation is *expressing* oneself to God.

Sometimes, however, as the young person noted,
prayer doesn't seem to fit any of these categories.
It is simply "love in search of a word."
"When it comes to prayer," said John Bunyan,
"it is better to have a heart without words
than words without a heart."

MEMORY PATTERNS

A number of proverbs follow a set form.
No doubt this facilitated memorizing them.
The form usually takes one of three patterns.
The first is *contrast*.

Peace of mind makes the body healthy,
but jealousy is like a cancer.

PROVERBS 14:30

A gentle answer quiets anger,
but a harsh one stirs it up.

PROVERBS 15:1

A second poetic pattern is *completion*.
Some point is made in the first half of a verse
and completed in the second half.

The start of an argument is like the first break
in a dam; stop it before it goes any further.

PROVERBS 17:14

When you give to the poor,
it is like lending to the LORD,
and the LORD will pay you back.

PROVERBS 19:17

A final poetic pattern
is that of the *simile* or *metaphor*.

A lazy person is as bad as someone
who is destructive.

PROVERBS 18:9

Kind words are like honey—
sweet to the taste and good for your health.

PROVERBS 16:24

SIMPLE PROSE

Not all the instructions in the Book of Proverbs
are put in these poetic patterns.
Some are merely expressed in vivid prose.
An example
is this caution against excessive drinking:

Don't let wine tempt you, even though
it is rich red, and it sparkles in the cup. . . .
The next morning you will feel
as if you had been bitten by a poisonous snake.
Weird sights will appear before your eyes,
and you will not be able to think
or speak clearly.
You will feel as if you were out on the ocean,
seasick, swinging high up in the rigging
of a tossing ship.
"I must have been hit," you will say . . .
"but I don't remember it.
Why can't I wake up? I need another drink."

PROVERBS 23:31–35

YOU WONDER

As you read these proverbs, you may wonder:
How do they relate to the rest of the Bible?
The answer lies in Israel's concept of religion.
Life and religion were inseparable.
Consequently, the biblical writer is concerned
about every phase of human existence.

Nevertheless, the editor of the Book of Proverbs
does attempt a specific connection between God
and the quest for knowledge.

To have knowledge, you must first
have reverence for the LORD.

PROVERBS 1:7

In other words, without an appreciation of God,
people cannot begin to appreciate God's creation.

LATER CONNECTION

New Testament writers found another connection.
Chapter 8 of the Book of Proverbs
speaks of wisdom as a person.

I was there when he set the sky in place . . .
when he laid the earth's foundations.
I was beside him like an architect.

PROVERBS 8:27–30

Compare this to John's description of Jesus.

Before the world was created,
the Word already existed. . . .
Through him God made all things.

JOHN 1:1–3

Paul linked Jesus and wisdom explicitly.
He called Jesus the wisdom of God
(1 Corinthians 1:24).

Thus, New Testament writers portrayed Jesus as the personification of the wisdom
that the ancient wisemen sought.

"I am the light of the world," he said.
"Whoever follows me will have the light of life
and will never walk in darkness."

JOHN 8:12

"If you obey my teaching . . .
you will know the truth,
and the truth will set you free."

JOHN 8:31–32

Early American Wisdom

Poor Richard's Almanac is a fine example
of early American *wisdom* literature.
A study of it helps us understand better
Israel's Book of Proverbs.
Benjamin Franklin, the *Almanac's* author, wrote:

I consider it a proper vehicle for conveying
instructions among the common people,
who bought scarcely any other books;
I therefore filled all the little spaces that occurred
between the remarkable days of the calendar
with proverbial sentences.

These proverbs were the "Sayings of Poor Richard."
Franklin collected them from all nations.
In this respect, his self-taught knowledge
of German, French, Italian, Latin, and Spanish
came in handy.

Franklin did not merely translate the proverbs,
but also simplified them for the common people.
An example is this saying:

Fresh fish and new-come guests smell,
but that after they are three days old.

Franklin shortened it to read:
Fish and visitors stink in three days.

After 25 years of publishing the *Almanac,*
Franklin put out an anniversary edition in 1757.
The preface describes a country auction,
where people are complaining of high taxes.
Franklin has a wise man address the people.
He tells them
that the taxes they lay upon themselves
are far heavier than those
imposed by the government.

We are taxed twice as much by our idleness,
three times as much by our pride,
and four times as much by our folly.

Throughout the wise man's speech
occurs a host of proverbs that had appeared
in earlier editions of the *Almanac.*

He who is good at making excuses
is seldom good for anything else.

If a man could have half his wishes,
he would double his trouble.

A plowman on his knees
is higher than a gentleman on his legs.

145

MACEDONIA

PHRYGIA

Black Sea

Mt. Ararat

MESOPOTAMIA

Mediterranean Sea

JERUSALEM

EGYPT

Red Sea

Time Chart

Jeroboam	Rehoboam	922 BC	
	Others	915	
Others		901	
		883	Ashurnasirpal II
Omri		876	
Ahab	Jehoshaphat	870	
		859	Shalmaneser III
Ahab's sons	Others	850	
Jehu		842	
		824	Others
Others		815	
Jeroboam II		786	
	Uzziah	783	
Others		745	Tiglath-pileser III
	Others	742	
Hosea		732	
		727	Shalmaneser V
North falls		722	Sargon II
	Hezekiah	715	
		705	Sennacherib
Others		687	
		680	Esarhaddon
		669	Others
Josiah		640	
		612	Assyria falls Nabopolassara
Others		609	
		605	Nebuchadnezzar
Jehoiachim		598	
First attack		597	
Zedekiah			
South falls		586	

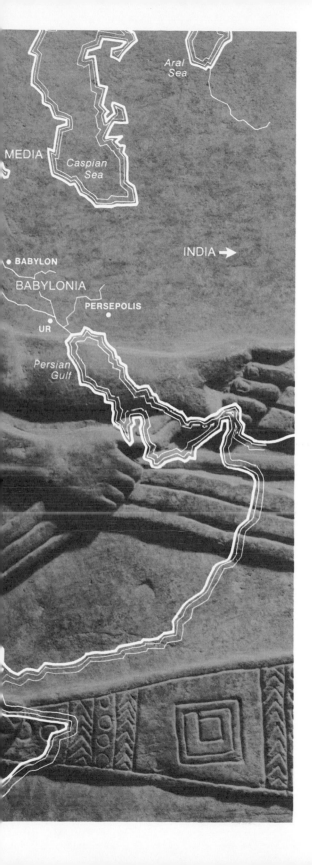

NATIONHOOD
EXILE

Books

1 Kings 11-22	Hosea
2 Kings	Amos
2 Chronicles 10-31	Micah
Isaiah 1-40	Nahum
Jeremiah	Habakkuk
Lamentations	Zephaniah
Baruch	

32

From Brothers to Rivals

Some years ago, a report was filed on Indians of South Dakota's Pine Ridge reservation.

Grim Poverty Stalks the Land of Red Cloud
JAMES FITZGERALD

Government studies show that the life expectancy
for the American Indian is 43 years,
while that of the white man is 67 years.
Of the 10,000 Indians on the Pine Ridge reservation,
800 families have no home of their own.
88 percent live in slum conditions.
Some of these people must live in tents and
abandoned automobile bodies even in midwinter.
Half of the reservation's population is unemployed,
largely because they must live 30 miles or more
from the nearest public transportation. . . .

Half of the people on the reservation are under 21.
Yet there are no public movie theaters,
drive-ins, bowling alleys. . . .
Only about one home in ten has electricity.
And of the 500 telephones on the reservation,
most are in government offices or at trading posts.

All of the government offices
and the 58 bed government hospital are located
on the far southwestern corner of the reservation.
Indians having business or needing medical help
must, in most cases, travel 90 to 100 miles. . . .
Nine out of ten lack proper dental care.
75 percent of them have no safe water supply.

VIOLENCE

In the light of situations like this,
it was not surprising that some Indians
responded with violence to dramatize their plight.
Concerning this kind of violence,
historian Arnold Toynbee said:

Human beings are committing acts of violence
because they feel that they are being treated
not as persons but as things . . .
and in many cases
they have found by infuriating experience
that recourse to violence is the only means
by which they can extort attention
to legitimate claims and genuine grievance.

Ignoring legitimate claims and genuine grievance
stirred up violence in Israel
at the death of Solomon.

During the latter half of his reign,
Solomon taxed the twelve tribes heavily in money
and manpower for national building projects.
There was always the whispered suspicion
that he favored the two southern tribes,
Benjamin and Judah.

When Solomon died and his son Rehoboam took
the throne, the suspicion broke into the open.
The angry northern tribes sent a delegation
to the new king and demanded reform.

NARRATOR   *King Rehoboam consulted*
the older men who had served
as his father Solomon's advisers.

KING   *What answer do you advise me*
to give these people?

ELDERS   *. . . Give a favorable answer*
to their request,
and they will always serve you
loyally.

NARRATOR	*But he ignored the advice . . .*
	and went instead to the young
	men who had grown up with him
	and who were now his advisers.
KING	*. . . What shall I say*
	to the people . . . ?
ADVISORS	*. . . Tell them, "My father placed*
	heavy burdens on you;
	I will make them even heavier.
	He beat you with whips;
	I'll flog you with bullwhips!"

1 KINGS 12:6-11

The king followed the advice of the young men.
The ten northern tribes reacted swiftly.
Uniting under a leader named Jeroboam,
they broke with the southern tribes.

David's work of unifying Israel
went pouring down the drain of history.
In 922 B.C. the kingdom split into two nations:
the South, Judah; and the North, Israel.

LIFE IN THE NORTH

The leaders of the North
set up religious centers at Bethel and Dan,
in opposition to Jerusalem.
These new centers not only crippled religious unity,
but also set the stage for idolatry later.

A crisis arose after Jeroboam's death.
As yet the North had no clear line of kingship,
and so the throne fell
to whoever was strong enough to seize it.

Not until the reign of Omri
did a definite line of kingship develop.
Thus, the 25 years
between Jeroboam's death and the rise of Omri
were checkered with plots and assassinations.

Omri finally stabilized the political situation.

First, he established Samaria as the North's capital.
Next, he arranged for his son, Ahab,
to marry a Phoenician princess named Jezebel.
Thus Phoenicia and the North became allies.

With his government stabilized, Omri expanded
his kingdom by subduing Mesha, king of Moab.
Omri's brilliant career ended with his death.

When Ahab mounted the throne, problems began.
Jezebel badgered him into allowing her
to bring altars and priests of Baal to Samaria.
Religious unity, already weakened by keeping
the people from Jerusalem, began to crumble.
Soon Baalism began to make inroads in the North.

CULT OF BAAL

Baalism has been clarified in recent years.
At modern Ras Shamra (site of ancient Ugarit
on the northern Mediterranean coast),
archaeologists found tablets relating to the cult.

Baal was one of many gods
worshiped by Israel's neighboring nations.
Following the rhythm of the changing seasons,
he died and revived each year.
His lovemaking with his female partner
revived all fertility of womb and field.
Baal worshipers imitated their God.

Since most Israelites
were uneducated herdspeople and farmers,
the cult of Baal held a fascinating appeal—
especially when Yahweh seemed to turn a deaf ear
to their prayers in time of famine.
After all, wasn't Yahweh a "desert" God?
Did he know about crops and flocks?
Perhaps they should turn to Baal for help in these.

It was this situation that caused the prophets
Elijah and Elisha to rise up during Ahab's reign.
With their appearance,
the Era of the Prophets dawned in Israel.

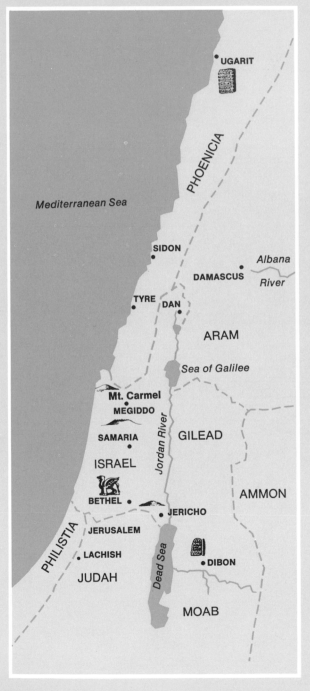

UGARIT
Inscribed tablets were found here (now Ras Shamra) and supply invaluable data about Baalism. The tablets are written in a Canaanite dialect somewhat similar to pre-Mosaic Hebrew.

MEGIDDO
Excavations at this location clarify biblical accounts relating to the era of Solomon and the North-South split of Israel in 922 B.C.

SAMARIA
The palace begun by Omri and completed by Ahab was unearthed by a team of Anglo-American archaeologists. Beautiful ivory carvings confirmed biblical reports about this "palace decorated with ivory" (1 Kings 22:39).

DIBON
The Moabite Stone, found here, tells of King Mesha's revolt against Israel. The stone is now housed in the Louvre in Paris.

33

Two Who Said "No"

No tourist who has read his guidebook carefully
can enter the port of Haifa
without thinking of Elijah, the prophet.
From the starboard side of incoming ships,
you get a striking view of Mount Carmel.

At that site, nearly 25 centuries ago,
Elijah made a dramatic stand against Baalism.
Before a standing-room-only crowd,
he took on 450 prophets of Baal all by himself.
The First Book of Kings describes the contest.

ELIJAH *I am the only prophet*
of the LORD still left,
but there are 450 prophets of Baal.
Bring two bulls;
let the prophets of Baal
take one . . .
and put it on the wood—
but don't light the fire.
I will do the same
with the other bull.
Then let the prophets of Baal
pray to their god,
and I will pray to the LORD,
and the god who answers
by sending fire—
he is God.

NARRATOR *The people*
shouted their approval. . . .
[The prophets began.]

They shouted,
"Answer us, Baal!"
and kept dancing around
the altar they had built.
But no answer came.
At noon,
Elijah started making fun of them.

ELIJAH *Pray louder! He is a god!*
Maybe he is day-dreaming. . . .
Or maybe he's sleeping,
and you've got to wake him up!

NARRATOR *So the prophets prayed louder*
and cut themselves
with knives and daggers,
according to their ritual . . .
but no answer came,
not a sound was heard.

Then Elijah . . .
approached the altar and prayed.

ELIJAH *O LORD, the God of Abraham,*
Isaac, and Jacob . . . answer me,
so that this people will know
that you, the LORD, are God
and that you are bringing them
back to yourself.

NARRATOR *The LORD sent fire down,*
and it burned up the sacrifice,
the wood, and the stones. . . .
When the people saw this, they
threw themselves on the ground.

PEOPLE *The LORD is God;*
the LORD alone is God!

1 KINGS 18:22–39

This story,
like others about Elijah,
was passed on orally for centuries.
Based on actual circumstances,
it was probably simplified to make its point:
the power of faith in Israel's prophets.

"Elijah climbed to the top of Mount Carmel. . . .
He said to his servant,
'Go and look toward the sea.'"

1 Kings 18:42–43

of Anne Frank *where the young Dutch Jew
affirmed her conviction that "in spite of everything,
I still believe that people are really good at heart."*

*"At our family seder Monday night,"
Rabbi Bronstein said,
"my own daughter read that passage
and the room became as silent as it could be."*

*The North Shore spiritual leader quickly added . . .
that the new seder rite
is not a memorial but a "redemptive experience,
a celebration of our deliverance. . . ."*

*He continued,
"Because the future may well be the greatest period
of Jewish spirituality, we have given prominence
to the tradition of the 'fifth cup.'"*

*The "fifth cup" is the ceremonial glass of wine
placed on the table for the prophet Elijah who,
it is believed, will usher in the messianic age.*

The Fifth Cup

Elijah is described as departing life
in a fiery chariot, amid a whirlwind (2 Kings 2:11).
Symbolic or not,
the description gave rise to Jewish belief
that Elijah would return some day.

Orthodox Jews still place an empty chair for Elijah
at each seder meal.
Reform Jews put new stress on the "cup of Elijah"
in their revised seder rite.

New Seder Celebration
ROY LARSON

*In an interview . . .
Rabbi Bronstein said a new seder rite
has long been overdue. . . .*

*In a collection of supplementary resources . . .
is the well-known passage from* The Diary

Already Come

Some New Testament Jews
thought Jesus was Elijah returned (Matthew 16:14).
Others thought John the Baptist was (John 1:21).
Jesus, however, said:

*"But I tell you that Elijah has already come
and people did not recognize him. . . ."*

*Then the disciples understood
that he was talking to them
about John the Baptist.*

MATTHEW 17:12–13

*"He will go ahead of the Lord,
strong and mighty like the prophet Elijah. . . .
He will turn disobedient people back
to the way of thinking of the righteous;
he will get the Lord's people ready for him."*

LUKE 1:17

152

ELISHA

After Elijah departed,
his prophetic charisma passed to Elisha, his disciple.
Elisha continued the fight against Baalism.

Elisha was also recalled in New Testament times.
Jesus referred to this incident (Luke 4:27).

NARRATOR *Naaman, the commander*
of the Syrian army,
was highly respected and esteemed
by the king of Syria . . .
but he suffered
from a dreaded skin disease.
In one of their raids against Israel,
the Syrians had carried off
a little Israelite girl,
who became a servant
of Naaman's wife.

GIRL *I wish that my master could go*
to the prophet who lives in Samaria!
He would cure him. . . .

NARRATOR *[Naaman] went to the king*
and told him
what the girl had said.

KING *Go to the king of Israel*
and take this letter to him.

NARRATOR *So Naaman set out. . . .*
The letter that he took read:
"This letter will introduce
my officer Naaman. I want you
to cure him of his disease."

When the king of Israel read
the letter, he tore his clothes. . . .

KING *. . . Does he think that I am God,*
with the power of life and death?
It's plain that he is trying
to start a quarrel with me!

ELISHA *Why are you so upset?*
Send the man to me, and I'll show
him that there is a prophet in Israel!

NARRATOR *So Naaman went. . . .*
[Elisha sent word to Naaman
to bathe seven times
in the Jordan River.]

NAAMAN *[angry] I thought that he would*
at least come out to me,
pray to the LORD his God,
wave his hand over the diseased spot,
and cure me! . . .
[Are not the rivers in Damascus]
better than any river in Israel?
I could have washed in them
and been cured!

SERVANTS *Sir, if the prophet had told you*
to do something difficult,
you would have done it.
Now why can't you
just wash yourself, as he said,
and be cured?

NARRATOR *So Naaman*
went down to the Jordan,
dipped himself in it seven times,
as Elisha had instructed,
and he was completely cured.
His flesh became firm
and healthy like that of a child.

2 KINGS 5:1–14

In the months that followed,
Elisha's reputation as a miracle worker soared.
In fact, some scholars believe
that many of the miracle stories about him
took on legendary proportions.

Regardless of how you interpret them, however,
the point the stories make remains unmistakable:
Elisha was a spiritual giant
whose religious and political importance
extended even beyond the borders of Israel.

This seventh-century B.C. relief
bears out the Assyrian king's boast:
"The heads of their warriors I cut off
and formed into a pillar over against their city."
Assyrians were masters of psychological warfare,
sending paid agents ahead to frighten people with tales
of the advancing army's size, strength, and brutality.

AHAB'S SUCCESSORS

When Ahab died, problems arose.
King Mesha of Moab revolted against Israel.
Moabite opposition to Israel is reported
not only in the Bible (2 Kings 3:1-5), but also
on the Moabite Stone found at Dibon. It reads:

As for Omri, king of Israel . . .
I [Mesha] have defeated him and his house.

Ahab's two sons followed their father to the throne,
but they were irresponsible kings.
Finally, Elisha put an end to the House of Omri.
He had Jehu, a military leader, anointed king.

JEHU

Jehu inherited problems
not only from within, but also from without.
One of these was the nation of Assyria,
which began to bully tiny nations in the Near East
about the time of the North-South split.

Excavated records provide a grim insight
into Assyrian battle tactics.
One inscription tells how the Assyrian king
(Ashurnasirpal II) treated defeated peoples.

Their young men and their maidens,
I burned in fire.

A second boast by the same king reads:

The heads of their warriors I cut off
and formed into a pillar over against their city.

An excavated stone carving
shows Assyrian soldiers doing precisely this.

A companion carving shows enemy soldiers
stripped and impaled on spikelike poles
outside the city walls.

Somehow Jehu and his immediate successors
survived the Assyrian menace.
But the day was not far off
when their luck would run out.

Behind wicker shields, archers shoot past
the bodies of prisoners impaled outside the city walls.
A battering ram is ready
to punch through the city wall or tunnel under it.

Found in Nimrud, an Assyrian palace site,
this black limestone pillar contains five panels of pictures.
Intended to be read horizontally around the four sides,
each panel is captioned above. The second panel
from the top depicts Jehu (842-815 B.C.) paying tribute to
Shalmaneser. The obelisk is now in the British Museum.

Buried Story

Back in the middle 1800s,
when archaeology was still in its infancy days,
an adventuresome young Englishman,
Austen Layard,
got excited about the treasures of the Near East
by reading the *Arabian Nights*.

He left England and journeyed to the Near East.
There he organized Arab work crews
and began digging into the desert sands
for lost treasures.

155

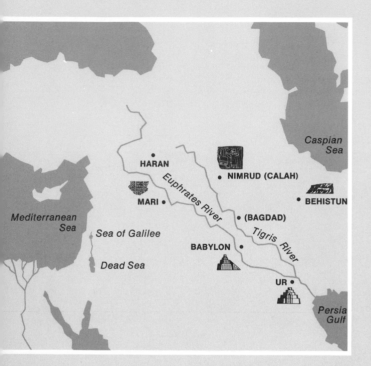

NIMRUD (CALAH)

Here diggers unearthed the Assyrian palace
of Ashurnasirpal II. A contemporary of Ahab,
he was succeeded by Shalmaneser III,
to whom Jehu paid tribute (see page 155).
Also found were wall panels carved in stone.
Some depict Assyrian battle practices;
one depicts Tiglath-pileser III, king of Assyria.

This remarkable relief found at Nimrud
shows the Assyrian king, Tiglath-pileser III, being driven
in his state chariot. An attendant holds an umbrella
to shield him from the hot desert sun.

One day
his searches paid off beyond his dreams.
The shovel of one of his workmen
struck something solid in the sand.

When the tons of sand around it were removed,
the object turned out to be a six-foot,
four-sided, black obelisk,
which once belonged to Shalmaneser III.

One of the obelisk panels
contained a captioned carving of Jehu,
kneeling in humble tribute
before the mighty Assyrian monarch.
The caption read:

Jehu, son of Omri.
I received from him silver, gold, and javelins.

156

34

More Voices of Protest

A UN study says
that 75 percent of the world's population
under the age of 15
lives in third-world countries.

It also says that every 30 seconds
100 more children are born in these countries.
Twenty of these children will die in childhood.
Of the 80 children who survive,
60 will never get any modern medical care
in their childhood years.

In his book *The Great Ascent,*
Robert Heilbroner probes what it means
to live in a third-world country. He asks:
What would we have to do to an American family
to reduce it to the level of a third-world family?
His answer is startling.

We would have to begin by emptying
the living room and bedrooms of all furnishings.
We may leave a few moth-eaten blankets
and some threadbare clothes for the family.
A pair of beaten-up shoes may be left
for the father, but for no one else.

Next, we would move to the kitchen.
Again, everything must go.
Some matches, a sack of flour, some salt,
and a little sugar may stay on a wooden shelf.
So may a few onions and dried beans.
A few potatoes—already in the garbage—
may be retrieved for tonight's meal.

Now, we take away the house itself.
The family may move into the garage—
providing it is not too good.
If it is, the family moves into the tool shed.
It is crowded, but it is not uncommon
for some third-world families
to live in a space the size of a large bed.

But now the real work begins.
We must remove all other houses on the street.
We must also rip up the streets and sidewalks.
Similarly, all forms of communication
and public service are discontinued—
all newspapers, magazines, radios
(except one for the entire community).
There is a two-room school three miles away.
There is also a makeshift medical station
staffed by an unskilled attendant ten miles away.

Finally, all money goes.
Each family may keep about five dollars
to guard against the kind of tragedy
reported in the *New York Times,*
where a third-world peasant went blind
because he did not have the small fee
he thought he needed for entry into a hospital.

Meanwhile, the father must work
for as little as $100 a year.
If he rents land to grow some small crops,
a third of his produce goes to the owner.
Food is a constant problem.
Some third-world children have been known to eat
the undigested oats picked out of horse droppings.

Our job is now complete.

POVERTY AND SPLENDOR

During the reign of Jeroboam II,
Israel enjoyed an era of prosperity.
But amid the glitter of Israel's great society
lay the telltale signs of decay.
Baalism was still bubbling up here and there.
There was also a wide gap between rich and poor.

157

Archaeological digs at Samaria
testify to the lopsided luxury that once existed there.
Excavators found palaces and hovels side by side.
They also discovered luxurious ivory carvings,
confirming biblical reports
of "houses decorated with ivory" (Amos 3:15).

CRIES OF PROTEST

Into this sick society
entered the first writing prophets, Amos and Hosea.
They are called "writing" prophets
because their words were collected together
and recorded in separate books of the Bible.

Included among these men are four major prophets
(long writings) and twelve minor prophets (short
writings). The major prophets are:

Isaiah   Ezekiel
Jeremiah   Daniel

The minor prophets include:

Hosea   Jonah   Zephaniah
Joel   Micah   Haggai
Amos   Nahum   Zechariah
Obadiah   Habakkuk   Malachi

Also included among the Prophetic Books
are two other works (associated with Jeremiah):
the Book of Lamentations and the Book of Baruch.

For the most part,
prophets and kings walk along together in the Bible.
Where you find one, you usually find the other.

The reason for this is that part of the prophet's job
was to advise and correct the king.
This dual function stands out clearly
in the case of King David and Nathan.

Nathan was both
a "foreteller" (he foretold to David God's promise)
and a "forthteller" (he condemned David's crime
against Uriah).

This double ivory comb (ca. 1200 B.C.),
dug up at Megiddo,
is not unlike ivory carvings found at Samaria.

PANDORA'S BOX

The event
that provoked the writing prophets into action
was not just exploitation of the poor.
Rather, it was a flood of evil
that now began to engulf both kingdoms.

Disunity between the two kingdoms
opened the lid of a giant Pandora's box.
From it poured out every kind of abuse:
idolatry, adultery, oppression of the poor,
and religious formalism.

Religious formalism was especially widespread.
Failing to serve Yahweh in their daily lives,
the people eased their consciences
by multiplying altars, sacrifices, and rituals.
Religion became a shell—all show and no soul.

Giants of Faith

Without the prophets
there would have been no apostles and martyrs;
Jesus of Nazareth
would have remained at his carpenter's bench,
unheard of and unsung;
there would have been no Judaism;
Mohammed
would have stayed an unknown camel driver.

This is another way of saying
that the prophets kept faith alive in Israel
when it flickered and almost went out.

The prophets disturbed the comfortable,
and comforted the disturbed.

35
God of Concern

A recent cartoon shows
a bearded fanatic in sackcloth and sandals
carrying a placard . . .
"Repent, for the end is at hand!"
Behind him the sky is criss-crossed
by rockets and war planes. . . .

In the caption,
a bystander remarks to his companion:
"Have you noticed?
No one's laughing at him any more!

The cartoon reflects . . .
what many people think of Old Testament prophets.
They feel that the prophets,
if they were alive today,
would be bearded fanatics
with no message for our times . . .
warning that the end is at hand.

AMOS

The prophets were not out of it.
They were very much with it.
They knew what was going on and they spoke out
against it. Such a man was Amos.

Born at Tekoa, near Bethlehem,
Amos was not a northerner, but a southerner.

159

Nor does he seem to have been especially prepared
for his prophetic mission.

I am a herdsman,
and I take care of fig trees.
But the LORD took me
from my work as a shepherd
and ordered me to come and prophesy
to his people Israel.

AMOS 7:14–15

Amos turned over his flocks and sycamores
to hired hands and left the ravines and hills
of Judah for the North.
After a 30-mile journey, he came to Bethel,
one of the religious centers
that Jeroboam had set up in the North.

This dust-covered farmer must have made
a strange impression on the crowds
milling about the temple grounds.
But his words probably seemed
even more quaint to the city dwellers.
Written portions of his prophetic message
are checkered with colorful rural images:

a prey in the mouth of a lion (Amos 3:4);
a bird caught in a snare (Amos 3:5);
a mangled sheep being carried home
by a weeping shepherd to prove to its owner
that it had been killed, not stolen (Amos 3:12);
a fig tree stripped bare by locusts (Amos 4:9).

But Amos' images in no way obscured his message.
Pointing his finger at the complacent rich,
he scorched their ears saying:

The LORD says . . .
"They sell into slavery
honest men who cannot pay their debts. . . .
They trample down the weak and helpless
and push the poor out of the way."

AMOS 2:6–7

If social injustice was bad in the North,
religious worship was even worse.

Ignoring Yahweh's covenant in the marketplace,
the people tried to bribe Yahweh in the temple.
Amos condemned this religious formalism.

The LORD says,
"I hate your religious festivals;
I cannot stand them! . . .
Stop your noisy songs;
I do not want to listen to your harps.
Instead,
let justice flow like a stream,
and righteousness
like a river that never goes dry."

AMOS 5:21–24

DAY OF DARKNESS

Referring to the "Day of the Lord,"
which people looked forward to
as a day of triumph for Israel over her enemies,
Amos said:

How terrible it will be for you
who long for the day of the LORD! . . .
For you it will be a day of darkness.

AMOS 5:18

"When I punish the people of Israel . . .
I will destroy the altars of Bethel.
The corners of every altar
will be broken off and will fall to the ground."

AMOS 3:14

PREDICTABLE RESPONSE

The reaction to Amos' words was swift and expected.

Amaziah, the priest of Bethel,
then sent a report to King Jeroboam of Israel:
"Amos is plotting against you among the people.
His speeches will destroy the country.
This is what he says:
'Jeroboam will die in battle, and the people
of Israel will be taken away from their land. . . .'"

Amaziah then said to Amos,
"That's enough, prophet! Go on back to Judah
and do your preaching there. . . .
Don't prophesy here at Bethel any more.
This is the king's place of worship."

AMOS 7:10-13

So Amos departed from Bethel.

POINT OF AMOS

The Bible doesn't say how Amos ended his days.
Presumably, he shook the dust from his feet
and returned to his farm in Tekoa.

Amos has been called the prophet of social justice.
This is a valid observation, but we would miss
the key point about Amos if we stopped here.

Amos didn't reveal any new, revolutionary doctrine;
he merely refocused attention on the commandments.
Israel had forgotten
that while three concerned their relationship to God,
seven concerned their relationship to each other.

HOSEA

Coming after Amos was Hosea.
He, too, was appalled by the evil in Israel
and spoke out against it fearlessly.
His words, however,
had a more compassionate ring
than did the words of Amos.
Perhaps this was because of the tragedy
in his own personal life.

Actually, little is known of Hosea,
except that he seems to have married an adultress.
He loved her deeply in spite of her infidelity.

Conditioned by this painful experience,
Hosea tried to draw Israel back to the covenant
by love rather than by threat.
He compared Yahweh's love for Israel
to that of a loyal husband for his disloyal wife.

God of Amos

The God of Amos was a God of concern.
He scorned those who burned incense one day a week
and exploited the poor on the other six days.
Yahweh's concern embraced all people,
especially the poor and the weak.
And he expected those who worshiped him
to share his concern.

In New Testament times,
Jesus fleshed out Amos' image of God.
Speaking to legalistic Pharisees, he said:

"You put onto people's backs loads
which are hard to carry, but you yourselves
will not stretch out a finger to help them
carry those loads."

LUKE 11:46

"I was hungry but you would not feed me,
thirsty but you would not give me a drink . . .
naked but you would not clothe me. . . .
Whenever you refused to help one of these
least important ones, you refused to help me."

MATTHEW 25:42-45

Basil, a fourth-century Christian bishop,
told wealthy Christians:

The bread that you store up
belongs to the hungry;
the cloak that lies in your chest
belongs to the naked;
the gold that you have hidden in the ground
belongs to the poor.

161

She will run after her lovers
but will not catch them. . . .
Then she will say,
"I am going back to my first husband—
I was better off then than I am now."

HOSEA 2:7

Hosea compared Yahweh to a loving father.

"When Israel was a child,
I loved him
and called him out of Egypt as my son.
But the more I called to him,
the more he turned away from me."

HOSEA 11:1–2

The prophets disturbed the comfortable,
but they also comforted the disturbed.
Hosea did both with delicate balance.

In New Testament times,
Jesus developed Hosea's image of God as father.
Nowhere is it better expressed
than in his Parable of the Prodigal Son.

NARRATOR   *He was still a long way from home*
                 when his father saw him;
                 his heart was filled with pity,
                 and he ran,
                 threw his arms around his son,
                 and kissed him. . . .

FATHER   *[to servants]*
                 Hurry! Bring the best robe
                 and put it on him.
                 Put a ring on his finger
                 and shoes on his feet. . . .

                 Let us celebrate with a feast!
                 For this son of mine was dead,
                 but now he is alive; he was lost,
                 but now he has been found.

LUKE 15:20–24

162

Night

Fire
PHILIP YANCEY

I was in an airplane, 30,000 feet above
Pennsylvania, reading Night, *by Elie Wiesel.*
It's a small book about Elie's teenage years.
He spent them in German concentration camps—
Elie was a Jew in World War II.

The Jews of Elie's town first heard of the German
holocaust through a man named Moche,
a likable fellow
who was physically as awkward as a clown.
Moche, a foreign Jew, was one of the first
to be expelled from the town. . . .
Several months passed before Moche returned.
He was changed.
There was no longer joy in his eyes.
He no longer sang.

Instead, he told of what had happened to him
and the other foreign Jews.
They were freighted far away into Poland,
made to get out and dig huge graves.
Then, one by one they were marched
before the Gestapo and machine-gunned. . . .
Moche was taken for dead and left behind.

Over and over Moche told the story.
The Jews refused to believe him.
Later, they stopped listening to him.

"They take me for a madman,"
Moche would whisper, and tears
like drops of wax, would flow from his eyes.

A whole year passed. It was Spring 1944,
and the German army's outlook appeared bleak.
The Jews' hopes rose. . . . Then came the news
that German units had entered Hungary. . . .

"I warned you," Moche cried to Elie's family.
And he fled.

Police confiscated all valuables in Jewish homes.
Jews were made to wear the yellow star.
Then they moved into a ghetto in the town's center.
Windows were blocked up and a barbed wire fence
separated Jews from the outside world. . . .

One day new faces showed in the ghetto—
two German officers from the Gestapo.
Fear spread among the Jews.
And that night the order was given—deportation.

The Jews were marched to a train station
and shoved into cattle cars—80 people to each car.
Then the cars were sealed. A whistle split the air.
The wheels began to grind. . . .

On the third night,
a piercing cry split the silence in Elie's wagon.
"Fire! I can see a fire! I can see a fire!"

Panic. Everyone awakened.
Madame Schachter was standing in the middle
of the wagon pointing to the window. . . .

Some of the men pressed against the window bars.
They saw nothing but darkness. . . .

Madame Schachter continued screaming "Fire!" . . .

Elie and the other Jews
tried to explain away her behavior,
talking about hallucinations caused by thirst. . . .

Finally they could stand it no longer.
Some of the young men forced her to sit down,
tied her up and put a gag in her mouth. . . .

Toward 11 o'clock, the train moved on slowly.
Elie pressed against the windows.
The train slowed and he could see barbed wire. . . .

And as the train stopped, Elie saw the flames
gushing out of a tall chimney into the black sky. . . .

An abominable odor floated in the air . . .
burning flesh. He had arrived at Birkenau—
reception area for Auschwitz.

I read Elie's story on the horror
he went through at Auschwitz. . . .
I looked up, out of the window
to the rolling countryside below me. . . .

I thought of a street corner in Philadelphia.
That morning, I had watched a man—
a grizzled street preacher—shout and rail . . .
of fire and coming judgment. . . .

Like Moche and Madame Schachter,
he was ignored. The onlookers . . .
thought him a fool.

36
Gloom without Brightness

There comes an hour of reckoning.
There comes a time when we must reap
what we have sown—perhaps unwittingly.

When this moment of truth comes,
we may cry, we may curse.
We may try to blame others,
or we may blame ourselves.
We may wish we could cram a lifetime of change
into a moment, but we can't.

The poet Whittier put it well:

For of all sad words of tongue or pen,
The saddest are these: "It might have been!"

Such a moment of reckoning came for the North.
In spite of Elijah and Elisha,
in spite of Amos and Hosea,
the North did not change its ways.
And so dawned the Day of the Lord,
the day of gloom without brightness (Amos 5:20).

The tool of God's justice was powerful Assyria.
Called the "Romans of Asia,"
the Assyrians conquered
because of superb weapons and organization.
Dominating the Near East from about 900
to 600 B.C., Assyria began intimidating the North
by demanding heavy tribute or taxes.

The North turned to Egypt and was promised
military help. It never came.
Finally, Assyria decided to crush the North.

The siege began under King Shalmaneser V.
It ended in 722, under his successor, Sargon II.

What the prophets tried to avert
was written into the pages of history:
It is the end of the North.

The event is described not only in the Bible,
but also in ancient Assyrian records.
The discovery of these records
came about in an interesting way.

In the 1840s, Paul-Emile Botta, a French diplomat,
bartered with a one-eyed pasha
for an excavating permit.
He got it; and the "dig" turned out to be a bonanza.
It unearthed the palace of Sargon II.
Until this discovery, Sargon was unknown to history,
except for a brief reference in Isaiah 20:1,
which referred to a general sent by Sargon.
Today, it is almost possible to reconstruct
from archaeological discoveries alone
a whole biography of Sargon.

Sargon II (left) conquered the North in 722 B.C.
Buried for 25 centuries beneath tons of desert sand,
this stone carving from Sargon's 209-room palace
was found by Botta at Khorsabad in 1843.
Garbed in ceremonial headdress, robe, and staff,
Sargon receives an official,
possibly one of his army commanders.

Among the palace ruins
were records of Assyria's victory over the North.

One entry says:

I attacked and conquered Samaria,
and led away as booty 27,290 inhabitants. . . .
And I installed over them one of my officers.

LOST TRIBES

Those inhabitants who were led away
were never heard from again.
Historians call them the lost tribes of Israel.

Some northern citizens, for reasons unknown,
were permitted to remain behind.
But their fate has forever fallen under a shadow.
These northerners socialized and intermarried
with the Assyrian occupation forces.
This drew down upon them
the disdain of other Jews forever.
The Samaritans, as they later became known,
were never again held in respect.

Jesus was an exception to the hatred
between Jews and Samaritans.
John records this incident:

NARRATOR   *A Samaritan woman came*
           to draw some water.

JESUS   *Give me a drink of water.*

WOMAN   *You are a Jew,*
           and I am a Samaritan—
           so how can you ask me
           for a drink?

NARRATOR   *[Jesus ignored her question.*
           Instead he told her of living water
           that would lead to eternal life.
           The woman was amazed.
           She ran back to the village
           to report what had happened.]

Assyrian soldiers lead prisoners to labor camps.
This stone relief was dug up at Nineveh
and dates from about the time
Assyria crushed the North.

WOMAN   *Come and see the man who told me*
           everything I have ever done.
           Could he be the Messiah?

NARRATOR   *So they left the town*
           and went to Jesus. . . .
           Jesus stayed there two days. . . .

VILLAGERS *[to woman]*
           We believe now,
           not because of what you said,
           but because we ourselves
           have heard him, and we know
           that he really is the Savior.

                            JOHN 4:7–9, 29–42

165

Samaritan elder wearing the distinctive white hat. Only a small remnant of this once prominent sect survives today.

Samaritans Today

What is the status of Samaritans today? A newspaper reporter files this report:

I Met a Samaritan
JANICE ROTHSCHILD

*I met a Samaritan,
but it was not on the road to Jericho.
It was at his place of business in Nablus. . . .
My husband and I stopped there
on our way from Jerusalem to Galilee. . . .*

*The Samaritans . . . are neither Arabs nor Jews,
although in some respects they resemble both.*

*They have kept to themselves, married only
among their own. . . .*

*Their number dwindled
from an estimated 40,000 at the time of Jesus
to a mere 152 at the beginning of the twentieth
century. Today improved economy and hygiene
have helped increase their population to 400. . . .*

*They tell you they are the true Jews . . .
who have the only authentic copy of the Pentateuch
written personally by Moses five days after
he descended Mount Sinai (they showed it to us!).
This is the whole of their Bible.
It differs from the first five books of our Bible
only in certain passages which they use
to support the validity of their beliefs.*

*Samaritan rites
have not changed since biblical times.
Whereas Judaism abolished the ritual sacrifice,
Samaritans still practice it
as an integral part of their Passover observance.
On Passover eve all the men come
in white garments and red fezzes,
to the house of the high priest on Mount Gerizim.
They then march in procession to a fenced-in area,
in the center of which stands an altar.
Their wives and children remain at a respectable
distance while they themselves
form two circles around the altar.*

*Twelve sheep are slaughtered. Then the men
break into joyous song and dance, some of them
dabbing blood from the sacrificed animals
onto their foreheads and their children's faces.*

*The service officially begins with the chanting
of prayers. Next the animals are prepared,
their entrails burned upon the altar,
their carcasses roasted on spits over open fires. . . .
The Samaritans schedule their ceremony so that
the festive meal may begin exactly at midnight.*

37

A Holy Remnant

Shock waves rumbled through the South
when they heard of the North's fall.
People clustered in excited groups
outside the temple and around the city gates.

Underlying the talk, however, was a complacency—
a naive belief
that no tragedy like this could strike the South.
Was not Judah ruled by David's successors?
Were they not heirs
to Yahweh's pledge of an unending kingship?

Perhaps this complacency explains
why the South began to drift into the same evils
that plagued the North: idolatry,
religious formalism, and oppression of the poor.

After the North's fall, two southern prophets,
Isaiah and Micah, intensified their preaching.
Both had been preaching reform before the fall.
In fact,
many of their warnings were aimed at the North.

MICAH

Micah is the lesser known of the two prophets.
His unpolished style suggests
that, like Amos, he was of humble origin.
Another prophet says of him:

"When Hezekiah was king of Judah,
the prophet Micah of Moresheth
told all the people

that the LORD Almighty had said,
'Zion will be plowed like a field;
Jerusalem will become a pile of ruins,
and the Temple hill will become a forest.'"

JEREMIAH 26:18

BETHLEHEM PROPHECY

Micah's prophecies, however,
were laced with hope. He said:

"Bethlehem Ephrathah,
you are one of the smallest towns in Judah,
but out of you I will bring a ruler for Israel. . . ."
His people will live in safety . . .
and he will bring peace.

MICAH 5:2–5

New Testament writers recalled this prophecy
shortly after Jesus' birth.

NARRATOR   *Some men who studied the stars*
came from the East to Jerusalem.

EASTERNERS   *Where is the baby*
born to be the king of the Jews?
We saw his star when it came up . . .
and we have come to worship him.

NARRATOR   *When King Herod heard about this,*
he was very upset, and so was
everyone else in Jerusalem.
He called together all the chief priests
and the teachers of the Law
and asked them,
"Where will the Messiah be born?"

TEACHERS   *In the town of Bethlehem in Judea.*
For this is what the prophet wrote:
"Bethlehem in the land of Judah,
you are by no means the least
of the leading cities of Judah;
for from you will come a leader
who will guide my people Israel."

MATTHEW 2:1–6

167

ISAIAH

No prophet is more highly esteemed
among Jews and Christians than Isaiah.
Born in Jerusalem, he was qualified
by birth and by education to walk with kings.
In contrast to the unpolished style of Micah,
Isaiah was elegant and aristocratic.

A copy of Isaiah's writings
was found among the Dead Sea Scrolls.
Dating back to the days of Jesus,
it is the world's oldest copy of any biblical book
written in Hebrew.

EXPERIENCE OF GOD

Scholars call Isaiah the prophet of God's holiness.
Throughout his life, Isaiah showed a deep
realization of the total otherness of God.
This resulted from his call in 740 B.C.,
when, for a fractional moment, he was gifted
with an insight into the mystery of God.

The experience produced in him
a feeling of fear and fascination—a paradox
that must be experienced to be understood.
Isaiah described the experience symbolically.

ISAIAH   *I saw the Lord.*
            He was sitting on his throne,
            high and exalted,
            and his robe filled the whole Temple.
            Around him flaming creatures
            were standing. . . .

CREATURES   *Holy, holy, holy!*
            The LORD Almighty is holy!
            His glory fills the world.

ISAIAH   *The sound of their voices*
            made the foundation of the Temple
            shake. . . .

Then one of the creatures
flew down to me,
carrying a burning coal. . . .
He touched my lips
with the burning coal.

CREATURE   *This has touched your lips,*
            and now your guilt is gone,
            and your sins are forgiven.

ISAIAH   *Then I heard the Lord . . .*

LORD   *Whom shall I send?*
            Who will be our messenger?

ISAIAH   *I answered,*
            "I will go! Send me!"

            So he told me to go.

ISAIAH 6:1–9

Isaiah's experience of God's holiness
affected his entire prophetic career.
No less than 29 times,
he referred to Yahweh as the Holy One of Israel.
And it was to holiness that Yahweh called Israel.
At Mount Sinai, Yahweh said:
"You shall be to me . . . a holy nation"
(Exodus 19:6, *New American Bible*).

The idea of biblical holiness
is not well understood by modern Christians.
It is not something reserved for the saints,
who go off to monasteries or desert hermitages
to spend days in penance and nights in prayer.

Perhaps holiness can be understood best
in terms of its opposite—sinfulness.
When sin entered human life,
it dehumanized people.
It alienated them
from themselves, their neighbor, and God.

The purpose of God's intervention in history
was to restore people to their original integrity.
New Testament writers saw this process
reach a new level of fulfillment in Jesus.

At the Last Supper,
Jesus addressed the Father in these words:

"I pray that they may all be one.
Father! . . . May they be one . . .
just as you and I are one:
I in them and you in me."

JOHN 17:21–23

In the final analysis,
holiness is reconciliation, oneness with oneself,
one's neighbor, and one's God.

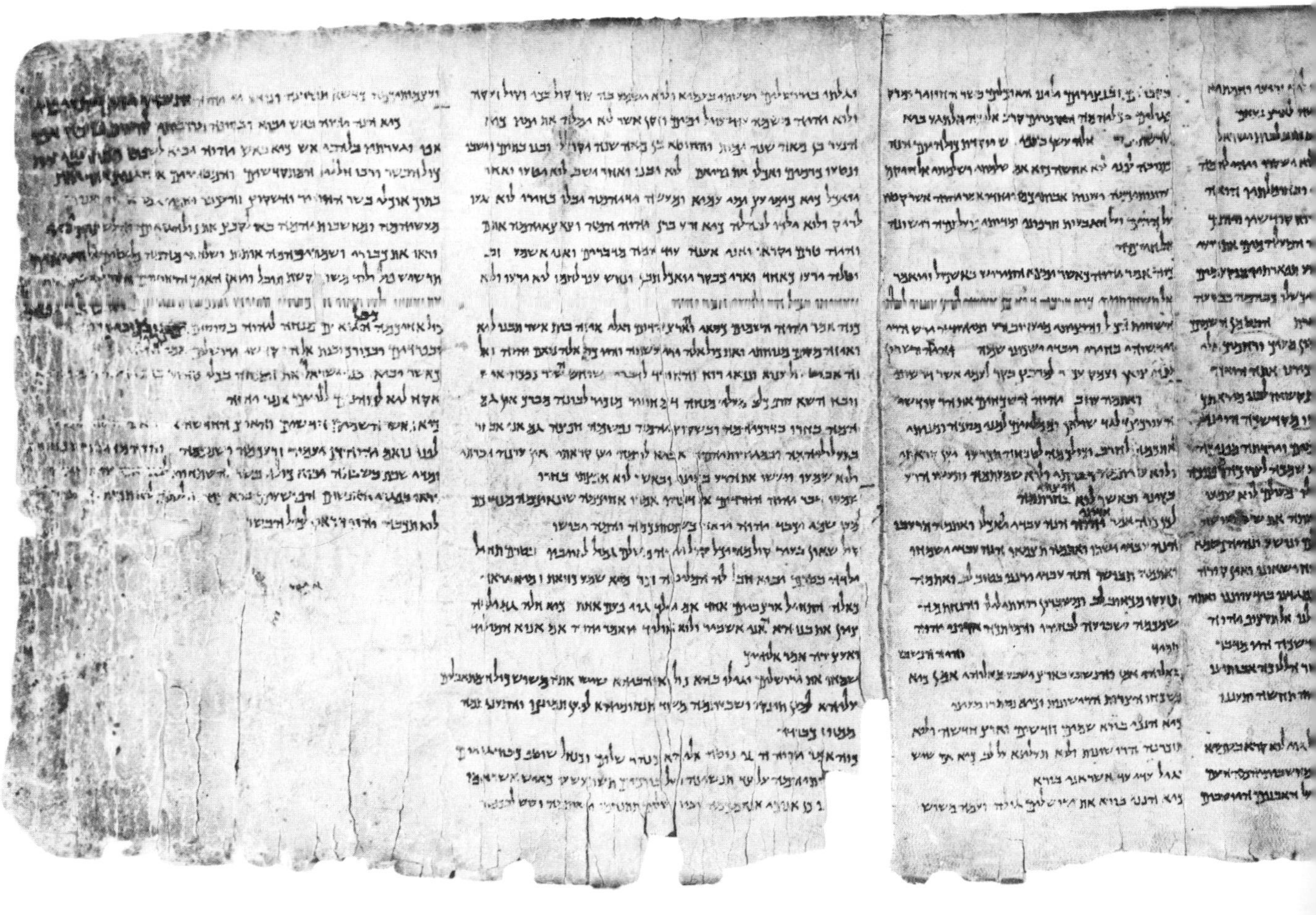

Portion of the Isaiah Scroll found at Qumran.

CALL TO CONVERSION

Isaiah's career arched like a great umbrella
over 40 stormy years of Judah's history.
Because of his keen sense of holiness,
Isaiah spoke out repeatedly wherever he found evil.
Condemning religious formalism, he said:

"I am tired of the blood of bulls and sheep
and goats. . . .
It's useless to bring your offerings.
I am disgusted with the smell of the incense
you burn."

ISAIAH 1:11–13

Isaiah's purpose was not to condemn the people, but to call them to conversion.

The LORD said . . .
"Stop all this evil that I see you doing. . . .
Help those who are oppressed,
give orphans their rights, and defend widows. . . .
Although your stains are deep red,
you will be as white as wool."

ISAIAH 1:2, 16–18

On the other hand, if Judah does not change, Isaiah says, "you are doomed to die" (1:20).

But what about Yahweh's promise?
Will Yahweh reject his people if they reject him?
Isaiah gave this answer:

The Lord will raise a signal flag
to show the nations
that he is gathering together again
the scattered people of Israel and Judah.

ISAIAH 11:12

REMNANT

This prophecy of Isaiah introduced a new dimension in Old Testament thought: the idea of the remnant. The concept was hinted at by prophets like Amos and Micah. Now, Isaiah develops it.

He warns the people
that it is not enough to belong to a chosen nation.
Yahweh's covenant is not a blanket pledge
to a nation, but only to its faithful members.

From this moment forward,
the idea of membership in God's chosen people
takes on a qualitative note: it involves more
than being born of Jewish parents.

New Testament writers identified
the remnant of Judah with the followers of Jesus.
Paul wrote:

Did God reject his own people?
Certainly not! I myself am an Israelite,
a descendant of Abraham. . . .

God has not rejected his people. . . .
There is a small number left of those
whom God has chosen because of his grace.

ROMANS 11:1–5

IMMANUEL PROPHECY

Delivered at a time
when Judah's existence was threatened,
this prophecy assured the people
that Yahweh would raise up a champion to save them.
The heart of the prophecy reads:

"The Lord himself will give you a sign:
a young woman who is pregnant
will have a son
and will name him 'Immanuel.'"

ISAIAH 7:14

Many interpreted this prophecy
as referring to Hezekiah, Judah's next king.
But New Testament writers interpreted it
as being ultimately fulfilled in Jesus.
Matthew says of Jesus' birth:

Now all this happened
in order to make come true
what the Lord had said through the prophet,
"A virgin will become pregnant
and have a son, and he will be called Immanuel"
(which means, "God is with us").

MATTHEW 1:22–23

Matthew ends his Gospel on the same theme:
"God is with us."
He reports Jesus' final words as being:

"And I will be with you always,
to the end of the age."

MATTHEW 28:20

Song of the Vineyard

One of Isaiah's most memorable prophecies
was expressed in song.

Listen while I sing you this song,
a song of my friend and his vineyard:
My friend had a vineyard
on a very fertile hill.
He dug the soil and cleared it of stones;
he planted the finest vines. . . .
He waited for the grapes to ripen,
but every grape was sour.

So now my friend says, "You people
who live in Jerusalem and Judah. . . .
Here is what I am going to do to my vineyard:
I will take away the hedge around it . . .
and let wild animals eat it and trample it. . . .
I will let briers and thorns cover it.
I will even forbid the clouds
to let rain fall on it."

Israel is the vineyard of the LORD Almighty;
the people of Judah
are the vines he planted.

ISAIAH 5:1–7

Isaiah's song began on a pleasant note,
but ended with the bitter truth.
Like an arrow, it pierced the hearer's heart.

In New Testament times,
Jesus carried Isaiah's image a step further, saying:

"There was once a landowner
who planted a vineyard. . . .
Then he rented the vineyard to tenants
and left home on a trip.
When the time came to gather the grapes,
he sent his slaves to the tenants
to receive his share of the harvest.
The tenants grabbed his slaves,
beat one, killed another, and stoned another.
Again the man sent other slaves,
more than the first time,
and the tenants treated them the same way.
Last of all he sent his son to them.
'Surely they will respect my son,' he said.
But when the tenants saw the son,
they said to themselves,
'This is the owner's son.
Come on, let's kill him,
and we will get his property!'
So they grabbed him, threw him out
of the vineyard, and killed him.

"Now, when the owner of the vineyard
comes, what will he do to those tenants?"
Jesus asked.

"He will certainly kill those evil men,"
they answered,
"and rent the vineyard out to other tenants,
who will give him his share of the harvest
at the right time."...

The chief priests and the Pharisees
heard Jesus' parables
and knew that he was talking about them.

MATTHEW 21:33–45

38

Bird in a Cage

In 715 B.C. Hezekiah became king of Judah.
One of the three great kings in Jewish history,
he gave solid backing to the reform efforts
of Isaiah and Micah.
But the South still failed to respond.
It became clear that only a shock
would jolt the people from their apathy.

The shock came in 705 B.C.
News arrived that Sargon II, the Assyrian king
who had crushed the North, was assassinated.
His successor was the dazzling Sennacherib.

Hezekiah began to fear for his people.
He knew that the new king was a warrior at heart.

Modern archaeology
has helped paint a colorful portrait of Sennacherib.
One excavated document records the king's
own reflections about travels with his armies.

Where the countryside was rugged,
I rode my horse and had my chariot carried.
Where it became steep,
I scrambled on foot, like an ox. . . .
When I grew tired,
I sat on a rock and drank from my waterskin.

FALSE FEAR

Hezekiah's fears turned out to be premature.
Sennacherib had other plans for the present.
He drafted slave labor and began making Nineveh,
his capital, the showplace of the Near East.

He even imported Egyptian obelisks
to enhance the grandeur of the city.
The job of transporting these giant stone slabs
must have been staggering,
since they were cut as single blocks
and weighed up to 325 tons.

Modern archaeologists are still exploring
the excavated remains of Nineveh.

SHOCKING NEWS

But Hezekiah's fears eventually materialized.
In 701 B.C. Sennacherib's armies
struck in lightning fashion against Judah.
Town after town fell.
Then came the fateful day when runners brought
the news to Jerusalem: "Sennacherib is coming!"

Warning horns sounded everywhere!
Farmers fled the fields and raced into the city.
The great bronze gates to the city were bolted.
Hezekiah and his generals awaited the inevitable.

When the Assyrians pitched camp outside the city,
they sent peace envoys to negotiate the surrender
of Jerusalem (2 Kings 18:17-37).

As soon as King Hezekiah heard their report,
he tore his clothes in grief, put on sackcloth,
and went to the Temple of the LORD. . . .

"Now, LORD our God,
rescue us from the Assyrians,
so that all the nations of the world will know
that only you, O LORD, are God."

Then Isaiah sent a message
telling King Hezekiah . . .
"This is what the LORD has said
about the Assyrian emperor:
'He will not enter this city
or shoot a single arrow against it.
No soldiers with shields will come near the city.'"

2 KINGS 19:1, 19–20, 32

172

Sennacherib Prism

This hexagonal "Prism of Sennacherib"
was unearthed by archaeologists at Nineveh.
Dating from the seventh century B.C.,
it tells how Sennacherib boasted
of his expedition into Judah.
A portion of it reads:

As for Hezekiah of Judah,
he did not submit to me.
So I laid siege to 46 of his strong cities . . .
and captured them. . . .
I shut him up in Jerusalem . . .
like a bird in a cage.

One of the growing number of examples of ancient records
that confirm events described in the Bible.

Night fell, and in spite of Isaiah's words,
a jittery Jerusalem laid awake in fear of the dawn.
When the sun rose, the people of Jerusalem
could hardly believe what they saw:
the Assyrians were withdrawing.

When the Assyrian armies had gone,
Hebrew patrols went out to the campsite
and found it littered with dead.

Three books of the Bible report the event.
Here's how the Second Book of Kings describes it:

An angel of the LORD went to the Assyrian
camp and killed 185,000 soldiers.
At dawn the next day
there they lay, all dead!

Then the Assyrian emperor Sennacherib
withdrew and returned to Nineveh.

2 KINGS 19:35-36

The Book of Sirach says simply that God struck
the Assyrian camp "with a plague" (48:21, NAB).

Ancient historians,
taking their lead from Sirach,
suggest the disaster was triggered by
a sudden outbreak of the bubonic plague.

After the Assyrians pulled out,
Jerusalem breathed a great sigh of relief.
Reluctantly, Hezekiah agreed to pay a tax to Assyria
for the cities that fell
prior to the ill-fated march on Jerusalem.

Hour to Remember

The remarkable event
that saved Israel from certain defeat
at the hands of Sennacherib
has been described in poetry by Lord Byron.

The Assyrian came down
like a wolf on the fold,
And his cohorts were gleaming
in purple and gold. . . .

Like the leaves of the forest
when Summer is green,
That host with their banners
at sunset were seen:
Like the leaves of the forest
when Autumn hath blown,
That host on the morrow
lay withered and strown. . . .

And the might of the Gentile,
unsmote by the sword,
Hath melted like snow
in the glance of the Lord!

SECRET TUNNEL

A remarkable monument to Hezekiah
remains to this day in Jerusalem.
It is an underground tunnel built by him
to pipe water from the spring of Gihon.
The discovery of the tunnel happened this way.

One hot day in 1880, a student exploring
Jerusalem's Old City came upon it accidentally.
Entering the tunnel, he slipped and fell.
Getting up, he noticed strange writing on the wall.
It turned out to be an inscription,
in ancient eighth-century B.C. Hebrew script,
telling how Hezekiah hastily built the tunnel
to insure a water supply for the city.
Part of the inscription reads:

Quarry men cut through the rock,
each man toward his fellow, axe against axe.

Water still flows in the tunnel
and venturesome tourists
still explore its near-1,800-foot length.

Equipped with a flashlight and hip boots,
you can make out how the two rows of workmen
advanced toward each other.
In the middle of the tunnel, you can see
the exact place where the work parties met.

The Bible mentions the tunnel in three different places
(2 Kings 20:20; 2 Chronicles 32:30; Sirach 48:17).
The Sirach text reads:

[Hezekiah]
had a tunnel built through solid rock
with iron tools
and had cisterns built to hold the water.

Hezekiah's tunnel stretches in an S-shape from the
spring at Gihon (outside the city)
to the pool of Siloam (inside the city).
The original wall inscription was removed in 1890 by Turks
and placed in an Istanbul museum.

This limestone panel inscribed in early cuneiform writing
dates back to the 18th century B.C.
It pictures Hammurabi, whose ancient Babylonian kingdom
stretched from the Persian Gulf to the Mediterranean Sea.

BABYLONIA

When Sennacherib returned to Assyria,
he ran into a storm of internal problems.
They ended in 680 B.C.
when his own sons murdered him (2 Kings 19:37).

The Assyrians enjoyed prosperity until 625 B.C.
Then things began to decline.
As the Assyrian star faded,
another nation began its rise to power: Babylonia.
The change took place in 612 B.C.
Babylonian troops invaded and crushed Assyria.
Clay tablets, called the Babylonian Chronicles,
describe the event.

Babylonia was not a newcomer among the nations.
It had been around since 2500 B.C.

Back in Abraham's time
it had produced the famous lawgiver, Hammurabi.

A stone pillar bearing Hammurabi's Code of Laws
was unearthed by archaeologists in 1902.
It once stood in a Babylonian marketplace,
telling the citizens their rights.
Inscribed in cuneiform, the writing on the pillar
reads from top to bottom—instead of left to right.
Typical of its laws is this one:

If a citizen has accused a fellow citizen,
and has indicted him for murder,
and has not substantiated the charge,
the accuser himself shall be put to death.

Babylon, Babylonia's capital, became the dream-city
of its age, dwarfing even Nineveh.
The city was surrounded by walls
decorated with magnificently colored animals.
Dominating the city was a giant ziggurat,
dedicated to the god Marduk.
According to Herodotus, it had seven tiers,
each constructed of different-colored brick.

Even more spectacular
were Babylon's amazing Hanging Gardens.
One of the seven wonders of the ancient world,
these gardens were built on a man-made mountain.
One tradition says the king built them
to please a princess who was homesick
for the mountain scenery of her own country.

175

"[Babylon,]
your wisdom and knowledge led you astray"
(Isaiah 47:10).
Reconstruction of ancient Babylon,
according to Unger. Oil painting by Maurice Bardin.

Star Watchers

The Babylonians were great star watchers.
They pictured the various constellations
as beasts and used them to foretell the future.
From this came our signs of the zodiac.

The Babylonians were also good historians.
They dated all important events
by noting the position of the moon and planets
when the event took place.

This is proving extremely helpful to us today,
as the following news report shows.

"[Babylon,]
ruin will come on you suddenly—
ruin you never dreamed of!" (Isaiah 47:11).
Ancient Babylon was
exhumed from its grave by modern archaeologists.

At International Business Machines Corp.,
one of the more complicated computers
recently spent 40 hours calculating the motions
of the moon, sun and planets for 600 years
as they cruised over ancient Babylon.

The Babylonians . . .
believed that the motions of the heavenly bodies
had an intimate influence on human affairs.
When they recorded current events . . .
they were likely to include
the position of the moon on that day,
or the location of a couple of planets.

Today, if a scholar
studying the clay tablets of ancient Babylon
wants to know the exact date of a given event,
all he has to do is to calculate the date
when the heavenly bodies were in their positions.

For years, scholars have known about this
dating system, but tracing astronomical motions
backward for more than 2,000 years
is forbiddingly time consuming. . . .

So mathematician Bryant Tuckerman of IBM
got time on a 704 computer.
In 40 hours of electronic calculation the 704 . . .
disgorged 301 tables of figures
showing the positions of the Moon, Venus,
and Mercury at five-day intervals,
and of Mars, Jupiter, Saturn, and the sun
at ten-day intervals between 601 B.C. and A.D. 1. . . .

Scholars who can read the cuneiform writing
of ancient Babylon are already hard at work
with Dr. Tuckerman's tables.
Eventually they may check the dates of such events
as Nebuchadnezzar's deportation of the Jews . . .
perhaps, to the very hour,
Babylonian Standard Time.

39

The Unheeded Prophet

When Isaiah and Hezekiah died,
tragedy struck Judah.
The throne passed to Manesseh, Hezekiah's son.
Historians consider Manesseh
Judah's worst king.

He sacrificed his son as a burnt offering.
He practiced divination and magic
and consulted fortunetellers and mediums.
He sinned greatly against the LORD
and stirred up his anger.

2 KINGS 21:6

Good citizens, therefore,
shed few tears when Manesseh died in 638 B.C.

BOY-KING

Eventually, the throne passed to an eight-year-old
boy-king, Josiah.
The youth turned out to be a remarkable ruler.
In his twenties, he ordered the temple remodeled.
During the work, an old book of the law was found.

Hilkiah told [Shaphan]
that he found the book of the Law in the Temple.
Hilkiah gave him the book, and Shaphan read it.
Then he went back to the king and reported . . .
"I have here a book that Hilkiah gave me."
And he read it aloud to the king.

When the king heard the book being read,
he tore his clothes in dismay.

2 KINGS 22:8-11

177

Immediately, Josiah ordered a reform to take place throughout Judah, in strict accord with the laws set down in the book.

At first, the reform was backed by an impressive cluster of prophets: Nahum, Zephaniah, Habakkuk, Baruch, and Jeremiah.

JEREMIAH

Of these five prophets, Jeremiah was the giant. Jeremiah's life is described in the book that bears his name. A mixture of history, biography, and prophecy, the book portrays a nation in crisis and the inner torture of a prophet who had to confront and challenge this nation.

Jeremiah appears to have been a deeply sensitive man. He never married. Therefore, he never had a family to fall back on. His closest friend was Baruch, his secretary.

Like Josiah, Jeremiah was called by God at a young age. He himself described his reaction to the call.

I answered, "Sovereign LORD,
I don't know how to speak;
I am too young."...
Then the LORD reached out,

touched my lips, and said to me...
"Today I give you authority over nations...
to uproot and to pull down...
to build and to plant."

JEREMIAH 1:6–10

SOLITARY FIGURE

At first, Jeremiah enjoyed the support of Josiah. But tragedy soon reversed the situation. The king was killed at Megiddo, when he personally tried to prevent Egyptian troops from passing through his country.

Toward the end of his career, Jeremiah stood alone. Stationing himself outside the temple gates, he preached fearlessly.

"Change the way you are living
and stop doing the things you are doing.
Be fair in your treatment of one another....
Stop killing innocent people in this land.
Stop worshiping other gods."

JEREMIAH 7:5–6

Over and over, Jeremiah tried to warn the people against the popular belief that the temple would never be destroyed.

Jeremiah also stationed himself outside the gates of the king's palace. He warned those who entered.

Found at Qumran, this scroll fragment
is from a commentary on the Book of Habakkuk.
It was the prophet Habakkuk who wrote:

"Even though the fig trees have no fruit
and no grapes grow on the vines,
even though the olive crop fails
and the fields produce no grain . . .
I will still be joyful and glad,
because the LORD God is my savior."

Habakkuk 3:17–18

The LORD said to me,
"Tell the king and his mother
to come down from their thrones. . . ."
Your enemies are coming down from the north!

JEREMIAH 13:18–20

The king grew anxious
as he saw Jeremiah point his finger to the north.
For in the north, Babylonia was beginning to pose
a real threat to tiny Judah.

Instead of urging religious reform, however,
the king hurriedly bolstered Judah's armies
and began to barter with Egypt for military support.

DAY OF JUDGMENT

Finally, the day came when Jeremiah
had to pass judgment on the nation he loved.

The LORD told me to go
and buy myself some linen shorts
and to put them on. . . .
So I bought them and put them on.
Then the LORD spoke to me again and said,
"Go to the Euphrates River
and hide the shorts in a hole in the rocks."
So I went and hid them near the Euphrates.

Some time later
the LORD told me to go back to the Euphrates
and get the shorts.
So I went back, and when I found the place
where I had hidden them,
I saw that they were ruined
and were no longer any good.

Then the LORD spoke to me again.
He said,
"This is how I will destroy the pride of Judah

and the great pride of Jerusalem.
These evil people have refused to obey me . . .
and have worshiped and served other gods.
So then, they will become like these shorts. . . .
Just as shorts fit tightly around the waist,
so I intended all the people
of Israel and Judah to hold tightly to me . . .
but they would not obey me."

JEREMIAH 13:1–11

The people were enraged at Jeremiah's words.
The prophet was whipped
and placed in the stocks (Jeremiah 20:1-2).
On another occasion, he was imprisoned, beaten,
and placed in a dungeon (Jeremiah 33:1; 37:15).

DEEP ANGUISH

This brutal treatment
deeply wounded the sensitive nature of Jeremiah.
In one part of his book, called the "Confessions,"
Jeremiah cried to Yahweh:

LORD, you have deceived me,
and I was deceived.
You are stronger than I am,
and you have overpowered me. . . .
I say, "I will forget the LORD
and no longer speak in his name,"
then your message is like a fire
burning deep within me.
I try my best to hold it in,
but can no longer keep it back. . . .

Curse the day I was born!
Forget the day my mother gave me birth!
Curse the man who made my father glad
when he brought him the news,
"It's a boy!
You have a son!"
May he be like those cities
that the LORD destroyed without mercy.

JEREMIAH 20:7-9, 14–16

179

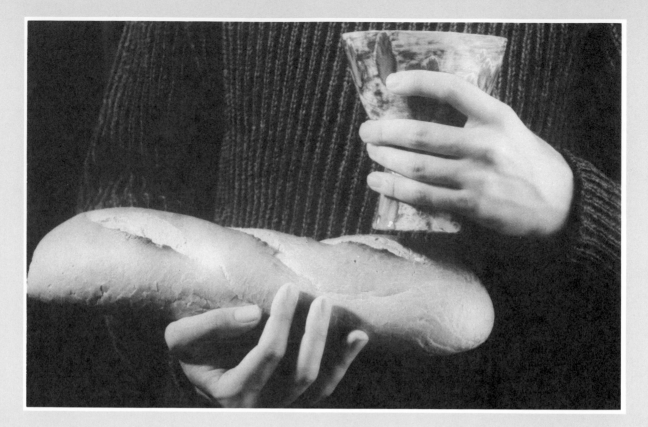

New Covenant

For those people who heeded his words,
Jeremiah had a prophecy of hope.

The LORD says, "The time is coming
when I will make a new covenant with the people
of Israel and with the people of Judah. . . .
The new covenant that I will make
with the people of Israel will be this:
I will put my law within them
and write it on their hearts.
I will be their God,
and they will be my people. . . .
I will no longer remember their wrongs."

JEREMIAH 31:31–34

New Testament writers
recalled Jeremiah's prophecy when Jesus

took a piece of bread, gave thanks to God,
broke it, and said,
"This is my body, which is for you.
Do this in memory of me."
In the same way,

after the supper he took the cup and said,
"This cup is God's new covenant,
sealed with my blood.
Whenever you drink it, do so in memory of me."

1 CORINTHIANS 11:23–25

From Jesus' viewpoint
the New Covenant did not destroy the Old Covenant
any more than adulthood destroys childhood.
The one was the outgrowth of the other.

The stress of the New Covenant
was a new law of love,
communicated to each person by the Spirit.
Paul wrote: "No longer
do we serve in the old way of a written law,
but in the new way of the Spirit" (Romans 7:6).

For Paul, the written law was no longer primary.
Rather, it was subordinated to the law of love.
The Christian should no longer ask:
"How far can I go before I break the law?"
but rather,
"How much more can I do, because I love?"

THE STORM BREAKS

Eventually, the day came
when Jeremiah's warnings became a reality.
Babylonian armies crossed the border into Judah.

The battle for Jerusalem took place in 597 B.C.
Quickly, the city was brought to its knees.
The Babylonian king (Nebuchadnezzar)
personally directed its purge.

Nebuchadnezzar
deported all the important men to Babylonia,
seven thousand in all,
and one thousand skilled workers.

2 KINGS 24:16

The downfall of Jerusalem in 597 B.C.
is also reported in the Babylonian Chronicles,
found by archaeologists at Babylon.

RUMBLE OF THUNDER

One might think that Babylon's action
would strike fear into the hearts of the people.
But it did not. Some even rejoiced, saying:
"The city and the temple are still untouched;
Yahweh is protecting us."

Jeremiah looked at the situation differently.
He saw it as only the first rumble of thunder.
The real storm may yet lie ahead.
Jeremiah warned Zedekiah, Judah's new king.

"I, the LORD,
command you to do what is just and right.
Protect the person who is being cheated. . . .
Do not mistreat or oppress
aliens, orphans, or widows. . . .
But if you do not obey my commands . . .
this palace will fall into ruins."

JEREMIAH 22:3–5

The king turned a deaf ear to Jeremiah.
Instead, he secretly began to seek Egypt's help.

40
Day of Drums

Judah's "day of drums" dawned in 586 B.C.
This date is branded on the heart of every Jew.
It marks the fall of the South
and the destruction of Jerusalem and the temple.

Angered by Zedekiah's Egyptian strategy,
Nebuchadnezzar decided to put an end to the South.
His armies marched back to Jerusalem
and reduced the city to rubble—temple and all.
Jeremiah records the tragedy.

In the tenth month of the ninth year
that Zedekiah was king of Judah,
King Nebuchadnezzar of Babylonia
came with his whole army and attacked Jerusalem.
On the ninth day of the fourth month
of Zedekiah's eleventh year as king,
the city walls were broken through. . . .

When King Zedekiah and all his soldiers
saw what was happening,
they tried to escape from the city
during the night. . . .
But the Babylonian army pursued them
and captured Zedekiah. . . .
[Nebuchadnezzar] put Zedekiah's sons to death
while Zedekiah was looking on,
and he also had the officials of Judah executed.
After that, he had Zedekiah's eyes put out
and had him placed in chains
to be taken to Babylonia.
Meanwhile, the Babylonians burned down

*the royal palace and the houses of the people
and tore down the walls of Jerusalem.
Finally Nebuzaradan, the commanding officer,
took away as prisoners to Babylonia
the people who were left in the city,
together with those who had deserted to him.
He left in the land of Judah
some of the poorest people, who owned no
property, and he gave them vineyards and fields.*

JEREMIAH 39:1–10

Contemplating the disaster of Jerusalem,
the Book of Lamentations says:

*How lonely lies Jerusalem,
once so full of people! . . .
All night long she cries. . . .
Of all her former friends,
not one is left to comfort her. . . .*

*Her children have been captured
and taken away.
The splendor of Jerusalem
is a thing of the past.*

LAMENTATIONS 1:1–6

LOST GLORY

It is impossible for us to imagine
what the fall of Jerusalem meant to devout Jews.
The three great pillars of Judah's existence,
inseparably linked to God's covenant with them,
now lay in smouldering ruins:

> the king,
> the temple,
> the nation.

The king was dethroned, the temple was in ashes,
and the nation was in exile.

The psalmist cried in anguish:

*By the rivers of Babylon we sat down;
there we wept when we remembered Zion.
On the willows near by we hung up our harps.
Those who captured us told us to sing;
they told us to entertain them:
"Sing us a song about Zion."*

*How can we sing a song to the LORD
in a foreign land?*

PSALM 137:1–4

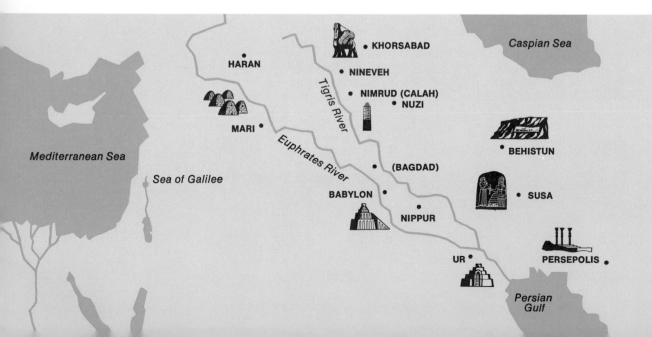

FRAGMENTED CITIZENRY

The fall of Jerusalem split the Jews into three groups.
The overwhelming segment of the citizenry
was deported as prisoners to Babylon.

A handful of poor peasant people,
who had no land or property,
was left behind to fend for themselves.

Another small group, Jeremiah among them,
managed to escape to Egypt.
The Egyptian refugees
began the so-called Jewish diaspora:
Jews dispersed from their homeland
and taking up residence in other parts of the world.

A large colony of these Jews
settled at Alexandria in Egypt.
Centuries later, Alexandrian Jews
translated the Old Testament into Greek.
Called the *Septuagint,* it became the official
Old Testament for Greek-speaking Christians.
Matthew, Mark, Luke, and John
all quoted from it.

Possibly some of the Jews who fled to Egypt
found their way to Elephantine,
an island in the Nile River,
opposite Egypt's modern Aswan Dam.
Archaeologists have found evidence
that a large colony of Jews once lived there.

How the original colony started is uncertain.
Some experts speculate
that the Elephantine Jews may have been part
of the ten lost tribes of the northern kingdom,
who vanished in 722 B.C.

Among the discoveries found at Elephantine
were papyrus scrolls from the fifth century B.C.
Written in Aramaic,
they included business documents
and letters from the colony.
The letters show that the Elephantine Jews
were in touch with the Jerusalem Jews.
They also show
that they celebrated the Passover
and held to Jewish traditions.

KHORSABAD
Giant slabs depicting cherubim (Genesis 3:24)
were found when the palace of Sargon II was excavated.
Records also tell of Assyria's victory over the North in 722 B.C.

NINEVEH
A prism found at this later Assyrian palace site
reports Sennacherib's expeditions against Judah in 701 B.C.
A library of over 20,000 clay tablets was also unearthed.

NIPPUR
Here archaeologists dug up asphalt-sealed jars
containing business records.
These documents
reveal how some Jews adjusted to everyday life in Babylon
after Jerusalem's fall in 586 B.C.

Time Chart

Judah in exile	586 BC	
	562	**Nebuchadnezzar dies**
		Others
	557	**Cyrus rises in Persia**
	555	**Nabonidus in Babylon**
Judah freed	536	**Cyrus defeats**
Exiles return		**Nabonidus**
	529	**Cambyses**
Temple reconstruction	522	**Darius I**
	486	**Xerxes**
	465	**Others**
	336	**Alexander the Great**
	335	**Darius III**
	331	**Alexander rules**
		Judah
		Alexander defeats
		Persia
	323	**Alexander dies**
	275	**Egypt rules Judah**

EXILE
REMNANT COMMUNITY

Books

Ezra	Joel
Nehemiah	Obadiah
Job	Jonah
Ecclesiastes	Haggai
Wisdom	Zechariah
Isaiah 40-66	Malachi
Ezekiel	

41

Can These Bones Live Again?

With Jerusalem in ashes,
the focus of Jewish history shifted to Babylon.
After the initial shock of exile wore off,
the Jews began to adjust to their new situation.
Many were given considerable freedom;
some even established themselves in trades.
In time, one group of Jews
became completely content with life in Babylon.

A second group, however,
began to think and reflect upon their past.
This group underwent a profound change.
They experienced a reawakening
of a faded, almost lost religious sensitivity.
In short, they experienced a religious conversion.

GOD'S WORD

With the temple miles away and in ruins,
devout Jews turned more and more to God's word
to keep their faith alive.
They gathered to hear it recited from memory,
or to hear read those sections
that had been written out on scrolls.

Two important developments
flowed from these weekly Sabbath meetings.

First, the meetings gave rise to a new worship place,
called the synagogue.
Prior to this time, all public worship took place
in the Jerusalem temple.

Now the synagogue came into being.
Synagogue worship focused on instruction and prayer,
in contrast to temple worship,
which focused on sacrificial offerings.

The second development was that Jewish scribes
began to write out those sections of God's word
that were preserved only in the memory of elders.
These sections were joined with other sections.
Later scribes
would edit them into a continuous whole.

EZEKIEL

The exiled Jews were guided also
by new revelation through new prophets.
One of these prophets was Ezekiel.
Along with Isaiah and Jeremiah,
he now ranks as one of Israel's greatest prophets.

Ezekiel grew up in Jerusalem.
After the first Babylonian invasion of the South,
he was deported to Babylon.
There he received his prophetic call.

Ezekiel's ministry divided into two periods:
before and after the final fall of Jerusalem.
Each period had its own special problems.

During his first days in exile,
Ezekiel warned Jews about their optimism.
Many Jews believed that no harm
could befall Jerusalem or the temple.
Anxiously, they awaited news from home—
news of Egyptian help,
or revolt against the forces of occupation.

Ezekiel warned that such optimism was folly.
As did previous prophets, he pointed out
that Israel's election as God's chosen people
involved moral obligations.
Only repentance would save the nation—
if not the nation, then a remnant of it.

Ezekiel's words fell on deaf ears.
The people persisted in their beliefs.

Finally, in 586 the fateful news arrived in Babylon:
"Jerusalem and the temple are in ashes!"
Refugees started to pour in from the fallen city.
The entire Jewish population
was plunged into unbelievable disillusionment.

Now Ezekiel's task was to save the people
from total despair.
Ezekiel the corrector became Ezekiel the comforter.
Ezekiel's message shifted to one of hope.
First, he prophesied the restoration of the people:

"I, the Sovereign LORD, say . . .
I will give you a new heart and a new mind.
I will take away your stubborn heart of stone
and give you an obedient heart.
I will put my spirit in you
and will see to it that you follow my laws. . . .
You will be my people,
and I will be your God."

EZEKIEL 36:13, 26–28

Closely related to this prophecy
was Ezekiel's famous allegory of the "dry bones."
Set to music by exiled black slaves in America,
it gave hope to them, as it did to exiled Jews.

EZEKIEL   *I felt the powerful presence*
of the LORD, and his spirit took me
and set me down in a valley
where the ground
was covered with bones. . . .

LORD   *Mortal man,*
can these bones come back to life?

EZEKIEL   *Sovereign LORD,*
only you can answer that!

LORD   *Prophesy to the bones.*
Tell these dry bones to listen
to the word of the LORD. . . .

EZEKIEL   *So I prophesied as I had been told.*
While I was speaking,

I heard a rattling noise,
and the bones began to join together.
While I watched, the bones
were covered with sinews and muscles,
and then with skin. . . .
Breath entered the bodies,
and they came to life. . . .

LORD   *Mortal man, the people of Israel*
are like these bones.
They say that they are dried up,
without any hope and with no future.
So prophesy to my people Israel. . . .
I will put my breath in them,
bring them back to life,
and let them live in their own land.
Then they will know that I am the LORD.
I have promised that I would do this—
and I will.
I, the LORD, have spoken.

EZEKIEL 37:1–14

Second, Ezekiel prophesied the restoration
of David's line.

"I, the Sovereign LORD, tell you . . .
I will rescue my sheep
and not let them be mistreated any more. . . .
I will give them a king like my servant David
to be their one shepherd,
and he will take care of them.
I, the LORD, will be their God,
and a king like my servant David
will be their ruler.
I have spoken."

EZEKIEL 34:20–24

Finally, Ezekiel prophesied the return of Yahweh
to the temple.

The man took me to the gate that faces east,
and there I saw coming from the east
the dazzling light
of the presence of the God of Israel.

187

God's voice sounded like the roar of the sea,
and the earth shone with the dazzling light. . . .
Then I threw myself face downward. . . .
The dazzling light passed through
the east gate and went into the Temple.

The LORD's spirit lifted me up
and took me into the inner courtyard,
where I saw that the Temple was filled
with the glory of the LORD. . . .
I heard the LORD speak to me
out of the Temple:
"Mortal man, here is my throne.
I will live here among the people of Israel
and rule them forever."

EZEKIEL 43:1–7

FULFILLMENT

New Testament writers
interpreted Jesus to be the final fulfillment
of all three of Ezekiel's prophecies.

new nation   Jesus sends the Holy Spirit,
who forms his followers into
a new holy nation of God (Acts 2).

new king   Jesus is the Good Shepherd,
the restored King of Israel
(John 10:11).

new temple   Jesus' followers became
the new living temple of
Yahweh's glory
(1 Corinthians 3:16-17).

Jesus and the New Testament, however,
were 500 years away.
For the present, any fulfillment
of Ezekiel's prophecies lay in the future.

Now, all that Israel could do was to wait
in silence and darkness.

Lost City

At the turn of the century,
a group called the German Oriental Society
equipped Professor Robert Koldewey
with a sizable archaeological team
to excavate a huge mound on the Euphrates River.

Eighteen years later,
Babylon, the most famous city of ancient history,
lay exposed in the grave of sand and rubble
that it had occupied for centuries.

42
Suffering Servant

Today, the ancient city of Babylon
has been resurrected from a grave of sand.
For the first time in centuries,
the desert sun shines on its walls and gateways.

Through the city's famous Isthar Gate
once passed Babylon's proud armies.
Carrying trophies of war,
they marched down the long parade street
that led to the center of the city.

An anonymous Jewish prophet of the exile
used to stand along this same street
and watch the great victory parades.
Known to history only as Second Isaiah,

Circling the ancient city
is an 11-mile-long wall.
Soaring to heights of 60 feet in places,
the wall has widths up to 15 feet.
Nearly 600 animals
decorate the wall's surface.

he prophesied in the spirit of the great Isaiah.
Thus, his works were appended to the earlier
prophet's writings.
Forming chapters 40-55,
they are often called the Book of Consolation.

PROPHET OF HOPE

Second Isaiah often walked through Babylon.
He saw the many idols in the city,
and thought how foolish idol worship is.

A man uses part of a tree for fuel. . . .
He roasts meat, eats it, and is satisfied.
He warms himself
and says, "How nice and warm!
What a beautiful fire!"
The rest of the wood he makes into an idol,
and then he bows down and worships it.
He prays to it and says,
"You are my god—save me!"

ISAIAH 44:15–17

How different was Yahweh, the Lord of Israel—
even though he seemed silent now!

The LORD *is the everlasting God;*
he created all the world. . . .
Those who trust in the LORD *for help*
will find their strength renewed.
They will rise on wings like eagles;
they will run and not get weary;
they will walk and not grow weak.

ISAIAH 40:28–31

With words like these, Second Isaiah
lifted the sagging spirit of Jewish exiles.

DAWN BREAKS

Then came a day of great excitement.
Rumors began filtering through to the exiles
of the spectacular feats of Cyrus, the king of Persia.
As the rumors multiplied,
so did the hopes of the people.

Was it possible?
Would the armies of Cyrus march on the city?
Would Cyrus be the instrument by which Yahweh
would reassert his presence in Israel's history?
Second Isaiah broke the silence.

189

The Isthar Gate
is one of eight passageways
into the city.
It opened onto
a wide parade street.
An inscription
found in Babylon reads:
"In this city
are 53 temples to chief gods,
55 chapels to Marduk,
and 180 altars to Isthar,"
the goddess of love and war.

"Comfort my people," says our God. . . .
"Tell them they have suffered long enough."

ISAIAH 40:1–2

To Cyrus the Lord says,
"I myself will prepare your way,
leveling mountains and hills. . . .
I appoint you to help my servant Israel,
the people that I have chosen. . . .

"I will send victory from the sky like rain;
the earth . . . will blossom with freedom
and justice."

ISAIAH 45:1–8

So it happened that, after 50 years of waiting,
Second Isaiah announced
that Yahweh was about to free his people,
as he once freed their ancestors from Egypt.

SOMETHING NEW

The people will soon go forth across the desert
in a new exodus. The prophet says:

A voice cries out,
"Prepare in the wilderness
a road for the Lord!
Clear the way in the desert for our God!"

ISAIAH 40:3

Israel's new exodus will culminate
in a new manifestation of God—
a new Sinai experience for all people.

"Then the glory of the Lord will be revealed,
and all mankind will see it."

ISAIAH 40:5

"All mankind will know that I am the Lord,
the one who saves you and sets you free.
They will know that I am Israel's powerful God."

ISAIAH 49:26

SERVANT SONGS

Second Isaiah does more than prophesy
Israel's freedom from Babylon.
He foretells a new Sinai experience for all people,

The Isthar Gate and the parade street
as they may have appeared in ancient times.

Proud griffins, fierce bulls,
and snarling lions with red and yellow manes
sparkle against a background of blue glazed tile.

and Israel's role in this great event.
The prophecy is called
"The Suffering Servant Songs."

These songs refer to the servant
sometimes as an individual person
and sometimes as a community of people.
Why this ambiguity?

Scholars say that this was the way the Israelites
saw themselves: sometimes as a community,
and sometimes as an individual,
represented in the person of a single figure,
like the king.

The fourth Servant Song
presents a new concept in Old Testament thought.
It portrays suffering
as the way the servant will reveal God's glory
and become a blessing for all people.

"We despised him and rejected him. . . .

*"But he endured the suffering
that should have been ours. . . .*

*All of us were like sheep that were lost,
each of us going his own way.
But the LORD
made the punishment fall on him,
the punishment all of us deserved."*

*The LORD says . . .
"His death was a sacrifice to bring forgiveness. . . .
For his sake I will forgive them."*

ISAIAH 53:3–11

New Testament writers
interpreted this song as referring to Jesus.

NARRATOR   *Now an Ethiopian . . .
was reading from the book
of the prophet Isaiah. . . .
He invited Philip to climb up
and sit in the carriage with him.
The passage of scripture
which he was reading was this:
"He was like a sheep
that is taken to be slaughtered. . . .
He did not say a word. . . ."*

191

ETHIOPIAN   *Tell me,*
             of whom is the prophet saying this?
             Of himself or of someone else?

NARRATOR   *Then Philip began to speak . . .*
             about Jesus.

                                        ACTS 8:27–35

Jesus also identified himself
with the "suffering servant."
On the third day after Jesus was crucified,
two downhearted disciples were returning home.
Jesus intercepted them,
but they failed to recognize him.
The disciples explained to the "stranger"
how Jesus was handed over and crucified.

DISCIPLES   *And we had hoped*
             that he would be the one
             who was going to set Israel free! . . .

JESUS   *How foolish you are,*
             how slow you are to believe
             everything the prophets said!
             Was it not necessary for the Messiah
             to suffer these things
             and then to enter his glory?

                                        LUKE 24:21–26

REJOICE

Second Isaiah ended his prophecies saying:

"You will leave Babylon with joy;
you will be led out of the city in peace.
The mountains and hills
will burst into singing,
and the trees will shout for joy."

                                        ISAIAH 55:12

43
Like Men Dreaming

As hope mounted among the exiled Jews,
so excitement mounted among Cyrus' troops
massing to attack Babylon.
Informers painted an ideal battle picture.
The popularity of Babylon's king, Nabonidus,
was plunging rapidly.
He was losing the support of his people.

Modern archaeologists
feel a strange kinship toward Nabonidus.
He too was fascinated by antiquity.
Sometimes called the world's first archaeologist,
he loved the past better than he ruled the present.
Excavated records report his interest in rebuilding
old temples.

Among his better-known reconstructions
was the famed Babylonian ziggurat,
which dated from before Abraham. We read:
"I restored this ziggurat to its former state
with mortar and baked bricks."
Twenty-five centuries later,
many of these bricks are still in good condition.
Arabs today occasionally load them on pack mules
and cart them off for use.

CYRUS II

In contrast to the unpopularity of Nabonidus
was the growing popularity of Cyrus.

Under his brilliant leadership,
the star of Persia began to ascend rapidly.
It reached its zenith under Darius the Great,
whose inscription on the cliffs of Behistun
provided the key for deciphering cuneiform.
Still standing in modern Iran are the remains
of the city of Persepolis, built by Darius.

The armies of Cyrus invaded Babylon,
and the city fell easily.
One record, called the Cyrus Cylinder,
says that Cyrus entered the city as a friend.

Unlike conquerors before him,
Cyrus did not deport defeated people for slave labor.
Nor did he suppress their religious traditions.
Rather,
he allowed them to remain in their homeland,
and Cyrus himself honored their gods.

Dating from the fifth century B.C.,
the Cyrus Cylinder was discovered at Babylon.
Speaking in the name of the great Persian king,
it boasts: "I am Cyrus, king of the world,
great king, mighty king."

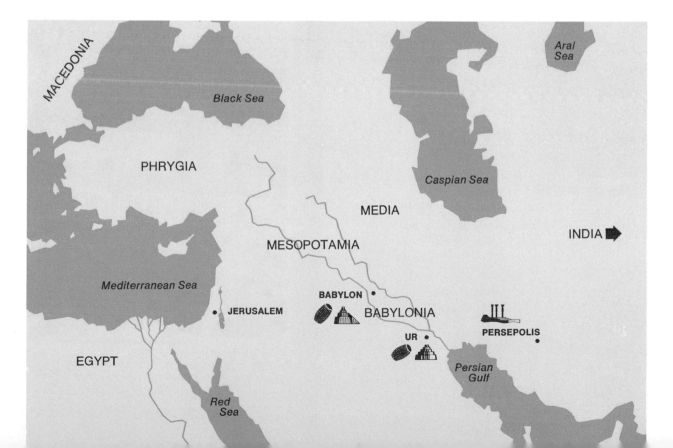

DECLARATION OF FREEDOM

In keeping with his policy toward defeated peoples,
Cyrus issued a proclamation to Jews in Babylon.
It read:

"This is the command of Cyrus,
Emperor of Persia.
The LORD, the God of Heaven,
has made me ruler over the whole world
and has given me the responsibility
of building a temple for him
in Jerusalem in Judah.
May God be with all of you
who are his people.
You are to go to Jerusalem
and rebuild the Temple of the LORD,
the God of Israel."

EZRA 1:2–3

The news of freedom was carried by runners
throughout Babylon.
For Jews who had lost hope and deserted their faith,
the news was embarrassing.
For Jews who had remained faithful to Yahweh,
the news brought joy beyond words.

LIKE MEN DREAMING

Even the former captors of the Jews
were caught up in the spirit.
They came forth with help in every way.
King Cyrus gave the exiles a farewell gift of
"the bowls and cups
that King Nebuchadnezzar had taken
from the Temple in Jerusalem" (Ezra 1:7).

The psalmist recalled Israel's day of freedom:

When the LORD brought us back to Jerusalem,
it was like a dream!
How we laughed, how we sang for joy! . . .
Indeed he did great things for us;
how happy we are!

PSALM 126:1–3

"I built Persepolis beautiful and secure," wrote the Persian King Darius I.

Darius' son, Xerxes, enlarged the city and royal palace. A portion of the excavated ground plan is shown here.

Persepolis

Neither snow, nor rain,
nor heat, nor gloom of night
stays these couriers
from the swift completion
of their appointed rounds.

This line, adapted from the historian Herodotus
and inscribed on the New York City post office,
was a tribute to the messenger service
established by Darius the Great in ancient Persia.
Darius' greatest monument, however,
was Persepolis, Greek meaning "Persian City."
Its ruins still stand in mute protest
to their destruction 2,500 years ago
by the armies of Alexander the Great.

The palace at Persepolis
ranks among the greatest examples
of ancient Persian art and architecture
known to modern archaeologists.

When news was announced that
the armies of Alexander the Great were not far off,
a frightened Darius III fled the palace,
leaving behind even his harem.

Alexander's armies carried off
the treasures of the palace
and left the magnificent site
in wreckage and flames.

Twenty-two centuries later,
University of Chicago archaeologists excavated the ruins
buried under the drifting sands of centuries of storms.

44

A Remnant Rebuilds

A plane packed with American POWs
returning home after imprisonment in Vietnam
approached the airport.
On the ground, crowds milled about excitedly.
Then it happened.

Home at Last
NEWSWEEK

In the control tower, a blip finally appeared
on the traffic controller's radarscope. . . .
"You are cleared for landing on Runway Zero Two,
repeat Zero Two. . . ."

When the white and grey Starlifter
settled onto the runway,
a tremendous cheer burst from the crowd—
a cheer echoed by the men on board.
While a phalanx of Air Force police
held back the onlookers,
the airplane taxied into position
and the crowd chanted over and over,
"Welcome home, welcome home."

DIFFERENT STORY

No such homecoming greeted the Jewish POWs.
All that greeted them was a desolate city
and the charred remains of a once beautiful temple.
Weeds grew where jubilant crowds once walked.
The site of the ghost city ripped open old wounds
and snuffed out homecoming joy.

The narrow, stepped streets of today's Jerusalem
still retain some of the flavor of the ancient city.
Inside hole-in-the-wall cafes, old men sit placidly
drawing smoke through the water-filled bowls
of their hookah pipes.

In the months ahead,
the people cleared the rubble and began to rebuild.
Top priority was given to the temple.

As soon as the Jews started working on it,
however, Samaritans from the North
tried to block their efforts.
At times, workmen found themselves
building with one hand and fighting with the other.

To add to the hardship,
farm crops failed during the first season back.
The people found themselves in serious trouble.
Joy and enthusiasm
gave way to depression and discouragement.
Soon, bickering broke out among individuals
and groups.

These stones of the Western (Wailing) Wall
are all that remain of the ancient temple.
Remodeled by Herod in Jesus' time,
it was destroyed by the Romans in A.D. 70.

He comes triumphant and victorious,
but humble and riding on a donkey—
on a colt, the foal of a donkey. . . .
"He will rule . . . to the ends of the earth."

ZECHARIAH 9:9–10

New Testament writers recalled this prophecy
when Jesus rode into Jerusalem on Palm Sunday.

"Tell the city of Zion,
Look, your king is coming to you . . .
on a colt, the foal of a donkey."

MATTHEW 21:5

NEHEMIAH AND EZRA

Then a big boost to morale occurred.
A second wave of exiles returned from Babylon.
Buoyed in spirit and strengthened in numbers,
the people finished building the temple.

Next, the people turned their attention
to rebuilding the city walls.
Under the dynamic leadership of Nehemiah,
who returned with a third wave of exiles,
the job was completed.

Finally, around 450 B.C.,
the day for celebration came.
Ezra assembled the faithful remnant of Jews
to renew their covenant with Yahweh.

On the first day of that month
they all assembled in Jerusalem,
in the square just inside the Water Gate. . . .
[Ezra] read the Law to them from dawn until noon,
and they all listened attentively. . . .

As Ezra stood there on the platform
high above the people,
they all kept their eyes fixed on him. . . .
Ezra said, "Praise the LORD, the great God!"

All the people raised their arms in the air
and answered, "Amen! Amen!"

NEHEMIAH 8:1–6

Into this critical situation stepped two prophets,
Haggai and Zechariah.
Haggai challenged the people:

"You have planted much grain,
but have harvested very little.
You have food to eat,
but not enough to make you full. . . .
Can't you see why this has happened?"

HAGGAI 1:6–7

Zechariah encouraged the people.
He reminded them of Yahweh's promise
that days of glory lay ahead.

Rejoice, rejoice, people of Zion!
Shout for joy, you people of Jerusalem!
Look, your king is coming to you!

45

The Reluctant Preacher

A man who is preoccupied with his own problems
tends to see only himself.
His vision shrinks and he forgets
there are other people in the world.

Something like this happened to the Jews
in the years after their return from exile.
They isolated themselves from the world.
The people made Yahweh
into their own image and likeness.
He became a nationalistic God
who was little concerned about the rest of the world
and mainly concerned about his chosen people.

Two prophets emerged to challenge this attitude.
Their words are recorded in the Book of Malachi
and in the Book of Jonah.

MALACHI

Far from showing unconcern
for the rest of the nations of the world,
the Book of Malachi praises them.
Speaking in God's name, the prophet says:

*"People from one end
of the world to the other honor me.
Everywhere they burn incense to me
and offer acceptable sacrifices. . . .
But you dishonor me."*

MALACHI 1:11–12

JONAH

The most forceful challenge to Jewish nationalism
comes in the Book of Jonah.
This book of four short chapters is still hotly debated.
Literalists regard it as a factual report.
Contextualists regard it as a book-length parable
containing an important religious message.

Here is the Book of Jonah in dialogue form.

Chapter One

NARRATOR *The LORD spoke to Jonah. . . .
He said, "Go to Nineveh,
that great city,
and speak out against it. . . ."
Jonah, however, set out
in the opposite direction in order
to get away from the LORD. . . .*

*But the LORD
sent a strong wind on the sea,
and the storm was so violent
that the ship
was in danger of breaking up.
The sailors were terrified
and cried out for help,
each one to his own god. . . .
Meanwhile, Jonah had gone below
and was lying in the ship's hold,
sound asleep. . . .*

SAILORS *Let's draw lots and find out
who is to blame
for getting us into this danger.*

NARRATOR *They did so,
and Jonah's name was drawn. . . .*

*Then they picked Jonah up
and threw him into the sea,
and it calmed down at once. . . .*

At the LORD's command
a large fish swallowed Jonah,
and he was inside the fish
for three days and three nights.

Chapter Two

NARRATOR   *From deep inside the fish*
Jonah prayed to the LORD . . .

JONAH   *O LORD . . .*
you threw me down into the depths,
to the very bottom of the sea,
where the waters were all around me,
and all your mighty waves
rolled over me. . . .
When I felt my life slipping away,
then, O LORD, I prayed to you,
and in your holy Temple
you heard me. . . .
I will sing praises to you;
I will offer you a sacrifice. . . .
Salvation comes from the LORD!

NARRATOR   *Then the LORD ordered the fish*
to spit Jonah up on the beach,
and it did.

Chapter Three

NARRATOR   *Once again*
the LORD spoke to Jonah.
He said,
"Go to Nineveh . . .
and proclaim to the people
the message I have given you."
So Jonah obeyed the LORD
and went to Nineveh,
a city so large that it took
three days to walk through it.
Jonah started through the city,
and after walking a whole day,

he proclaimed, "In forty days
Nineveh will be destroyed!"

The people of Nineveh
believed God's message.
So they decided
that everyone should fast. . . .

God saw what they did. . . .
So he changed his mind
and did not punish them
as he had said he would.

Modern Tel Aviv, viewed from adjoining Joppa,
where Jonah boarded a ship for Tarshish.
Centuries later, Crusaders,
commanded by Richard the Lionhearted,
used this same port
to reconquer the Holy Land.

Chapter Four

NARRATOR   *Jonah was very unhappy*
about this and became angry.

JONAH   *LORD,*
didn't I say before I left home
that this is just what you would do?
That's why I did my best
to run away to Spain!
I knew that you are a loving
and merciful God, always patient. . . .

NARRATOR   *Jonah went out east of the city. . . .*
He made a shelter for himself
and sat in its shade,
waiting to see
what would happen to Nineveh.
Then the LORD God
made a plant grow up over Jonah
to give him some shade. . . .
Jonah was extremely pleased
with the plant.
But at dawn the next day,
at God's command, a worm
attacked the plant, and it died.
After the sun had risen,
God sent a hot east wind,
and Jonah was about to faint
from the heat of the sun. . . .

JONAH   *I am better off dead than alive.*

LORD   *What right do you have*
to be angry about the plant?

JONAH   *I have every right to be angry—*
angry enough to die!

LORD   *This plant grew up in one night*
and disappeared the next;
you didn't do anything for it
and you didn't make it grow—
yet you feel sorry for it!
How much more, then,

should I have pity on Nineveh,
that great city.
After all, it has more than
120,000 innocent children in it,
as well as many animals!

The point of the Book of Jonah
is contained in its ending.
After the humor subsides,
a serious question is left hanging in the air.
The author has God put it to Jonah this way:

"You feel sorry for the plant!
How much more,
then, should I have pity on Nineveh."

The point is clear: God is concerned
not just about Jews, but all people.
Moreover, God's concern
must become the Jews' concern also.

The Book of Jonah
reveals to Jews a new universalism
concerning God's activity in human history.

NEW TESTAMENT TIMES

Jesus referred to the story of Jonah to clarify
his own mission and message. Luke writes:

As the people crowded around Jesus,
he went on to say,
"How evil are the people of this day!
They ask for a miracle, but none will be given
them except the miracle of Jonah.
In the same way that the prophet Jonah
was a sign for the people of Nineveh,
so the Son of Man will be a sign for the people
of this day. . . . On the Judgment Day
the people of Nineveh will stand up
and accuse you,
because they turned from their sins
when they heard Jonah preach."

LUKE 11:29–32

46
Voice in the Storm

Judah's ghetto years ended
when the armies of Alexander the Great
invaded the Near East.

Alexander was not a power-mad egotist.
A student of the great Aristotle,
he saw himself as a disciple of Hellenic culture.
He wanted to bring its blessings to all the world.

The Roman historian Plutarch
says Alexander's joy of victory was sobered
when he read the inscription on Cyrus' tomb:

*O man, whoever you are
and wherever you came from—
for I know you will come—
I am Cyrus, son of Cambyses,
who gave the Persians their empire.
Do not begrudge me
this tiny plot of earth
where my body rests.*

Alexander marched his armies to India
before he stopped to solidify his gains.
At the age of 32, he headed the largest empire
ever ruled by one man.

But death, the ultimate tyrant,
closed the door on his brilliant career.
Alexander died without an heir.
Three bickering generals divided his empire.

Two powerful kingdoms developed from it:
the Syrian (Seleucid) and the Egyptian (Ptolemy).
The Jews found themselves controlled first by one,
then the other.

NAGGING INCOMPLETENESS

This pawnlike existence jolted Jewish pride.
It shattered their dreams of political independence.
What chance did a tiny nation have
in a world of giants?

Now, a disturbing sense of incompleteness
began to nag at Jewish hearts. It is reflected
in the Book of Ecclesiastes.

"Their graves are their homes forever;
there they stay for all time,
though they once had lands of their own."
Psalm 49:11

This 30-foot-high limestone tomb of Cyrus
is in modern Iran.

But After All That

In a meditation on Alexander the Great
the First Book of Maccabees says:

He fought many battles,
captured fortified cities,
and put the kings of the region to death. . . .
When he had conquered the world,
he became proud and arrogant. (1:2-3)

This portrait of Alexander
is part of a larger mosaic unearthed at Pompeii.
Containing over a million pieces of marble,
it is patterned after a painting
of Alexander's victory
over the Persian king, Darius III.

Everything leads to weariness. . . .
I have seen everything done in this world,
and I tell you, it is all useless.
It is like chasing the wind.

ECCLESIASTES 1:8, 14

Sensing that Judah has reached its day of drums,
the book's author, Qoheleth, writes:

Fast runners do not always win the races,
and the brave do not always win the battles.
Wise men do not always earn a living. . . .
Bad luck happens to everyone.

ECCLESIASTES 9:11

Repeatedly, the author raises the question:
What is the purpose of life?
His inability to answer the question
gives his work a tinge of sadness—the kind of
sadness that trademarks so many great works.

Classic writers see human moments of joy
and peaks of glory, but deep in their hearts
they know that these things are like the dawn dew—
doomed to disappear.
It is this affirmation of people's fragility
that gives great literature its timeless appeal.

Occasionally Qoheleth counterpoints his sadness
with flights of advice to enjoy life.

Go ahead—eat your food and be happy;
drink your wine and be cheerful.

ECCLESIASTES 9:7

But in the end all things are vanity.
Human life moves in a monotonous, tragic cycle.

Television viewers caught this feeling
as they listened to the reading from Ecclesiastes
during the funeral services for John F. Kennedy
on November 25, 1963.

203

Is It All Useless?

Remember your Creator in the days of your youth,
before the evil days come....

When the guardians of the house tremble...

and the grinders are idle because they are few,
and they who look through the windows grow blind;

when the doors to the street are shut,
and the sound of the mill is low...

when the almond tree blooms,
and the locust grows sluggish
and the caper berry is without effect...

before the silver cord is snapped
and the golden bowl is broken...

and the dust returns to the earth as it once was,
and the life breath returns to God
who gave it.

Vanity of vanities, says Qoheleth,
all things are vanity!

ECCLESIASTES 12:1–8
New American Bible

Remember your Creator while you are still young,
before those dismal days and years come....

Then your arms, that protect you, will tremble....

Your teeth will be too few to chew your food,
and your eyes too dim to see clearly.

Your ears will be deaf to the noise of the street.
You will barely be able to hear the mill as it grinds....

Your hair will turn white;
you will hardly be able to drag yourself along,
and all desire will be gone....

The silver chain will snap,
and the golden lamp will fall and break....

Our bodies will return to the dust of the earth,
and the breath of life will go back to God,
who gave it to us.

Useless, useless, said the Philosopher.
It is all useless.

ECCLESIASTES 12:1–8
Today's English Version

[God] sets the time for birth
and the time for death ...
the time for sorrow and the time for joy,
the time for mourning
and the time for dancing ...
the time for silence and the time for talk ...
the time for war and the time for peace.

ECCLESIASTES 3:2–8

WHAT'S THE ANSWER?

Ecclesiastes contains none of the certainty
of the Book of Proverbs.
The book asks all the big questions,
but comes up only with the admission
that it doesn't know the answers.
"Somewhere out there," the author seems to admit,
"there is an answer, but I don't know what it is."

The Book of Ecclesiastes helps us enter
the heart of a Jew waiting for more revelation.
Early Jews had little or no idea of an afterlife.
True, they believed in a nether world, *Sheol.*
But they thought it was just a place for the dead,
good and bad alike.
What happened there, they did not know.

The question emerged:
If God is good, and if this is man's only home,
why do so many good people go unrewarded?
Worse yet, why do so many suffer so much?

THREE SUGGESTED ANSWERS

One proposal was that such people suffered
because of secret sins.

A second suggestion was that they suffered
because they belonged to the total community
of Israel.
The Book of Deuteronomy seemed to indicate
that God treated Israel as a total community.
Thus, an innocent man might suffer
because he was a member of a guilty whole.

A third proposal was that innocent people suffered
because of the sins of their parents or children.
Thus, one person or the whole community
might suffer because of the sins of another.

A CORRECTION

Later prophets, like Ezekiel, corrected this view.

"What is this proverb
people keep repeating in the land of Israel?
'The parents ate the sour grapes,
but the children got the sour taste.'

"As surely as I am the living God,"
says the Sovereign LORD, "you will not repeat
this proverb in Israel any more. ...

"A son is not to suffer
because of his father's sins,
nor a father because of the sins of his son.
A good man will be rewarded for doing good,
and an evil man will suffer for the evil he does."

EZEKIEL 18:2–3, 20

But in spite of this revelation,
many Jews continued to be influenced
by the older view,
even into New Testament times.
One day the disciples saw a man
who had been born blind,
and they asked Jesus who was to blame
for his blindness, the man or his parents.

Jesus answered,
"His blindness has nothing to do
with his sins or his parents' sins.

JOHN 9:3

Jews who accepted Ezekiel's new revelation
were forced to examine the question:
Why do good people suffer?
For the answer to this question,
we must turn to the Book of Job.

Cast of Characters

NARRATOR	ELIPHAZ	⎫
LORD	BILDAD	⎬ FRIENDS OF JOB
SATAN	ZOPHAR	⎭
JOB	ELIHU, YOUNG BYSTANDER	

NARRATOR *There was a man named Job,*
living in the land of Uz,
who worshiped God
and was faithful to him.
He was a good man,
careful not to do anything evil.
He had seven sons and three daughters,
and owned 7,000 sheep, 3,000 camels,
1,000 head of cattle, and 500 donkeys.
He also had a large number
of servants and was
the richest man in the East.

ACT 1

Scene i

NARRATOR *When the day came*
for the heavenly beings
to appear before the LORD,
Satan was there among them.

LORD *What have you been doing?*

SATAN *I have been walking here and there,*
roaming around the earth.

LORD *Did you notice my servant Job?*
There is no one on earth
as faithful and good as he is.
He worships me and is careful
not to do anything evil.

SATAN *Would Job worship you*
if he got nothing out of it?
You have protected him and his family
and everything he owns.

You bless everything he does,
and you have given him enough cattle
to fill the whole country.
But now suppose
you take away everything he has—
he will curse you to your face!

LORD *All right, everything he has*
is in your power,
but you must not hurt Job himself.

[Exit Satan]

Scene ii

NARRATOR *[Misfortune strikes Job's household.*
Enemies steal his cattle and kill his
servants. Lightning destroys his sheep.
Outlaws carry off his camels.
A wind flattens his house,
killing his sons and daughters.]

Called "ships of the desert," camels
made trade possible across Middle East deserts.
Camel milk delighted the nomad's taste;
camel skin was used for clothing and tent coverings.

Job tore his clothes in grief.
He shaved his head
and threw himself face downward
on the ground.

JOB *I was born with nothing,*
and I will die with nothing.
The LORD gave,
and now he has taken away.
May his name be praised!

NARRATOR *In spite of everything*
that had happened,
Job did not sin by blaming God.

Scene iii

NARRATOR *When the day came*
for the heavenly beings
to appear before the LORD again,
Satan was there among them.

LORD *Where have you been?*

SATAN *I have been walking here and there,*
roaming around the earth.

LORD *Did you notice my servant Job?*
There is no one on earth
as faithful and good as he is.
He worships me and is careful
not to do anything evil.
You persuaded me to let you
attack him for no reason at all,
but Job is still as faithful as ever.

SATAN *A man will give up everything*
in order to stay alive.
But now suppose you hurt his body—
he will curse you to your face!

LORD *All right, he is in your power,*
but you are not to kill him.

[Exit Satan]

Scene iv

NARRATOR *[Severe boils blanket Job's body.*
He suffers in deep torment.]

[Enter three friends of Job]

[At the sight of Job, his three friends]
began to weep and wail,
tearing their clothes in grief. . . .
Finally Job broke the silence
and cursed
the day on which he had been born.

JOB *. . . Turn that day into darkness, God.*
Never again remember that day;
never again let light shine on it. . . .

ELIPHAZ *Job, will you be annoyed if I speak? . . .*
Evil does not grow in the soil. . . .
Man brings trouble on himself,
as surely as sparks fly up
from a fire. . . .
Do not resent it
when God rebukes you. . . .

JOB *I have never opposed what God*
commands. . . . In trouble like this
I need loyal friends. . . .
Don't condemn me. . . .

ZOPHAR *Put your heart right, Job.*
Reach out to God.
Put away evil and wrong
from your home.
Then face the world again,
firm and courageous. . . .

JOB *You hit a man who is about to fall. . . .*
I am in the right.
Are you coming to accuse me, God?
If you do,
I am ready to be silent and die. . . .
Why do you treat me
like an enemy? . . .

207

ELIPHAZ   *Can any man be really pure?*
          Can anyone be right with God?
          Why, God does not trust even
          his angels;
          even they are not pure in his sight.
          And man drinks evil as if it were
          water; yes, man is corrupt. . . .

JOB   *The comfort you give*
          is only torment. . . .
          I want someone to plead with God
          for me,
          as a man pleads for his friend. . . .

BILDAD   *You are only hurting yourself*
          with your anger. . . .

JOB   *Why do you keep tormenting me . . .*
          and regard my troubles
          as proof of my guilt?
          Can't you see it is God
          who has done this? . . .
          He has taken away all my wealth
          and destroyed my reputation.

ZOPHAR   *Job, you upset me. . . .*
          What you have said is an insult. . . .

JOB   *Listen to what I am saying;*
          that is all the comfort I ask. . . .

ELIPHAZ   *Now, Job, make peace with God*
          and stop treating him like an enemy. . . .
          Put an end to all the evil
          that is done in your house. . . .

JOB   *I will never give up my claim*
          to be right; my conscience is clear. . . .
          I swear every word is true. . . .

NARRATOR *Because Job was convinced*
          of his own innocence, the three men
          gave up trying to answer him.
          [Then a bystander, Elihu, spoke up.]

ELIHU   *I am young, and you are old,*
          so I was afraid
          to tell you what I think. . . .
          But I tell you, Job, you are wrong. . . .
          Be careful not to turn to evil;
          your suffering was sent to keep you
          from it. . . .
          No one can tell God what to do
          or accuse him of doing evil. . . .

                                    [Curtain]

ACT 2

Scene i

NARRATOR *[Suddenly, a violent storm blows up:*
          wind, lightning, and thunder.]
          Then out of the storm
          the LORD spoke to Job.

LORD   *Answer the questions I ask you.*
          Were you there when I made the world?
          If you know so much, tell me about it.
          Who decided how large it would be?
          Who stretched the measuring line
          over it?
          Do you know all the answers?
          What holds up the pillars
          that support the earth? Who laid
          the cornerstone of the world? . . .

          Have you ever visited the storerooms,
          where I keep the snow? . . .
          Who is the mother of the ice . . .
          which turns the waters to stone . . . ?

          Have you watched wild deer . . . ?
          Do you know how long
          they carry their young? Do you
          know the time for their birth? . . .

          Was it you, Job,
          who made horses so strong? . . .
          They eagerly paw the ground
          in the valley;

208

The Horse

In ancient times,
horses were reserved mainly for war purposes.
Battle chariots were usually pulled by two steeds,
with a third running alongside for quick change.

they rush into battle
with all their strength.
They do not know
the meaning of fear,
and no sword can turn them back. . . .
Does a hawk
learn from you how to fly?
Does an eagle wait for your command
to build its nest? If so . . .
I will be the first to praise you
and admit
that you won the victory yourself. . . .

JOB   *Lord, I talked about things*
     I did not understand. . . .

I knew only
what others had told me,
but now I have seen you
with my own eyes.
So I am ashamed of all I have said
and repent in dust and ashes.

[Curtain]

Epilogue

NARRATOR   *After the Lord had finished speaking . . .*
          he blessed the last part of Job's life
          even more
          than he had blessed the first.

209

Unfathomable

The God who emerges from the Book of Job
is a God beyond human comprehension.
The greatest blunder a person can make,
the book seems to say,
is to try to reduce God to the level
of human definition and comprehension.

Augustine, the great fifth-century Christian,
put it this way:

God is inexpressible.
It is easier for us to say what he is not
than what he is. . . .
Nothing is comparable to him. . . .
If you could conceive him,
you would conceive something other than God.
He is not at all
what you have conceived him to be.

TRADITIONAL VIEW

If we approach the Book of Job
as *wisdom* literature, several points emerge.

Job's three friends answer Job's questions
in the traditional way,
presupposing that he is being punished for sin.
Their understanding of God,
that he rewards and punishes people in *this* life,
demands that they adopt this view.
To take the opposite view
would be to accuse God of being unjust.

ALTERNATE VIEW

Knowing in his heart that he is innocent,
Job is forced to search for an answer himself.

First, he toys with the idea
that God regards him as some kind of enemy.
But this seems unconvincing, even to Job.

Second, Job speaks the celebrated lines:

While still in this body I will see God.
I will see him with my own eyes. (19:26-27)

Some Bible readers cite this passage
as one of the first Old Testament indications
of a belief in the resurrection of the body.
Thus, Job will be rewarded in a life to come.

Others say that Job's statement
should not be interpreted
as referring to an afterlife.
For Job himself says earlier:

I will call the grave my father,
and the worms that eat me
I will call my mother and my sisters. (17:14)

In any event, Job continues to search
for an answer to his suffering.
When he can find none, he cries out:
"Let Almighty God answer me." (31:35)

At this point, young Elihu enters the picture.
Some suggest
that Elihu will grant Job's innocence (36:21).
Perhaps God is inflicting pain on Job
to keep him from sinning gravely in the future.

But Job's suffering is so great
that Job cannot accept this explanation.
Punishment for the greatest sin in the world
could not be any worse than his present pain.

*Then out of the storm
the LORD spoke to Job.* (38:1)

NEW VIEW

God's words to Job
take the form of a recital of the wonders of nature.
God reminds Job,
in a dramatic series of rhetorical questions,
that Job neither created, manages,
nor understands the universe.

This doesn't answer Job's question directly,
but it does suggest a new line of thought.
It is this:
If Job admits God's wisdom greatly surpasses his,
why does he question God's fairness to him?
If he can't understand other things,
why does he expect to understand this?

Expressed in *wisdom literature* terms,
it comes down to this:
Job's wisdom falls so short of God's wisdom
that it is folly for Job to challenge God.
To challenge God
is the posture of a fool, not a *wise* man.

In any event, Job's experience of God
changes him from a sage into a saint.
It transforms him
from a man who walked by the light of reason
to a man who walked by the light of faith.

The Door Opens

Later Old Testament books
made further inroads into the vexing question
posed in the Book of Job.

The Book of Wisdom
broke new ground in the second century B.C.
It reads:

*Wicked people
are wrong when they say to themselves . . .
"We were born by chance, and after life is over,
we will be as if we had never been born. . . .*

*"Come on, then,
let's enjoy the good things of life. . . .
Let's drink the most expensive wines
and use the finest perfumes.
Let's not miss
a single flower in the springtime! . . ."*

*That is how evil people think,
but they are wrong. . . .
When God created us, he did not intend for us
to die; he made us like himself. . . .*

*Righteous people are protected by God
and will never suffer torment.
It is a foolish mistake
to think that righteous people die
and that their death is a terrible evil. . . .
In fact, the righteous are at peace.
It might appear
that they have suffered punishment,
but they have the confident hope of immortality.
Their sufferings were minor
compared with the blessings they will receive.
God has tested them, like gold in a furnace,
and found them worthy to be with him.*

WISDOM 2:1–3:5

Time Chart

	198 BC	Syria defeats Egypt Syria rules Judah
	167	Antiochus persecutes Judah Antiochus desecrates temple
Judas	166	Maccabean revolt
	164	Maccabees recapture temple
Jonathan	160	
Simon	142	Judah wins independence
John Hyrcanus I	135	Hasmonean era begins
Others	104	
Hyrcanus II	63	Romans enter Jerusalem
Herod the Great	40	Hasmonean era ends
	29	Augustus Caesar rules Rome
Others	4	Old Testament era ends

TODAY'S BIBLELAND

Mediterranean Sea

Suez Canal

EGYPT

• CAIRO

SUEZ •

Nile River

Sinai Pennisula

Gulf of Suez

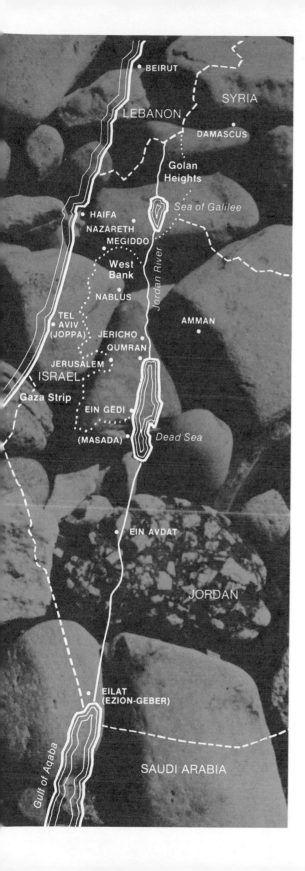

REMNANT COMMUNITY

Books

Tobit	2 Maccabees
Judith	Sirach
Esther	Daniel
1 Maccabees	

47

Dreams and Visions

The sense of incompleteness in Jewish hearts
exploded into agony in 167 B.C.
The stage was set this way.

Around 200 B.C., Syrian armies conquered Egypt.
Judah passed from Egyptian hands to Syrian hands.
At first, Judah's status remained about the same.
But then a Hellenic-minded tyrant, Antiochus IV,
took over the Syrian throne.

Calling himself Epiphanes, he fancied himself
an incarnation of the Greek god Zeus.
Coins bearing his name
were found by American archaeologists in 1931,
in a dig west of the Dead Sea.
It was this king who decided
to make Greeks out of his Jewish subjects.

The king . . .
sent messengers with a decree to Jerusalem
and all the towns of Judea,
ordering the people to follow customs
that were foreign to their country. . . .
They were commanded to build pagan altars,
temples, and shrines. . . .

The king . . . appointed officials
to supervise the people and commanded
each town in Judea to offer pagan sacrifices. . . .

Any books of the Law which were found
were torn up and burned.

1 MACCABEES 1:44–56

This decree created an impossible situation.
Those who disobeyed it were persecuted brutally.
Typical was the martyrdom of seven brothers,
while their mother looked on (2 Maccabees 7).

FAITH CRISIS

This reign of terror shook Judah's faith to the roots.
Devout Jews cried out to God:

How long will your anger burn like fire? . . .
Lord, where are the former proofs of your love?
Where are the promises you made to David?

PSALM 89:46–49

Into this crisis
stepped the unknown prophet of the Book of Daniel.
Like prophets before him, he faced the problem
of communicating a profound religious message
to a simple, uneducated people.
He had decided upon two literary devices to do it:
folktales and visions.
These he centered around a Jewish hero, Daniel.

BOOK OF DANIEL

The Book of Daniel divides into two parts:
the first half narrates a series of folktales;
the second half describes a series of visions.

The book opens on the eve of Jewish exile in 586 B.C.,
just after Babylon destroys Jerusalem.
The king of Babylon instructs his officers
to take young Israelites prisoner.

They had to be handsome, intelligent,
well-trained, quick to learn . . .
so that they would be qualified to serve
in the royal court.
Ashpenaz was to teach them to read and write
the Babylonian language. . . .
After three years of this training
they were to appear before the king.

DANIEL 1:4–5

The Syrian (Seleucid) ruler
Antiochus I.

The god Zeus
poised to hurl a thunderbolt
with his mighty right arm.

Antiochus IV

This 2,000-year-old coin portrays Antiochus I.
From his line came Antiochus IV,
who called himself Epiphanes (god-manifest).
In mocking hatred,
Jews dubbed him Epimanes (madman).

Antiochus thought himself
to be a manifestation of the Greek god Zeus,
pictured on the fifth-century B.C. coin
at the right, above.

He ordered Zeus' statue to be erected
in the place of honor in the Jerusalem temple.
Jews condemned the act,
calling it the "abomination of desolation"
or the "terrible sin" (Daniel 8:13).

It is interesting to note
that it was in honor of the same god, Zeus,
that the Olympic games were begun in 776 B.C.
and celebrated thereafter at four-year intervals.

FOLKTALES

The first tale describes how the king
orders the young men to be fed
the same food and drink as the royal court.

NARRATOR   *Daniel made up his mind*
not to let himself become
ritually unclean . . .
so he asked Ashpenaz
to help him. . . .

ASHPENAZ   *The king has decided*
what you are to eat and drink,
and if you don't look as fit
as the other young men,
he may kill me. . . .

DANIEL   *Test us for ten days.*
Give us vegetables to eat
and water to drink.

Then compare us with
the young men who are eating
the food of the royal court,
and base your decision
on how we look.

NARRATOR   *[The guard placed in charge]*
agreed to let them try it
for ten days.
When the time was up,
they looked healthier and stronger
than all those who had been eating
the royal food. . . .

God gave the four young men
knowledge and skill in literature
and philosophy. In addition,
he gave Daniel skill in interpreting
visions and dreams.

DANIEL 1:8–17

215

UNHEWN STONE

A second tale concerns a disturbing dream
that the king had.
When the king's wise men show ignorance about it,
Daniel is called in.

KING   *Can you tell me what I dreamed*
                and what it means? . . .

DANIEL   *Your Majesty, in your vision*
                you saw standing before you
                a giant statue, bright and shining,
                and terrifying to look at.
                Its head was made of the finest gold;
                its chest and arms
                were made of silver;
                its waist and hips of bronze,
                its legs of iron,
                and its feet partly of iron
                and partly of clay.
                While you were looking at it,
                a great stone
                broke loose from a cliff
                without anyone touching it,
                struck the iron and clay feet
                of the statue, and shattered them. . . .
                The stone grew to be a mountain
                that covered the whole earth.

This was the dream.
Now I will tell Your Majesty
what it means. . . .
You are the head of gold.
After you there will be another
empire, not as great as yours,
and after that a third,
an empire of bronze,
which will rule the whole earth.
And then there will be a fourth empire,
as strong as iron, which shatters
and breaks everything.
And just as iron shatters everything,
it will shatter and crush

all the earlier empires. . . .
You also saw
that the feet and the toes
were partly clay and partly iron.
This means
that it will be a divided empire. . . .
The rulers of that empire
will try to unite their families . . .
but will not be able to. . . .
At the time of those rulers
the God of heaven
will establish a kingdom. . . .
It will . . .
destroy all those empires
and then last forever.
You saw how a stone broke loose
from a cliff without anyone
touching it and how it struck
the statue. . . .
The great God
is telling Your Majesty
what will happen in the future.
I have told you exactly
what you dreamed,
and have given you its true meaning.

DANIEL 2:26, 31–45

The four kingdoms are the great empires
(Babylonian, Median, Persian, Greek)
that dominated the Near East
from the time of the Jewish exile
to the era of Jewish persecution.

Daniel's message is one of hope.
God will soon destroy the last of these empires.

New Testament writers
interpreted Jesus to be the unhewn stone,
rejected by human builders (Luke 20:18).

New Testament writers also
interpreted the kingdom of God, preached by Jesus,
to be the eternal kingdom foretold in this vision.

Darius and the Lion

King Darius I of Persia
takes aim at the head of a wounded lion.
Once the target
of a popular, ancient sport,
the lion is now extinct in the Near East.

The winged emblem above the carving
symbolizes Ahurmazka,
the national god of ancient Persia.

Made from a fifth-century B.C. cylinder,
this seal measures
two inches by four inches.

Darius' name appears to the right in three languages.
It was this same Darius whose Behistun inscription
(same three languages) solved the riddle of cuneiform.

LIONS' DEN

A third tale concerns Daniel's fidelity to prayer.
As Daniel grew older, King Darius the Mede
made him one of his chief administrators.
The other administrators grew jealous of Daniel.
They connived to have the king issue a decree
forbidding prayer to anyone but the king.
Daniel ignored the decree.

NARRATOR   *When Daniel's enemies*
observed him praying to God,
all of them went together
to the king to accuse Daniel.

ENEMIES   *Your Majesty, you signed an order*
that for the next thirty days
anyone who requested anything
from any god or from any man
except you, would be thrown
into a pit filled with lions.

KING   *Yes, that is a strict order. . . .*

ENEMIES   *Daniel . . .*
does not respect Your Majesty. . . .

NARRATOR   *When the king heard this,*
he was upset. . . .
[He liked Daniel but had no choice.]

So the king gave orders for Daniel
to be . . . thrown into the pit. . . .

The king returned to the palace
and spent a sleepless night,
without food
or any form of entertainment.

At dawn the king got up
and hurried to the pit.
When he got there,
he called out anxiously.

KING   *Daniel,*
servant of the living God!

217

Was the God you serve so loyally
able to save you from the lions?

DANIEL *May Your Majesty live forever!*
God sent his angel
to shut the mouths of the lions
so that they would not hurt me. . . .

NARRATOR *The king was overjoyed*
and gave orders for Daniel
to be pulled up out of the pit. . . .
Then the king gave orders
to arrest all the men
who had accused Daniel.

DANIEL 6:11-24

The message, again, is one of hope.
Yahweh will save his people
just as he saved Daniel from the jaws of the lions.

VISIONS

The visions of Daniel
begin in the second half of the book.
They are filled with strange images and symbols.
This kind of colorful writing style
is often referred to as apocalyptic writing.
The author's purpose is to communicate,
in a veiled (apocalyptic) way, things to come.

Apocalyptic writing is similar to prophetic writing,
but there are differences.
Prophetic writing
stresses human cooperation with God's plan;
apocalyptic writing
stresses God's final control over his plan.
Prophetic writing calls for action;
apocalyptic writing calls for patience.

The apocalyptic writer tells his readers
that God's action in the present is nothing
compared to what will happen in the future.
People must therefore be patient and trust in God.

THE SON OF MAN

Daniel's first vision is regarded by many experts
as the most important.
Daniel sees four beasts emerge from the sea.

While I was looking, thrones were put in place.
One who had been living forever sat down. . . .
There were many thousands of people there
to serve him,
and millions of people stood before him.
The court began its session,
and the books were opened.

DANIEL 7:9-10

The Ancient One and the court then pass judgment
on the four beasts.
After the judgment is passed, the visions continue.
Daniel says:

I saw what looked like a human being.
He was approaching me,
surrounded by clouds,
and he went to the one
who had been living forever
and was presented to him.
He was given authority,
honor, and royal power,
so that the people of all nations, races,
and languages would serve him.
His authority would last forever,
and his kingdom would never end.

The visions I saw alarmed me,
and I was deeply disturbed.
I went up to one of those standing there
and asked him to explain it all.
So he told me the meaning. He said,
"These four huge beasts
are four empires which will arise on earth.
And the people of the Supreme God
will receive royal power
and keep it forever and ever."

DANIEL 7:13-18

INTERPRETATION

For most readers these verses
reaffirm Nathan's prophecy to David
of an eternal kingship.

A new image, however, is the "son of man."
Daniel's vision equates the "son of man" (king)
with the "holy ones" (nation).
Thus, the king and nation
are combined in one figure.

New Testament writers referred to Jesus
as the "Son of Man" no less than 69 times.
The most striking reference
came when Jesus stood trial for his life.

HIGH PRIEST   *Are you the Messiah,*
               the Son of the Blessed God?

JESUS   *I am,*
               and you will all see the Son of Man
               seated at the right side
               of the Almighty
               and coming with the clouds
               of heaven!

HIGH PRIEST   *We don't need*
               any more witnesses!
               You heard his blasphemy.

                                    MARK 14:61-63

For New Testament writers,
the descriptive expression "the Son of Man
seated at the right hand of the Power"
captured the mysteriousness of Jesus' personality.

On the one hand,
it recalled that he was David's offspring.
On the other hand,
it recalled that he was Yahweh's servant.

In other words,
the expression captured the polarity of Jesus:
related to David,
and related to Yahweh.

Both the humble and the exalted aspects
of Jesus' personality were served.

No other title could have identified better
Jesus' person and mission.
He is both,
a humble member of the "holy ones" (nation)
and the exalted servant
of the "mighty one" (Yahweh).
His suffering will establish an eternal kingdom
not just for Israel, but for all peoples.

Referring to Jesus
as Son of Man and Suffering Servant, Paul said:

Christ is himself
the Savior of the church, his body.

                                    EPHESIANS 5:23

DAY OF JUDGMENT

The Book of Daniel ends dramatically.
Concerning the day of Yahweh's final judgment,
Daniel is told in a final vision:

"When that time comes,
all the people of your nation
whose names are written in God's book
will be saved.
Many of those who have already died
will live again:
some will enjoy eternal life,
and some will suffer eternal disgrace.
The wise leaders will shine
with all the brightness of the sky.
And those who have taught many people
to do what is right
will shine like the stars forever."

. . . "And now, Daniel, close the book
and put a seal on it until the end of the world."

                                    DANIEL 12:1-4

Esther

Three other pieces of Old Testament literature
belong to this era: Tobit, Judith, and Esther.
Each of these books centers around a Jewish hero
who remains faithful to Yahweh in time of trial.
As such, the books exhort persecuted Jews
to hold fast to their faith.

The Book of Esther is typical.
It is named after a beautiful Jewish girl
who was raised in exile by her uncle, Mordecai.
A Persian king, not knowing her nationality,
makes her his wife and queen.
Haman, an ambitious Persian leader,
convinces the king
to destroy the Jews of the kingdom.
Esther intervenes to outwit the evil Haman
and save her people.

Modern Jews celebrate the event on Purim.
The holiday is also known as the Feast of Lots,
after the way Haman chose the day
for exterminating all the Jews.

Ancient caves still honeycomb the rugged ravine
country of Palestine.
The Maccabees launched
their counteroffensive from sites like this.
Heroines like Esther inspired them.

THE MACCABEES

Fired with the spirit of the Book of Daniel,
loyal Jews came alive.

Soon a resistance movement was mounted
under the leadership of three Jewish brothers:
Judas, Jonathan, and Simon.

Called the Maccabees, they formed a guerrilla army.
From rocky ravines and hills,
they set in motion a counteroffensive.

Judas would make sudden attacks
on towns and villages and burn them.
He captured strategic positions
and routed many enemy troops,
finding that he was most successful at night.
People everywhere spoke of his bravery.

2 MACCABEES 8:6–7

Jewish poetry recalls Judas this way:

He advanced the cause of freedom
by what he did.
He made life miserable for many kings,
but brought joy to the people of Israel.
We will praise him forever
for what he did.

1 MACCABEES 3:6–7

The revolt gained momentum
when the ragged freedom fighters
stormed the temple and reclaimed it.
Modern Jews still celebrate the event
with the Feast of Lights, known as Hanukkah.

The tide finally turned in favor of the revolutionaries
when Antiochus overextended his army on other
battlefronts and ran into economic problems.

Typical of so many leaders,
Judas and Jonathan were killed in the process
of bringing victory to their people.
It fell to their brother, Simon,
to bring the revolt to a successful conclusion.

Life after Death

Taking cue from the Book of Daniel,
a new attitude toward life after death emerged
among many Jews in this period.
We see it reflected in the martyr stories
of the seven brothers.
The first brother says to his tormentors:

*"You may kill us,
but the King of the universe
will raise us from the dead
and give us eternal life."*

2 MACCABEES 7:9

The fourth brother echoes the same idea:

*"I am glad to die at your hands,
because we have the assurance
that God will raise us from death."*

2 MACCABEES 7:14

Similarly, a new attitude about the relationship
between the living and the dead emerged.

On one occasion Judas had his men
pray for the dead and took up a collection
to offer sacrifice for them.

*Judas did this noble thing
because he believed in the resurrection
of the dead.
If he had not believed
that the dead would be raised,
it would have been foolish and useless
to pray for them.
In his firm and devout conviction
that all of God's faithful people
would receive a wonderful reward,
Judas made provision for a sin offering
to set free from their sin
those who had died.*

2 MACCABEES 12:43-45

48
Threat from Within

The Persecution Era
was followed by the Hasmonean Era.
Simon, the last of the Maccabees brothers, died
and leadership passed to his son John.

If Jewish existence was threatened from without
during the Persecution Era,
it was now threatened from within.
The Hasmoneans (probably named for John's
grandfather) used the office of high priest
for political purposes.

During this era, three religious groups polarized:
Sadducees, Pharisees, and Essenes.

SADDUCEES

All three groups claimed loyalty to the Torah,
but took different religious stances.
The Sadducees, composed of priestly
and wealthy families, supported the Hasmoneans.

Opposing the Sadducees
were Jews of very strict observance, called Hasidim.
From this group emerged the Essenes and Pharisees.

ESSENES

The Essenes were so opposed to Hasmonean rule
that they broke with conventional Jewish society
and lived apart in the desert.
They believed that God's great intervention
in human history was close at hand.

Greek customs became widespread
among Near Eastern nations during this period.
Baths and gymnasiums appeared in Jerusalem.
Pharisees and Essenes found Greek customs offensive,
especially the cult of the body
and nudity in athletic games.

Thus, marriage meant little to them
and most of them lived as "monks."

It was their scrolls
that were found in the Dead Sea caves.
Some scholars speculate
that John the Baptist once belonged to this group.

PHARISEES

The Pharisees remained within the mainstream
of Jewish society.
Unlike the conservative Sadducees,
they accepted later prophetic revelation
concerning immortality, judgment after death,
and the resurrection of the body.

On the other hand,
they so stressed the letter of the law
that legalism became a constant threat in their lives.
In New Testament times,
this brought them into open conflict with Jesus.

ROMAN EAGLE

The clock began to strike midnight
for the Hasmonean Era in 63 B.C.
Then, Roman armies occupied Jerusalem.
A vivid story is told in connection with the event.

Witnesses to God
LEONARD JOHNSTON

*When the Roman general Pompey
captured Jerusalem in 63 B.C.
he determined to see its famous temple.
It was widely known
that the Jews would not worship any of the gods
which Rome received . . .
but there was some mystery
about the sort of God they did worship.
Now he would find out.*

*So he made his way up the hill
on which the Temple stood,
and crossed the courtyard which surrounded it.
Passing under the great doors
and through an outer hall,
he found himself in a long room with,
at the far end, shut off by a curtain,
a little secret room.*

*This was the sanctuary of the god.
And as he advanced toward it,
with no sound but the echo of his footsteps,
even the conqueror
could not prevent a feeling of awe.
What lay beyond those curtains?
Some strange and terrible animal?
A mysterious presence aglow with flame?*

*Pompey swept back the curtains and gazed in—
and burst into a bellow of laughter.*

*For there was nothing there.
This was the famous secret of the Jews.
No wonder they made a mystery of it;
no wonder no one had seen their god.
There was nothing to see.*

The curtain finally fell on the Hasmonean Era around 40 B.C., when the Romans installed Herod the Great as king of Judah.

Herod catered to the Romans and used terror tactics to control Jews who opposed him. Here's how one writer described him:

The Years of Galilee
HOWARD LAFAY

He murdered members of his own family—
yet scrupulously observed Mosaic dietary laws
and would eat no pork.
This provoked his Roman master Augustus
into jesting:
"I would rather be Herod's pig than Herod's son."

Another writer completed the portrait of Herod this way:

Who Was the Man Jesus?
ROBERT COUGHLAN

Herod was a brilliant, scheming, ruthless,
bloody man who reigned from 40 to 4 B.C. . . .

One of the few things
that recommended him to his subjects was . . .
that he began rebuilding the Temple
according to the grandiose plans of Solomon.

It was this ruler who served as the bridge between the Old and the New Testament periods.

Augustus Caesar

After occupying Jerusalem in 63 B.C.,
Pompey returned to Rome
and struck up a political friendship
with a young military genius, Julius Caesar.

But Pompey's ties with Julius were doomed.
A corrupt Roman Senate
turned the two leaders against each other.
Pompey met death in Egypt in 48 B.C.

By 44 B.C., Julius was Rome's undisputed boss;
but his days were numbered, also.
On March 15, Julius Caesar was assassinated.

Into his shoes stepped Octavian (photo),
his 18-year-old adopted son.
In 27 B.C., Octavian became Rome's first emperor,
taking the name Augustus Caesar.
It was during his reign that Jesus was born.

49

The Unfinished Story

The early American writer
Nathaniel Hawthorne was dead.
On his desk lay the outline to a play
that he never got a chance to write.

The play centered around a person
who never appeared on stage.
Everyone talked excitedly about the person,
everyone dreamed about him,
everyone wanted to meet him,
everyone waited eagerly for his arrival.

All kinds of minor characters
discussed the arrival of the main character.
But the play ended without the main character
ever putting in an appearance.

The Old Testament
is something like Hawthorne's unfinished play.
It, too, ends
without the main character appearing.

The Book of Sirach
rings down the curtain on ancient literature
from Old Testament times.
Fitting the category of *wisdom* literature,
it divides into two main themes:
meditations on how to live
and eulogies of Old Testament heroes.

MEDITATIONS

The tone of the meditations reminds us
of a departing parent addressing a child.

Son, if you are going to serve the Lord,
be prepared for times
when you will be put to the test. (2:1)

Give your help to the poor. . . .
Be generous to every living soul. . . .
Do not hesitate to visit the sick. . . .
Whatever you do, remember that some day
you must die. (7:32-36)

EULOGIES

Next, the Book of Sirach contains a review
of Old Testament history.
It does this in the form of eulogies to the giants
of Israel's past.
One by one, it parades before the reader
the great persons who peopled its pages.

ABRAHAM

Abraham was the great ancestor
of many nations;
his reputation was faultless.
He kept the Law of the Most High
and made a covenant with him. . . .
And so the Lord made him a solemn promise
that his descendants . . . would be countless,
like the dust of the earth. (44:19-21)

MOSES

The Lord
chose Moses out of all mankind. . . .
He let him hear his voice
and led him into the dark cloud,
where, face-to-face, he gave him . . .
the Law that gives life. (45:4-5)

Meditation on God

He sends the snow fluttering down
like birds. . . .
We marvel at its beautiful whiteness,
and in fascination we watch it fall.

He sprinkles frost over the ground like salt,
and it freezes into thorny flowers of ice.
He sends the cold north wind blowing
and the water hardens into ice;
every lake and pond freezes over,
putting on a coat of icy armor. . . .

Though you do your best to praise him,
he is greater than you can ever express.
Though you honor him tirelessly
and with all your strength,
you still cannot praise him enough.

SIRACH 43:18–20, 30

Meditation on Friendship

A loyal friend is like a safe shelter;
find one, and you have found a treasure.
Nothing else is as valuable;
there is no way of putting a price on it. . . .

If you touch tar, it will stick to you,
and if you keep company with arrogant people,
you will come to be just like them. . . .
You cannot keep a clay pot
next to an iron kettle;
the pot will break if it hits the kettle. . . .

If you insult a friend,
you will break up the friendship.
Even if you have a violent argument
with a friend, and speak sharply,
all is not lost. You can still make up.

SIRACH 6:14–15; 13:1–2; 22:20–22

A tenth-century frieze of David and Goliath from church near Lake Van, Turkey.

DAVID

When he was still a boy,
he killed a giant to rescue his people. . . .
He loved his Creator
and sang praises to him with all his heart.
He put singers at the altar
to provide beautiful music. . . .
The Lord forgave David's sin
and established his power forever. (47:4-11)

ELIJAH

Elijah, your miracles were marvelous! . . .
You were taken up to heaven
in a fiery whirlwind,
a chariot drawn by fiery horses.

The scripture says that you are ready
to appear at the designated time,
to cool God's anger . . .
and restore the tribes of Israel. (48:4-10)

HEZEKIAH AND ISAIAH

During his reign
Sennacherib attacked the city. . . .
The people lost their courage and shook
with fear. . . .
But they prayed to the merciful Lord . . .
who quickly answered their prayers
and sent Isaiah to save them. . . .
Yes, Hezekiah
did what was pleasing to the Lord. . . .
This was what was commanded
by the great prophet Isaiah,
whose visions were trusted. (48:18-22)

JOSIAH AND JEREMIAH

The memory of Josiah is as sweet as
the fragrance of expertly blended incense,
sweet as honey to the taste,
like music with wine at a banquet. . . .
All the kings, except David, Hezekiah,
and Josiah, were terrible sinners. . . .
They surrendered their power and honor
to foreigners, who set fire to the holy city
and left its streets deserted,
just as Jeremiah had predicted.
Jeremiah . . . was chosen as a prophet
before he was born, "to uproot and to pull
down . . . to build and to plant." (49:1-7)

EZEKIEL AND OTHERS

It was Ezekiel
who was shown the vision of the divine glory
over the chariot and the living creatures.

He also referred to the prophet Job,
who always did the right thing.

May the bones of the twelve prophets
rise to new life, because these men
encouraged the people of Israel. (49:8-10)

NEHEMIAH

The memory of Nehemiah is also great.
He rebuilt the ruined walls of Jerusalem,
installing the gates and bars.
He rebuilt our homes. (49:13)

SIMON

He was like the morning star
shining through the clouds. . . .
He stood beside the altar with his assistants
circling him like a wreath. . . .
Then Simon came down from the altar,
raised his hands . . .
and reverently pronounced
the blessing from the Lord. (50:6, 12, 20)

CONCLUSION

The Book of Sirach ends with these thoughts:

May God bless everyone
who gives attention to these teachings. . . .
Whoever lives by them
will be strong enough for any occasion,
because he will be walking in the light
of the Lord. (50:28-29)

Be joyfully grateful
for the Lord's mercy,
and never be ashamed to praise him.
Do your duty at the proper time,
and the Lord, at the time he thinks proper,
will give you your reward. (51:29-30)

ISRAEL IN WAITING

By its own admission
the Old Testament is an unfinished story.
It ends with faithful Jews
waiting for the return of Elijah,
waiting for the "Day of the Lord,"
waiting for "hidden things yet to be fulfilled."

The Old Testament drama closes with old Jews,
like Zechariah and Simeon,
watching, praying—waiting!
(Luke 1:67; 2:25)

Perhaps the most appropriate signature
to our study of God's chosen people is this image
by a modern novelist.

The Source
JAMES A. MICHENER

Rabbi Asher
wandered among the gnarled olive trees;
his attention was arrested
by one so ancient that its interior was rotted away,
leaving an empty shell
through which one could see;
but somehow the remaining fragments
held contact with the roots,
and the old tree was still vital,
sending forth branches that bore good fruit;
and as he studied this patriarch of the grove
Asher thought that it well summarized
the state of the Jewish people:
an old society
much of whose interior had rotted away,
but whose fragments
still held vital connection with the roots of God,
and it was through these roots of law
that Jews could ascertain the will of God
and produce good fruit.

REFERENCE NOTES

Part One

John T. Scopes, "The Trial That Rocked the Nation," *Reader's Digest,* March 1961, pp. 136–44.

"The Lutheran Pope," *Newsweek,* July 23, 1973, p. 50.

Charles Clayton Morrison, "Protestant Misuse of the Bible," *The Christian Century,* June 5, 1946.

Robert E. Gentet, "Dinosaurs Before Adam?" *Tract #670* (Pasadena, Calif.: Ambassador College, 1963).

Watch Tower Bible and Tract Society, *Is the Bible Really the Word of God?* (Watch Tower Bible and Tract Society of Pennsylvania, 1969), pp. 21–22.

William F. Dankenbring, "Why the New Creation-Evolution Controversy?" *Plain Truth,* June 1973, pp. 24–27.

Loren Eiseley, "In Darwin's Century," from *Adventures of the Mind* in *The Saturday Evening Post,* April 26, 1958.

Ronald Kotulak, "Deadend for Expanding Universe?" *Chicago Tribune,* 1973.

Ronald Kotulak, "End Only 100 Billion Years Away," *Chicago Tribune,* May 1, 1979.

D. J. Wiseman, *Illustrations from Biblical Archaeology* (Grand Rapids, Mich.: Wm. B. Eerdmans Publishing Co., 1959).

Feodor Dostoevski, *The Brothers Karamazov,* trans. by Constance Garnett (New York: Random House, Modern Library, 1950), pp. 436–37.

James Weldon Johnson, "Creation," from *God's Trombones* (New York: Viking Press, 1955).

Nikos Kazantzakis, *The Last Temptation of Christ* (New York: Simon & Schuster, 1960), pp. 391–92.

Watch Tower Bible and Tract Society, *Is the Bible Really the Word of God?* pp. 30–32.

Bill Barry, "Carbon Copy Man," *Chicago Sun-Times Midwest Magazine,* March 11, 1973.

"The Mind," *Time,* April 19, 1971, pp. 46–47.

Albert Rosenfeld, *The Second Genesis: The Coming Control of Life* (Englewood Cliffs, N.J.: Prentice-Hall, 1969), p. 135.

Ronald Kotulak, ". . . Half Plant, Half Animal," *Chicago Tribune,* March 21, 1976.

William Hines, "Fierce DNA Debate . . . ," *Chicago Sun-Times,* March 13, 1977.

Martin Luther King, Jr., *Strength to Love* (New York: Harper & Row, 1963).

Arthur J. Snider, "Man's a Born Killer . . . ," *Chicago Daily News,* September 1–2, 1973.

Paul Horn, "A Visit with India's High-Powered New Prophet," *Look,* February 6, 1968.

Thomas Merton, *The Seven Storey Mountain* (New York: Harcourt, Brace & Co., 1948), p. 111.

James T. Farrell, *Studs Lonigan* (New York: Vanguard Press, 1962), p. 385.

James Weldon Johnson, "Noah Built the Ark," from *God's Trombones* (New York: Viking Press, 1955).

Werner Keller, *The Bible as History: A Confirmation of the Book of Books,* trans. by William Neil (New York: William Morrow & Co., 1956), pp. 35–36.

Watch Tower Bible and Tract Society, *Is the Bible Really the Word of God?* pp. 35–36.

Editors, *Science News,* March 26, 1977.

John J. Dougherty, *Searching the Scriptures* (New York: Doubleday & Co., 1959), p. 52.

George Higgins, "Sin Comes Back on the Scene" (Washington, D.C.: National Catholic News Service, 1974).

Dorothy Thompson, "The Lesson of Dachau," *Ladies' Home Journal,* September 1945.

Edith Sitwell, "Still Falls the Rain," from *Street Song* (New York: A. Watkins, 1940).

Avery Corman, *Oh, God!* (New York: Simon & Schuster, 1971), pp. 21, 22, 24–25.

Part Two

Samuel Noah Kramer, "The World of Abraham," in *Everyday Life in Bible Times* (Washington, D.C.: National Geographic Society, 1967), p. 44.

James A. Michener, *The Source* (New York: Random House, 1965), pp. 112–13.

Morris West, *The Devil's Advocate* (New York: William Morrow & Co., 1959), p. 294.

Carlo Carretto, *Letters from the Desert,* trans. by Rose Mary Hancock (New York: Pillar Books, 1976), pp. 12–15, 30, 121–22, 125–26.

Sholem Asch, *Moses* (New York: G. P. Putnam Sons, 1951).

Bernhard W. Anderson, *Understanding the Old Testament* (Englewood Cliffs, N.J.: Prentice-Hall, 1966), p. 37.

National Geographic Society, *Everyday Life in Bible Times,* p. 179.

David N. Nichol, "Biblical Eighth Plague Hits Again," *Chicago Daily News,* March 7, 1969.

Mordecai Kaplan, Eugene Kohn, and Ira Eisenstein, eds., *The New Haggadah* (New York: Behrman House, 1941), pp. 11–13.

John Putnam, "To Sinai and the Promised Land," in *Everyday Life in Bible Times,* pp. 178–204.

David S. Boyer, "Geographical Twins a World Apart," *National Geographic Magazine,* December 1958, p. 852.

Gordon Gaskill, "Which Mountain Did Moses Climb?" *Reader's Digest,* June 1973, pp. 209–16.

Will Herberg, "Jewish Existence and Survival: A Theological View," *Judaism,* Vol. I (1952), p. 20.

Herodotus, *Histories IV,* The Penguin Classics, p. 264.

Barnabas Ahern, "The Biblical Way of Life," *The Critic,* September 1965, pp. 38–46.

Carl Sandburg, as quoted by Ralph McGill in "The Most Unforgettable Character I've Met," *Reader's Digest,* May 1954, p. 110.

Philip S. Bernstein, "What the Jews Believe," *Life,* September 11, 1950.

George Kent, "Happily Ever After with the Brothers Grimm," *Reader's Digest,* January 1965.

Roland de Vaux, "The Qumran Story," *The Bible Today Reader* (Collegeville, Minn.: The Order of St. Benedict, Inc., 1973), p. 42.

"Geiger Counters Prove Age of Biblical Scrolls," *Catholic Universe Bulletin,* December 7, 1951.

Robert Aron, *The Jewish Jesus* (Maryknoll, N.Y.: Orbis Books, 1971), p. 83.

Part Three

Werner Keller, *The Bible as History,* p. 74.

G. Ernest Wright, "The World of David and Solomon," in *Everyday Life in Bible Times,* pp. 209–13.

Charlotte D. Lofgreen, "From the Volunteer's Viewpoint: History by the Bucketful," *The Biblical Archaeology Review,* March 1976, pp. 35–37.

James A. Michener, *The Source,* pp. 281, 284–87.

Stuart E. Rosenberg, *Judaism* (New York: Paulist Press, 1966), pp. 61–63, 147–49.

Robert Wallace, "Kingly Glory and Ordeal," *Life,* December 25, 1964, p. 63.

Philip Yancey, "Ordeal on Mt. Hood," *Campus Life,* February 1978, pp. 77–78.

James Daniel, "The Psalms: Hymnbook of Humanity," *Christianity Today,* April 15, 1966.

George W. Cornell, "Salvation: PWs Say God Didn't Help—He Pulled Them Through," *Chicago Daily News,* March 10–11, 1973, p. 24.

Part Four

James Fitzgerald, "Grim Poverty Stalks the Land of Red Cloud," *Our Sunday Visitor,* May 19, 1968, pp. 4–5.

Roy Larson, "Reform Rabbis Will Vote on New Seder Celebration," *Chicago Sun-Times,* April 21, 1973, p. 14.

Emil G. Kraeling, "The Prophets," *Life,* December 25, 1964, p. 75.

Eamonn O'Doherty, "Ezekiel Today," *The Bible Today,* April 1963, p. 387.

Philip Yancey, "Fire," *Campus Life,* September 20, 1970.

Janice Rothschild, "I Met a Samaritan," *The Atlanta Journal-Constitution,* September 20, 1970.

Lord Byron, "The Destruction of Sennacherib."

"History by Computer," *Time,* April 27, 1962.

Part Five

"Home at Last," *Newsweek,* February 26, 1973, p. 26.

Ecclesiastes 12:1–8, *New American Bible* (Washington, D.C.: Confraternity of Christian Doctrine, 1970).

Part Six

Leonard Johnston, *Witnesses to God* (New York: Paulist Press, 1963), p. 109.

Howard LaFay, "The Years in Galilee," in *Everyday Life in Bible Times,* p. 328.

Robert Coughlan, "Who Was the Man Jesus?" *Life,* December 25, 1964, p. 92.

James A. Michener, *The Source,* p. 431.

INDEX (selective listing)

Biblical Persons

INDEX OF BIBLICAL CITATIONS AND PASSAGES

233

234

ACKNOWLEDGMENTS *(Continued from page 2)*

Excerpt from *Searching the Scriptures* by John T. Dougherty. Copyright 1959 by Doubleday & Co., Inc. Reprinted by permission of Doubleday & Co., Inc.

Excerpt from "Still Falls the Rain" by Edith Sitwell. Copyright 1942 by Edith Sitwell. Reprinted from *Street Song* by permission of A. Watkins, Inc. Reprinted from *Collected Poems* (Macmillan) by permission of David Higham Associates Limited, London.

Excerpt from "Sin Comes Back on the Scene" by George Higgins. Copyright 1974, by the National Catholic News Service. Reprinted with permission.

Excerpt from *Oh, God!* by Avery Corman. Copyright © 1971 by Avery Corman. Published by Simon & Schuster. Reprinted by permission of Avery Corman.

Excerpts from "The World of Abraham" by Samuel Noah Kramer, "To Sinai and the Promised Land" by John Putnam, "The World of David and Solomon" by G. Ernest Wright, "The Years in Galilee" by Howard LaFay, from *Everyday Life in Bible Times* by the National Geographic Society. Copyright 1967. Reprinted by permission of the National Geographic Society.

Excerpts from *The Source* by James A. Michener. Copyright © 1965 by Marjay Productions, Inc. Reprinted by permission of Random House, Inc., and Martin Secker & Warburg Limited, London.

Excerpt from *The Devil's Advocate* by Morris West. Copyright © 1959 by Morris West. Reprinted by permission of William Morrow & Co., Inc., and William Heinemann Ltd., London.

Excerpts from *Letters from the Desert* by Carlo Carretto, trans. by Rose Mary Hancock. Published and © 1972 by Orbis Books and Darton Longman & Todd Ltd. Reprinted by permission of Orbis Books and Darton Longman & Todd Ltd.

Excerpt from "Biblical Eighth Plague Hits Again" by David N. Nichol, *Chicago Daily News*, March 7, 1969. Reprinted with permission from Field Enterprises, Inc.

Excerpt from *The New Haggadah* by Mordecai Kaplan, Eugene Kohn, and Ira Eisenstein, eds., on page 77, reprinted with permission of the Publisher, Behrman House Inc., 1261 Broadway, New York, N.Y.

Excerpt from "Geographical Twins a World Apart" by David S. Boyer, *National Geographic Magazine*, December 1958. Reprinted by permission.

Excerpt from "Which Mountain Did Moses Climb?" by Gordon Gaskill, *Reader's Digest*, June 1973. Reprinted by permission.

Excerpt from "The Biblical Way of Life" by Barnabas Ahern, *The Critic*, September 1965. © *The Critic*, September 1965. Published by the Thomas More Association, Chicago, Illinois. Reprinted by permission of the Thomas More Association.

Excerpt from "The Qumran Story" by Roland de Vaux, *The Bible Today Reader*. Copyright 1973 by The Order of St. Benedict, Collegeville, Minnesota. Used with permission.

Excerpt from *The Jewish Jesus* by Robert Aron. Copyright © 1971 by Orbis Books. Reprinted by permission of Orbis Books.

Excerpt from "From the Volunteer's Viewpoint: History by the Bucketful" by Charlotte D. Lofgreen, *Biblical Archaeology Review*, March 1976, pp. 35–37. Reprinted by permission of *Biblical Archaeology Review*.

Excerpts from *Judaism* by Stuart E. Rosenberg. Copyright © 1966 by the Missionary Society of St. Paul. Reprinted by permission of Paulist Press.

Excerpt from "Grim Poverty Stalks the Land of Red Cloud" by James Fitzgerald, *Our Sunday Visitor*, May 19, 1968. Reprinted by permission of *Our Sunday Visitor*.

Excerpt from "Reform Rabbis Will Vote on New Seder Celebration" by Roy Larson. Excerpted with permission from the *Chicago Sun-Times*, April 21, 1973.

Excerpt from "Fire" by Philip Yancey. Used by permission from *Campus Life* Magazine, September 20, 1970. Copyright 1970, Youth for Christ International, Wheaton, Illinois.

Excerpt from "I Met a Samaritan" by Janice Rothschild, *The Atlanta Journal-Constitution*, September 20, 1970. Reprinted by permission of Janice Rothschild Blumberg.

Excerpt from "History by Computer," *Time*, April 27, 1962. Reprinted by permission from *Time*, The Weekly Newsmagazine; Copyright Time Inc. 1962.

Excerpt from "Home at Last," *Newsweek*, February 26, 1973. Copyright 1973 by Newsweek, Inc. All rights reserved. Reprinted by permission.

Excerpt from *Witnesses to God* by Leonard Johnston. Published by Paulist Press. Reprinted by permission of the author.